Bugger off and L

Vernon Coleman's Diaries (Book 3)

Vernon Coleman

Published by Blue Books

CONTENTS

Preface

Everything in this book is true except for any bits which might get me into very special trouble and they were made up, your Honour, and may I say that the wig you are wearing really suits you. I should point out, however, that the events that take place in this book did not necessarily take place on the dates mentioned. This is solely because I hardly ever know what date it is or, indeed, what day of the week it is when I'm making notes about things that have happened. I realise that I could buy a diary but that really wouldn't solve my problem. One of the small, pocket diaries wouldn't have enough space. And one of the big, desk diaries wouldn't fit in my pocket. So I write things down in little notebooks, on envelopes, on receipts or on my shirt. The basic problem is that I have earned my living as a full-time professional author for over 30 years and I long ago realised that it makes no difference to me whether it is Tuesday or Sunday, June or August. I am adept at identifying the seasons (in spring the leaves are appearing, in summer they are there, in autumn they are falling off and in winter they are gone) but that is about all. If I'm in a shop and need to sign a cheque (assuming that the shop will take a cheque) I have to ask the date. The assistant will tell me it's the 14th or the 19th but they won't tell me the month. I then have to ask the month. And the year. I am no longer embarrassed by this.

January

1

Antoinette has decided that she isn't going to read newspapers or watch the television news this year. She says, quite reasonably, that she's fed up of all the scary, depressing news and is, in future, only going to read and watch bright and jolly things. I told her that I understand her feelings but that I will still have to keep an eye on what is happening just in case the end of the world is announced and we don't know about it.

'I don't know want to know about wars and bombs or Nick Clegg,' said Antoinette. 'But you must tell me if anything happens to any of the Royal family. The main ones anyway. The Queen, Prince Philip, Charles, Camilla, William, Kate, George and Harry. Just those.'

I told her I'd let her know.

'And I want to know if any major celebrities die. Film stars, singers, authors – proper celebrities, not manufactured ones.'

I nodded.

'And I want to know if it turns out that Elvis is still alive.'

'And Michael Jackson?' I asked.

'Oh yes. Elvis or Michael Jackson. And you must tell me if they find a way to grow teeth. I've got that wonky tooth at the back. If they can find a way to help me grow a new one I want to know about that.'

I said I would.

'And if anyone invents a no calorie chocolate I want to know about that. Or if they invent something safe and permanent that stops hair going grey.' She paused and thought. 'And I want to know if they make a decent, vegetarian pork pie.'

I said I'd let her know if I heard about any of these items of news.

'Oh, and I want to know if they manage to find life on Mars.'

'I think you'd better make me a list,' I told her, having rather lost my way.

2

I am not paranoid, I'm really not. And I am not anti-social in a hermit sort of way. But I constantly feel as though I am under siege; forever being attacked by forces I don't understand and whose aims I find incomprehensible. Nothing makes much sense any more. Nothing is predictable. I find it difficult, nay impossible, to tell the difference between art, graffiti and vandalism. The world seems to become un-friendlier by the hour. Is this just me? A good deal of what I find alarming is blamed on progress but is it really progress when it takes the television longer to warm up than it did 40 years ago? Is it really progress when I have to fish out the manual to find out how to turn on my car's fog lights?

'We can't stand still!' people say.

'Why not?' I think to myself. Standing still is rather satisfying; even though I confess I do rather like to do my standing still while leaning on a five barred gate, watching sheep prong and frolic, rather than standing in a queue while a security guard with an IQ the wrong side of 100 checks to see if I have a rocket launcher tucked into my socks or an economy sized pack of hand grenades hidden among the books in my suitcase. Incidentally, watching farm animals is a very under-rated activity. Sheep, cows and pigs have fascinating social lives and television natural history programmes would do well to spend a little time and money filming their habits and relationships. The meteorological office (which specialises in predicting that it will shortly be wet and dry, not necessarily in that order and not necessarily today) could, for example, dump all their computers and all those smarmy forecasters with neat hair if they would invest instead in a ten acre field and a few sheep. Sheep are the best weather forecasters there are. Long before rain starts they find whatever cover they can and sit down on a nice piece of dry grass. Pigs are very bright animals too; brighter than dogs. I would say they are at about the level of a Parliamentary Under-Secretary. You could train pigs to work in banks but they would get bored and anyway this is never likely to happen because the powerful meat industry would not like us to know just how intelligent these animals really are. It's difficult to sit down and eat a slice of an animal which is far more intelligent than the average estate agent.

The trouble with progress, of course, is that most of it isn't progress at all; it is change for the sake of change, or it is change that

5

benefits someone else (usually a government department or a large company such as a bank or a utility company) but buggers up my life completely. Every day seems to bring more demands, more instructions, more threats and more warnings and I have to say that I am absolutely full up with worry. Change can be exciting but it can also be destructive, unnerving and frightening – especially if there is a good deal of it. Change saps energy and focus and when the change is unnecessary and senseless the damage it does is even greater.

The problem is, of course, that the endless torrent of change from which we now suffer, and which affects every aspect of our lives, produces great fear, instability, misdirected anger and whole swathes of superficiality and all that, of course, means power to those politicians and eurocrats producing the changes. Personally, I have no room left for fresh anxieties, however exotic they may be, and threats really don't work anymore because just what are they going to do to me? Telling me in capital letters (which is shouting by another name) that I must not under any circumstances throw away the tag on my new quilt has no more effect on me than telling me that HMRC is now entitled to demand that I produce all my bank statements and receipts for the last 60 years. It has all gone beyond absurd and I can no longer take any of it seriously. They may call it progress but I've had enough of it.

I wish all these people who keep writing to tell me what I must or must not do would just bugger off and leave me alone.

3

I had an email today from a company offering to look after my social media. For a fee they will write eight tweets a day for me and manage my Facebook and LinkedIn pages, and heaven knows what else besides. Having a presence on the social media is considered essential for writers these days and I'm told that book sales depend heavily on constant twittering and such like. Publishers doubtless do the twittering for some of their big name authors but many celebrity authors of the Stephen Fry variety love it so much that they never stop twittering, some even do it when they're in the bath, on the loo or making love. However, I am far too much of a recluse and far too independent to be keen on social media of any hue. I've never even visited anyone's Facebook page and although there is, I am told one of these things in my name I have never visited it. I regard Facebook as one of the world's most evil companies. It is entirely worthless and has done infinitely more harm than good.

The idea of having someone writing and publishing comments in my name eight times a day terrifies me. They might make me say: 'Vince Cable is a wonderful human being and I'm a great fan.' Or the idiot in charge of my daily outpourings might report that I'm travelling everywhere by roller skates in order to reduce my carbon footprint. But this is, presumably, how the world operates these days. Press relations officers have always put words into the mouths of their employers (through speeches and press releases) but this is far, far worse than that. The company which emailed me is offering to create a persona and a life for me. They are offering to take over my world. The deal is that I give them money and some unknown teenager, probably sitting in his bedroom, creates a new me to replace the old, original me that I thought I was and had just about got used to.

I was shivering at the prospect of this when I suddenly realised that it reminded me of the way the studios used to manage the lives of their big stars back in the 1930s and 1940s. Whole lives were created out of nothing. Big stars were given new names, new backgrounds, new friends, new hobbies, new relationships and, in every other respect, new lives. So, perhaps, nothing much is new. The company which wants to write tweets in my name is, presumably, now offering this service to everyone who wants a 'vibrant and exciting online presence' but can't find the energy or the time to constantly serve up irrelevant daily trivia for mass consumption. Every reality television 'star', every would-be singer, every television actor, everyone who has written, or would like to write a book, will have a manufactured life. How will any of us know who anyone really is?

I'm glad my writing career is in its autumn days.

4

A little while ago I wrote a novel called *Revolt*. Most newspapers and magazines won't review any of my books. This isn't personal in that I have a load of enemies, but is a result of the fact that my books are known to be self-published. Literary editors hate and fear self-publishers just as much as they hate authors whose books sell more than 10 copies a year and which cannot, therefore, be officially described as 'literary fiction'. Reviewers, like agents, live on the fringes of publishing and are totally opposed to anything which threatens their status. I published *Revolt* under the pen name Robina Hood.

I described the tale as a 'true story that hasn't happened yet' and, on the flap of the book, described Robina Hood as the pseudonym of one of Britain's best known and best loved television presenters. I don't know why I did this. It just seemed rather fun.

(I was going to say that Robina was a disabled, black, teenage lesbian with two children to support, since that seemed the most likely way to attract sympathetic reviews, but when I thought about it I realised that this was likely to get me into too much trouble. I'd actually written quite a nice biography for her in which I explained that Robina, born in Nigeria, was a paraplegic as a result of the car accident which killed both her parents when she was eleven. She had, I wrote, written short stories for hospital radio stations in her home country and had won the prestigious Keith Messenger award while still a student. She had returned to Nigeria to work with people less fortunate than herself. Agents would have fought to represent her and *The Guardian* and *The Independent* would have published huge features about her.)

I sent copies of the book to the usual reviewers and on the dedication page of many of the books wrote a personal note. 'Wonderful to meet you the other day. Hope you like my book. Love Robina x.' was pretty typical. The ploy worked reasonably well. Nigel Farage, leader of UKIP, sent me a really lovely postcard with a highly quotable handwritten note. Quite a few reviewers wrote pieces about the book. Most notably an unpleasant sounding fellow called Rod Liddle wrote a full page piece in *The Spectator* in which he tried to work out which television presenter had written the book.

(Actually, I'm not entirely sure that 'Rod Liddle' is a real person, either. Perhaps it is one of those cod names which are used when no one wants to take responsibility for something they've done; a rubbish bin name for second rate articles no one wants to admit to having written. Film directors who don't want to take the credit, or blame, for a film they've worked on but which hasn't quite worked out, will list the director as 'Alan Smithee'. Maybe journalists who feel embarrassed about something they've written put it down as by 'Rod Liddle'.)

Sadly, however, since *Revolt* was a first novel by an unknown author (and a pseudonymous one at that, who couldn't do any promotional interviews) the sales weren't too exciting. I've just published *Revolt* by Vernon Coleman as a kindle book on Amazon and, oddly enough, it's now doing quite nicely thank you.

5

It has been officially confirmed by the Organisation for Economic Cooperation and Development that the UK has fewer hospital beds per person than almost any country in the Western world. So much of the available money is being spent on administration that there is very little money available for the stuff that matters. I've been warning about this for years but no one takes any notice because to improve things would mean spending less on administration and administrators decide how the money is spent and turkeys don't vote for Christmas. Despite the fact that the population is soaring, the number of hospital beds in the UK has been steadily falling for decades. France and Germany now have two or three times as many beds per head as Britain. Hospitals in Estonia, Slovenia and Poland all have far more beds than the UK. Japan and South Korea have four or five times as many beds per citizen.

Some NHS spokespersons have tried to excuse this inexcusable state of affairs by pointing out, quite accurately, that many patients are better off at home, because hospitals are such dangerous places. This convenient truth ignores the inconvenient truth that if hospitals were not so overcrowded they would not be such dangerous places. It is the overcrowding in our hospitals which has led to the risk of superbugs (a problem which is almost exclusive to the National Health Service) and to the enthusiasm of politicians and doctors for mass slaughter of elderly patients under the auspices of the Liverpool Care Pathway (whereby elderly patients who are occupying valuable beds and who think their doctors and nurses are looking after them are secretly killed off by being denied food and water).

Operations are cancelled because there are no beds available and many patients, particularly elderly patients, are forced to spend hours lying on trolleys. Only India and Chile and one or two other countries are in a worse state than Britain. The problem, I fear, is the National Health Service itself. It was never a good idea and it should now be put to sleep. The bare fact is that the NHS, a bureaucratic giant, kills more people than it saves. There is far too much administration and far too few doctors, nurses and beds. The NHS encourages waste, misdirected resources and patronising and nannying behaviour by its state trained, state employed staff who see themselves as primarily servants of the State, behold to the State rather than the patients they care for and who, too often, offer their services with all the supercilious graciousness of Victorian soup kitchen operators 'serving' the needy poor. The end result is that Britain has one of the worst health care services in the world. Britain's infant mortality rate is horrifyingly high and Britain is second worst in the world (to the USA) for avoidable deaths and a healthy life expectancy at the age of 60. In Britain, 60-year-olds may survive for a while but, in general, they do so in a poor state of health, stumbling from one health crisis to the next. The NHS patches people up but it doesn't cure them; it is the medical equivalent of a dodgy backstreet garage which seals radiator leaks with chewing gum and replaces broken fan belts with nylon stockings.

Doctors used to be brave and the vast majority used to speak honestly and honourably. And then two bad things happened. First, the medical establishment was bought by the drug industry. It didn't cost much. A few ridiculously high speaking fees for leading members of the establishment, some posh meals and an endless supply of cheap pens did the job. Second, doctors became civil servants. Working for the government changed everything. In the old, old days doctors would not have allowed things to get so bad. Today, I'd trust the average British doctor about as much as I'd trust Nick Clegg or an estate agent. No other country in the world has waiting times or waiting lists for patients with cancer. No other country in the world has hospitals which are as dirty and as chronically infected with killer bugs. No other country in the world gives priority to women wanting breast enhancement surgery over women needing treatment for breast cancer. No other country in the world forces male and female patients to share a ward. No other country in the world has hospitals where so many members of staff seem to go to work each day with the aim of making life difficult,

10

embarrassing, uncomfortable and challenging for their 'customers'. (I suspect some NHS employees are trained by the same people who train Post Office employees.) And, worst of all, survival rates for almost all common cancers are worse in Britain than just about anywhere else in Europe. If you live in Britain and develop cancer of the stomach, colon, rectum, lung, breast, ovary, prostate, kidney or blood then your survival chances are worse than the European average. It is no wonder that I get depressed when I hear people saying how wonderful the NHS is. The NHS isn't wonderful. It is a deadly, murderous organisation which should be put to sleep – permanently.

6

Doctors are now pushing for everyone over the age of 50 to take cholesterol lowering drugs every day. There are already eight million Britons taking the damned things and now the medical establishment (much of which receives big chunks of cash from the drug industry) wants that doubling to sixteen million. How long before taking these drugs becomes compulsory? Doctors are keen on prescribing these drugs because, for reasons which are quite beyond me, they now receive a hefty cash bonus if they manage to persuade enough of their patients to take them.

(Doctors working in the NHS have contracts which give them bonuses for identifying patients with a number of specific diseases. It is no coincidence that the incidence of these diseases has been soaring since the payment bonuses were introduced. Similarly, of course, doctors are given bonuses if they vaccinate enough of their patients – despite the absence of evidence showing that vaccination is safe and effective and the existence of much evidence suggesting that it is dangerous and ineffective.)

Many of the patients taking these drugs have absolutely nothing wrong with them. The drugs are being handed out as a preventative. It is, I suppose, much easier for doctors to write out prescriptions than it is to sit people down and explain that heart disease and other killer diseases are often caused by eating the wrong sort of foods (hamburgers and chips for example) and by being obese.

Several things about all this worry me. First, no one really knows for certain whether or not lowering blood cholesterol does any good at all. It's perfectly possible that it does more harm than good.

Second, the side effects from the pills which are most commonly prescribed are horrendous. At least one in five patients taking these drugs develops side effects. And the side effects aren't trivial. They include diabetes, cataracts and memory disturbances. I first wrote about the danger of these drugs in my book *How to Stop Your Doctor Killing You*, the first edition of which came out nearly 20 years ago. At the time doctors were just beginning to hand out cholesterol lowering drugs to healthy patients. The questions which I asked in that book have still not been answered and I still have the same doubts.

It was once said that doctors prescribe medicines of which they know little to treat illnesses of which they know less while treating people of whom they know nothing at all. These days, doctors do the same but they're not treating sick people, they're giving the medicines about which they know little to perfectly healthy individuals. It's crazy and wicked. Is that really what all those doctors dreamt of doing when they were young?

7

It always used to be said that crooks would not be allowed to profit from their crimes. And yet I see that war criminals Blair and Brown are making vast amounts of money by explaining how they screwed Britain and the British. Hopefully, all the loot these two make will be confiscated and used to help pay off the nation's debts. At the rate at which war criminal Blair is raking it in he should be able to make Britain solvent by 2018. I feel no satisfaction from the fact that early on in his premiership I predicted in one of my books that (the not yet a war criminal but soon to be one) Blair was sucking up to the Americans so that he could make truckloads of cash when he'd finished with politics. It was, I said, the main reason he took Britain into illegal wars. I wonder if anyone still thinks I was wrong about that.

8

From time to time Antoinette buys me a magazine dealing with a subject about which I know absolutely nothing. It's a wonderful way to venture into other people's worlds for an hour or two. For example, in the last few months she's bought me magazines about carriage driving, caravanning, horse racing, model railways and whisky. She bought me a magazine called *Practical Pigs* and one called, simply, *Parrots*. Each magazine gave me an insight into the way other people live their lives; with small groups of dedicated, and sometimes obsessed, individuals often creating remarkable worlds within worlds; worlds about which I previously knew nothing; worlds I hardly knew existed. Today, Antoinette gave me a magazine entitled *Carving*. I found absolutely fascinating to see what amazing things people can do with nifty fingers, sharp tools and pieces of wood.

Inevitably, perhaps, the magazine contains this warning: 'Woodcarving is an inherently dangerous pursuit. Readers should not attempt the procedures described herein without seeking training and information on the safe use of tools and machines, and all readers should observe current safety legislation.'

I was going to whittle a stick but I've put my penknife away until I can check on the regulations. I hope, however, that my good lady continues to hunt down curious magazines. There are endless new worlds to explore and reading a magazine is an excellent way to do this. I find the advertisements (particularly the classified ads) are often just as revealing as the articles, editorials and news stories. My only rule is that I really don't want to see any of those magazines dealing with celebrities who are famous simply for being famous or who are exposing their private worlds purely for propaganda purposes. If those magazines had existed in the 1930s they would have doubtless featured photographs of Adolf and Eva in their lovely home in the mountains.

9

I read today that internet giant Yahoo is now creating Web magazines which contain advertisements embedded in among the articles written by journalists. The advertisements are written as though they were news stories or features. I very much doubt if they will carry the words 'advertisement' or 'advertorial' to warn readers that what they're perusing has been placed on the site by a company with a product to sell. There's a lot of this on the internet these days, and since it is impossible to tell which items are genuine and which are plugs or promotions I find it is safest to assume that everything I read on the Web is an advertisement. Even if the stuff I'm reading isn't a paid for advertisement (masquerading as a piece of journalism) the chances are high that it is nothing more than a rewritten press release or a piece put in place in response to the efforts of professional lobbyists.

The internet, better known as the valley of the trolls, has destroyed journalism; and journalists, editors and proprietors have, to their eternal shame, allowed it to happen. Internet journalists are, as a breed, so shallow that if they were puddles you could paddle in them without getting your socks wet. Every day around 1,500 people in Britain stop buying a daily newspaper. Most of them will never buy a paper again. I fear that as more and more newspapers abandon their printed selves and go online so honest, independent journalism will disappear. And the truth will become increasingly difficult to find. Whatever their faults (and there were many) it was newspaper journalists who investigated and exposed much wrong doing in our world. Some newspapers are biased and prejudiced (few worse than the *Financial Times* which rivals even the BBC for bias towards the fascist European Union and which can now be best regarded as a share price sheet with a few bent articles tacked on to make it look like a newspaper) but crooked politicians and business folk would have got away with a hell of a lot more without journalists poking their noses into their lives. What will replace investigative journalists? It certainly won't be the internet, though many newspaper groups clearly hope it will. The newspaper industry is hoping that what they call 'millennial readers' (those born between 1980 and 2000) will subscribe to their online newspapers and save their industry from the most potent and widely disruptive technology ever invented. They claim that the millennial readers will do this because they don't have the print habit and will, therefore, feel comfortable with a newspaper that comes on a screen. They may be right about that but they're wrong about the millennial readers saving their industry because the readers they're aiming at don't have the paying habit either. They're accustomed to getting their news and their gossip and their sports without paying for it. Why should they subscribe to an internet newspaper when they can get all the news they want without paying a cent for it? Not even Rupert Murdoch has been able to make a digital newspaper work. In 2011 he launched a paper called *The Daily*, designed for tablet users, and although his company spent $30 million a year on it the paper folded within two years. The taxpayer-funded BBC website alone will ensure that paid for versions of digital newspapers will never succeed. The BBC, using licence fee payers' money, has eradicated free choice, destroyed competition, made 'free' the default position and created a world in which it can pretty well control political debate in the United Kingdom.

A reader recently told me that she measures the world as either being B.I. or A.I. The letters stand for Before Internet and After Internet. She argues that the internet has changed the world far more than anything else for a century or so. She should know. She is 94-years-old. Sadly, however, most people seem curiously uncritical of the internet. The young constantly praise it, extolling its virtues without any idea of the damage it has done to the world. Only those who can remember what life was like B.I. really understand just how much damage Sir Tim Berners-Lee has done to our world. Why couldn't he content himself with inventing a new bagless, cordless vacuum cleaner or, better still, a genuinely squirrel proof bird feeder? Nothing, no war, no bomb, has changed life in such crucial and invasive and damaging ways as the World-Wide Web. The internet has encouraged hypochondriasis (forums for those suffering from specific illnesses invariably do far more harm than good, by spreading rumour, terror and confusion and creating panic and fear), it has made life unbelievably easy and profitable for thieves and confidence tricksters (so far today I have received three fake emails telling me that my Pay Pal account will be closed if I do not immediately send along my bank and personal details) and it has enabled lobbyists and public relations experts to control the spread of information. I'm afraid that anyone who claims that the internet helps broaden our knowledge or power simply doesn't understand how the internet works and how much harm it is doing. The only people who can truly claim to have gained from the internet are pornographers and thieves. And, boy, are they having a good time.

10

I'm not much of a DIY man so when the radiator and towel rail in our downstairs shower room started to lean forward, and was about to fall off, I could see that the support brackets holding it up had sheared but I didn't really know what to do about them. When I looked closely I could see that the brackets, which appeared to be chromium plated metal, had sheared because they were made of plastic and the heat of the radiator they were holding up had proved too much of a strain. I found some thick fencing wire, tied the radiator to a nearby sturdy downpipe and telephoned the central heating people who look after our boiler and central heating system. The engineer came today and to my astonishment told me that instead of being able to replace the brackets he would have to replace the whole radiator. The health and safety experts who cause so much confusion, distress and waste in our lives have apparently ruled that if a radiator support bracket breaks it must be replaced with exactly the same bracket that had been used originally. Since the radiator is a few years old finding the old original brackets would be impossible. So the whole radiator (which is working perfectly well and has absolutely nothing wrong with it) has to be taken out, thrown onto a radiator mountain somewhere and replaced. Useless plastic brackets would be acceptable if they were the brackets that had been originally sold with the towel rail but sturdy, steel brackets that might do a decent job would not be acceptable. Once again the European Union does serious harm to our planet. And yet, oddly enough, no one in authority seems to give a damn about the fact that radiator brackets are being made out of plastic which isn't heat resistant.

That was all a couple of weeks ago.

Today, the engineer returned to fit the new radiator and towel rail. He removed the broken brackets and the perfectly serviceable radiator and towel rail, drilled new holes (because, of course, the new brackets don't fit the holes the old brackets used), made a huge hole in the plaster (which will now need to be redecorated) and fitted the new brackets and the new radiator and towel rail.

'It looks fine,' I said. Then I leant forward and examined one of the brand new supporting brackets holding up the radiator and towel rail. 'What are these made of?'

The engineer muttered something I didn't quite catch. I asked him to repeat what he'd said. 'Plastic,' he told me. 'They're plastic.'

It seems that the radiator manufacturer, with the EU's blessing, is still making support brackets out of plastic which can't cope with heat.

So, in a couple of years' time the engineer will be back to replace the radiator and Europe's used and worthless radiator mountain will be even bigger.

11

Every town in England used to have a wonderful variety of small, specialist shops which were invariably owned and staffed by experts who knew their subject inside out, back to front and upside down as well. There were music shops, art shops, model shops, shops for people with dolls houses, craft shops, needlework shops, ironmongers and stationers where even if you didn't know what you were looking for it was possible to find someone who could tell you exactly what you needed and where it was kept in the shop. If you wanted a piano tuner, someone to teach you how to play the violin or an artist to paint your dog a local shopkeeper would know who to contact. Today, most of those shops have gone. The ones which survive do so because they are owned by individuals who don't have to pay rent and are of an age when they don't know what else they would do if they retired. When those folk do eventually call it a day their shops will close and a good deal of knowledge will be lost forever. The shops have gone for two reasons. First, the soulless internet, a boon for mail order businesses, has enabled large American corporations to sell violin strings, cat litter and staples at rock bottom prices. Small shops, doomed to buy from wholesalers, simply cannot compete. So now we all buy things which probably won't fit, or which will break down because they are shoddily made for price rather than for quality. And if we want a piano tuner or a violin teacher we have to rely on the internet rather than the recommendation of someone who knows someone. Second, greedy local councils, desperate to feed their ever-growing pension deficits, have put up business rates to the point where it is nigh on impossible for any small business to make a profit. All this has been done in the name of progress: making our lives richer. And so our town centres are now full of charity shops (which don't pay rent, rates or salaries and which are, therefore, of no value to the communities in which they sit) and nail parlours which last for a year, until the hopeful owners give up because their grants have run out.

12

I read today that when the earthquake and tsunami hit Japan in 2011, and damaged the nuclear power station at Fukushima, the disaster was worse than it might have been because the safety systems relied on electricity. The plan seems to have been that in the case of an emergency the nuclear plant would be dowsed with water provided by electrically driven water pumps. Sadly, the designers of the system hadn't allowed for the fact that in the case of a major emergency there probably wouldn't be any electricity available.

Chinese reactor designers are much smarter. In the nuclear power plants now being built in China, cooling water will be stored in huge tanks on the roof. In the event of a problem water will automatically pour down onto the hot reactor for 72 hours without the need for any electricity or human action. And that is, surely, as brilliantly simple as the Japanese method was staggeringly stupid.

13

The EU has devised a brilliant way to get rid of economic deficits in European countries. Eurocrats, the new European aristocracy, constantly exercising their droit de seigneur over every aspect of our lives, have decided that in future countries can include illegal and black market figures when working out their Gross Domestic Product figures. By making GDPs bigger, countries can make themselves look much better off – even though the income they are now including isn't legal or taxable. So, from now on, economists will guess the money raised by illegal drug sales, smuggling and prostitution and include the totals in their budget figures. If a country's citizens sell more cocaine, smuggle more cigarettes or run more brothels their country will become richer and more successful. It can't be long before the EU produces helpful films and booklets explaining how Europeans can get involved in these enormously profitable activities. Who can fail to be proud of the European Union?

14

Unemployed workers in France are demanding higher benefits payments and are threatening to go on strike though just what they're not going to do if they don't get their way isn't yet clear. Presumably, they will threaten to refuse to stop doing nothing if they don't get their own way.

15

We will never find out what the unemployed workers of France would have done (or not done) had their demands not been met. The

French Government always backs down in the face of any sort of threat and it has followed tradition and bowed to superior forces yet again. The unemployed of France will doubtless be celebrating tonight. I hope they are tactful enough to keep the popping of champagne corks to a minimum.

16

We desperately need a roofer to glue back bits of our roof. But, sadly, the days when it was possible to find workmen living in our village have long gone. City dwellers probably imagine that the Cotswolds are stuffed with wheelwrights, basket weavers, shepherds and blacksmiths. Hah. Sadly, nothing could be further from the truth. The seven nearest cottages to us are occupied by an IT specialist, a software developer, a mobile telephone sales person, someone who catches the train to London every day and does things in a bank, a director of a company which does something no one understands, a man who owns a car dealership and someone who does unspeakable things with currencies and comes to the country two or three times a year to hold noisy gin and tonic parties on his patio. None of these people is of any practical use to us or, probably, anyone else. After spending the morning on the telephone I eventually managed to find a roofing company in Wolverhampton which is prepared to send us two men and some ladders. Heaven knows how much this is going to cost us. The round trip journey will be around 175 miles.

It used to be said that people who lived in towns were generally unhappy unless something specific made them happy whereas people who lived in the country were generally happy unless something specific made them sad but I don't think this is true anymore. Life in the country is infinitely more difficult than it used to be a generation or two ago.

Since our neighbours are far more trouble than they are worth, Antoinette says that we should have bought a house at least 100 miles away from the nearest house in any direction and I am beginning to think that she is right. A lighthouse maybe?

17

We've decided to sell the old Publishing House, a property which is proving to be tiring and time consuming. Inevitably, the estate agent demands copies of passports, driving licences and utility bills so that they can reassure the authorities that we are not laundering money. Since the estate agents will not handle any money it is difficult to see the sense in this. You can't launder money unless you handle money, any more than you can launder dirty socks without handling dirty socks. As usual we declined to provide the estate agent with any of our private documents and as usual the estate agent decided that he could, after all, manage perfectly well without them since we were, very kindly, offering to pay him several thousand pounds for doing very little indeed.

I suspect that we are unusual in refusing to hand over our sensitive documents to people who really don't need to see them. Most people happily allow their passports and driving licences to be photocopied and the copies stuffed in a drawer. Then, in a year's time, they wonder why and how their identity has been stolen and how it has come to pass that a stranger in Morocco has invested their hard earned money in fast cars and even faster Columbian sneezing powder.

(I recently had to convert my old driving licence, which I'd had had since Boadicea was a road hog. At the advice of the Post Office I sent my old driving licence to DVLA by special delivery. I put in a note asking them to send the new EU photo-card licence the same way. They ignored my note, however, and sent the new licence in an ordinary brown envelope with the DVLA return address on the back. I'm amazed that the licence arrived. I had foolishly thought that the idea of the little plastic card was that I could carry it in my wallet. I was wrong. There is a notice on the top of the paper part of the licence, just under the pointless words 'Keep this safe', which states 'the photo-card and paper counterpart should be kept together'. Together the two documents are far more cumbersome than my old, frayed, paper licence.)

Banks, estate agencies and others talk incessantly about being 'forced' to collect and store confidential information. Most of them are, most of the time, talking cobblers. The most recent, relevant advice I know of came from the Financial Conduct Authority in April 2014 which stated: 'Firms must identify their customers and, where applicable, their beneficial owners, and then verify their identities. Firms must also understand the purpose and intended nature of the customer's relationship with the firm and collect information about the customer and, where relevant, beneficial

20

owner.' There is nothing there about taking photocopies and storing them. The FCA has also said: 'We expect firms to apply the guidance proportionately based on the riskiness of their clients.' And they have said that it is only if a customer is a 'politically exposed' person, identified as a 'higher risk' that a company needs to establish the source of wealth or funds. Finally, the FCA says that any clients who do not wish to give certain information to a financial company can complain to the company in question. 'If they are unhappy with the response, they should take their complaint to the Financial Ombudsman Service.'

No bank, finance company or other organisation, should ever require more than a national insurance number and a physical address. Those two pieces of information are perfectly adequate evidence of identity and address. The problem is that at banks and so on we tend to come face to face with low grade clerks who handle the paperwork and who simply do what their ill-informed managers tell them to do.

Curiously, anyone trying to purchase £40,000 worth of premium bonds, or any number of government gilts, can do so without providing any evidence of identity or address. It seems that the Government, at least, knows that all this data collecting is indeed nothing more than pointless nonsense.

18
A survey of 19,000 people in 10 countries shows that only one in ten internet users is willing to pay for digital news. An hour's hard work with a calculator, and some specially prepared software, tells me that this means that nine out ten internet users prefer to read news they haven't paid for. Here is solid proof that newspapers which are planning to move online, and to charge readers subscription fees, are doomed. It's difficult to blame the reluctant subscribers. Whenever you go hunting for news on the internet, and whether you pay for it or not, you are probably going to be fed material that was written by a public relations company or a lobbyist, promoting a specific product or attitude. Whether you pay for news or not it is now impossible to trust anything you read on the internet so what's the point of paying so that you can read public relations bullshit? There is no longer any such thing as 'a journal of record'. If an online newspaper contains 50 articles and just 10 of them are bent – but you

don't know which 10 are bent – then you have to assume that all 50 are untrustworthy.

In the old days, when councils used to fill potholes and politicians resigned when caught lying, newspapers used to make it clear which bits were editorial and which were paid for by advertisers. Editors beat journalists with a cat'o'nine tails if they caught them copying out chunks of promotional prose. But progress has changed all that and these days it's as hard to find a piece of hard news on a Web based publication as it is to find a ready-made sandwich without more than its fair share of escherichia.coli.

19

The Government says it is thinking of forcing local councils to go back to collecting rubbish once a week instead of once a fortnight. Apparently someone in authority has noticed that when rubbish is left lying around in gardens (or in the street) it attracts rats and flies and becomes a health hazard. Maybe a politician or civil servant has found his or her wine cellar crawling with rats. I am impressed to see that to accompany this piece of pleasant and over-ambitious nonsense the Government has published a guidebook (known as the *Bins Bible*) which offers tips to local authorities 'on how to replace fortnightly collections with weekly bin emptying'. I have long suspected that the people working for local councils are not the brightest in the land but even I am surprised that they need written advice on how to replace a fortnightly bin emptying service with a weekly bin emptying service. Send the bin men round every seven days instead of every fourteen days would have been my advice and I hardly think that merits a guidebook. Still, the authorities already publish booklets on how to eat vegetables and how to blow your nose so I suppose a guidebook on how to change from a fortnightly collection to a weekly collection isn't all that much of a surprise. All this is a complete waste of time and effort, of course, and is merely a piece of electioneering. The EU won't let councils collect the rubbish once a week (or will punish them severely if they do) and since the eurocrats rule our world we must restrain our cheers and cram our hopes and expectations in at the back of the sock drawer.

Meanwhile, our streets and lanes will continue to be awash with discarded litter.

Just this morning I watched in horror as a large, black Audi cruised to a halt in the narrow lane a few yards from our front door. The only passengers were an elderly couple. I could hardly believe what happened next. The driver, a man in his sixties or thereabouts, lowered his window and then proceeded to throw all the rubbish he could find in his car into the hedgerow. Before I could rush out and beat on his car roof with a stick he raised his window and drove off sedately; ostensibly the very picture of middle class probity.

20

A stupid woman ran out in front of the car today. She was, of course, busy texting and far too involved in her imaginary world to take any notice of the real world. I just managed to avoid her. 'What a crazy woman!' cried Antoinette. 'She could have been killed.'

'She would have been the lucky one,' I replied. 'She'd have been dead. I'd have been filling in insurance forms for a year.'

I wonder what the daft woman was texting? 'Am running across busy road and about to be run…'

21

I suspect that the people at Amazon have a tendency to treat books in exactly the same way that they treat dishwasher tablets and soap dish holders. And why should they care? They're all commodities; items for sale. Books were, I suspect, merely the first step in what is clearly going to be a long journey. The company's ill-disguised aim seems to me to be to take over the retail world and within the world of books this means convincing all book readers to buy Kindle devices so that readers will read e-Books and thus Amazon will eventually control the e-Books books business – and by extension, the book business. And so, for now, Amazon puts all its effort into making consumers feel important and very little into making authors feel loved. So, customers can write inaccurate and libellous 'reviews' of books which they haven't even read (or wish to destroy in order to help the sales of another book written by themselves or a friend) and Amazon will not only publish these reviews but will put the worst of them in pride of place so that every potential buyer will see them. Naturally, this means that a single one star review will destroy a book's sales immediately. Amazon doesn't give a fig about this because if the book buyer doesn't buy that book they will probably buy another. And the reviewer who wrote the nasty review will feel (and, indeed, be) powerful and important. The living author whose book sales have crashed, and whose income has declined, will suffer agonies of doubt, anger and misery that dead authors are spared.

Big publishers (who have about as big a future as the blotting paper manufacturers but who are hanging on to their rapidly disappearing power, status and wealth) counter this author unfriendly policy by arranging for all their new books to be greeted with a dozen five star reviews written by tame reviewers. If a bad review appears the sting can be removed by arranging for a friendly reviewer to produce a one star review that praises the book, and to arrange for that review to be the most popular 'bad' review by telling staff members to mark it as 'helpful'.

Small publishers and self-publishers (ostensibly the beneficiaries of the e-Book revolution) are the ones who are most likely to be destroyed by the mean, the ignorant and the self-important individuals who are now the world's most important book reviewers.

In the days of yore a big name reviewer, commonly a successful author in his own right, could, if he wrote a critical review for a large circulation newspaper, put a big hole in the sales of an author's new book. However, whatever he wrote he would not be able to destroy a book completely simply because not every reader would see his review. These days an unemployed and illiterate half-wit with access to an internet enhanced mobile telephone can completely destroy a book's sales in thirty seconds. All it takes is a one star review and a few brutish and dismissive words of contempt.

In principle, the idea of allowing readers to 'mark' books in the same way that teachers mark exams is fair enough but in practice the system fails because so many reviewers give books bad marks for the wrong reasons. To dismiss a book as worthless because it arrived late or because it is the book the author wrote and not the book you hoped it might be is unfair. To attack an author without bothering to read a book (because you disapprove of the book's content or because you don't like the author) is grossly unreasonable. To skip through a few pages of a book you've downloaded free of charge and then give it one star because you've realised it is not your 'cup of tea' is terribly unjust. A book will often have taken a year to write, and taken up much of an author's life. I suspect that many sensitive authors (the ones who invariably write the best books) will be frightened away from writing because they simply cannot face the prospect of their first book being unfairly demolished within seconds of it being published.

22

There was a time when athletes did what they did for the fun of it, and for the honour of representing their country. They ran around, jumped and threw big lumps of metal because it was what they wanted to do and what they were good at. The carried their kit around with them in a rucksack and if they were lucky they had their expenses paid. These days, athletics is a business, like football and cricket, and none the better for it. Athletes earn huge amounts by being sponsored by companies who have absolutely no interest in them or their sport, and most of them stand there mute and puzzled when their national anthem is being played. Bizarre rules mean that many of those who represent a country have never even visited the place until a few months before they are chosen to represent it.

Still, representing a country other than your own isn't entirely new. Consider, for example, the amazing Major D. G. Astley, who was surely one of the most remarkable sportsmen of all time. He was a member of the British gold medal winning curling team at the 1924 Olympics and, for reasons which are lost in the murk of time, he was also allowed to play for Sweden against France in the play off for the silver medal. Sweden won the match and so our Major Astley won gold and silver medals in the same event at the same Olympics. I bet none of today's overpaid, over-sponsored, over-honoured superstars ever beats that record.

23

Television pundits (most of them not old enough to have read a book, let alone written one), politicians and economists are puzzled by the fact that productivity in the UK keeps falling. They are particularly confused because they believe that the internet has (or should have) made business more efficient – and productive. Enormously expensive think tanks are struggling to find the answer to this conundrum. They keep coming up with ever more complex and unbelievable explanations. The truth is that if any of these people had any common sense at all they would realise instantly what is happening. The trouble is that politicians, senior civil servants and eurocrats are where they are because they are greedy, self-serving and concerned only with their own advancement and glorification. They, therefore, make a complete hash of everything they do.

There are, in reality, two reasons why productivity is falling.

First, employees spend several hours a day updating their social media entries. When staff members are fiddling with the ghastly Twitter and the equally absurd Facebook, and adding to the already existing mountains of incomprehensibly un-navigable ego based trivia and irrelevance, they aren't producing whatever they are being paid to produce. I discovered today that even the police in Scotland, who have such a huge chip on their collective shoulders that they now actually call themselves Police Scotland, have a twitter account so that they can entertain Web users with the force's official bleatings. (There is, of course, no Police England.) The average 22-year-old Briton has over 1,000 Facebook friends. Apart from the absurdity of any human being having over 1,000 friends (a number which reminds me of one of those Z list celebrity weddings where, in desperation, the bride and groom accept as guests a random assortment of other Z list celebrities who are notorious not for their achievements but because they are prepared to expose themselves in any way required, in the hope that their photographs will appear in a magazine) this figure suggests that most Facebook users must spend a huge part of their lives simply keeping up with what is going on with all their 'friends', and keeping them updated with information about what they had for breakfast and just how they felt when the number 69 bus was seven minutes late again.

Second, red tape from the European Union, ensures that when people are working they spend most of their time filling in forms or providing information for other people filling in forms.

I offer these conclusions free of charge to the pundits, politicians and economists. Sadly, I suspect that none of them will take any notice.

24

We drove to Ebbsfleet to catch the Eurostar train to Paris. We always used to catch the train from St Pancras (and, before that, from Waterloo) but the train journey to London from the countryside has become more like a lottery than a train service. In order to make sure that we arrived in London in time to join the taxi queue at Paddington Station we had to catch earlier and earlier trains.

The only snag with travelling from Ebbsfleet is that it seems to me that the staff who man the machines X-raying luggage don't really know what they are looking for and so I invariably end up having my bits and pieces pored over by one of the guards protecting Europe from elderly, white terrorists. There is, I have no doubt, a much higher bag-search rate at Ebbsfleet than there is at St Pancras. A bag which will sail through the X-ray examination at St Pancras will, when filled with pretty much the same contents, have to be opened and searched at Ebbsfleet. I made this point to a supervisor once and he became very defensive, looked as though he were ready to ride off into the sunset on his high horse, and announced ponderously that he took umbrage at my remarks. I think he felt that anyone who doesn't believe that leafing through assorted lingerie is going to save the civilised world must be a dangerous anarchist. He wanted my name for his report and insisted that if the people at his station did more searches it was because they could be more thorough because they weren't as busy. Neither argument seemed to me to offer much in the way of reassurance or explanation. And do the border guards really think that it might be possible to hijack a train with a small penknife? Where would I take the train? 'Drive this train to South America' just doesn't make much sense. And why does no one bother to search the cars and lorries which use the Channel Tunnel? Would it not be possible to hide more explosives in a ten ton lorry than in my suitcase? Just asking. Far too few people make the effort to complain about all the nonsense that goes on. At the Gare du Nord recently a bag fell off a trolley being pushed by a woman ahead of Antoinette in the queue to go through the customs check. Antoinette moved forward to pick up the bag and put it back into place. 'Don't touch it!' screeched the woman, who was clearly terrified that Antoinette might stuff her bag with drugs. Most people have spent so much of their lives being thugged by bullying civil servants and rule hugging bureaucrats that they live on the defensive. As I went through the barrier a female guard told me to remove the train tickets from my shirt pocket. Ye gods, are train tickets now a threat to the security of our weak and feeble nation?

After having my stuff pored over (as now seems usual) I put my bits and pieces back into my suitcase and wondered if anyone had ever thought that terrorists might actually pack their invisible Semtex into the frame of their suitcase. They never really examine suitcases properly and often miss one of the zipped compartments completely. (Here's an odd thought: the people doing the searching will sometimes claim that they're looking for drugs. What do we care if people are smuggling drugs out of England?)

I then joined Antoinette at the customs desk. 'Where are you going?' demanded the man in the uniform. Since there was only one train we could be catching and since it was going straight to Paris, without a stop, I was reminded that the people hired for this work are not the brightest in the world.

The whole customs/border/search/security farce is now an industry, doubtless with its own lobbyists, so it will now never end. Has there ever been a Government department as incompetent and as replete with self-important bullies as the UK Border Agency? Why hasn't the entire staff been fired for gross incompetence?

No one in authority seems capable of rational thought when it comes to questions of security. I remember the idiot Blunkett, who was Home Secretary at the time, sending tanks to Heathrow airport to prevent planes being hijacked. And during the Olympics a gunboat was moored on the river Thames and missile launchers were erected on top of East End tower blocks. Were the army really planning to shoot down planes over London?

The truth is that at airports and railway stations, the whole intimidating ordeal helps to keep us all frightened and compliant, and though I expect that some who have not yet worked out what is going on in our society will regard that as a sign of paranoia I would point out that paranoia is only one step up from suspicious and that suspicious is one step away from having men in uniforms kick down your front door at four in the morning.

Next time we travel I think I'll put a disarticulated skeleton in my case. That should cause some entertainment. Or maybe a blow-up doll, folded to fit into the case and filled with helium would be more fun.

25
We're in Paris.

I ran a bath this evening, while sorting through some of the mail which had been awaiting us and stepped into the water without checking the temperature. This was a mistake. I yelped with surprise and I pulled my foot out so quickly that I nearly fell over backwards. The water was stone cold. I told Antoinette the bad news. 'The boiler has gone on strike.'

Boilers, like most things, invariably break down within seconds of the warranty running out and the problem is nearly always something exceptional and mysteriously expensive. It really is very clever the way manufacturers do this. I think they fit a tiny clock somewhere inside and when this has ticked its way to a day or two after the end of the warranty period it triggers a small explosion which does something damaging and expensive. In the last decade or so we seem to have done very little but buy new boilers. In one twelve month period we bought four new boilers for four different properties. None of the machines which was replaced was old enough to go to playschool but all ended up making a one way journey to the knacker's yard.

We don't have a boiler service contract in France because the last company we paid was always unwilling to satisfy their end of the bargain. They were excellent at reminding us that we owed them money but far less enthusiastic about sending a man out whenever we had a boiler or plumbing problem. I wasn't too worried about not having a contract because every time I empty our mailbox it seems packed to the brim with little cards promoting the services of electricians, plumbers, central heating engineers, carpenters and experts who will open your front door if you've lost your key (and who, presumably, turn up carrying their tools in bags marked 'butin' which a French burglar friend tells us is the French for swag).

I picked out one of the recent cards and dialled the appropriate number. The man who answered the telephone was very helpful and promised to send an engineer around within the hour.

When they arrived there were two of them and the minute I saw them standing in the hallway I knew we were in trouble. Generally speaking I am probably the most naïve person I know. I believe people when they tell me things. When the garage told me that we needed a new petrol tank for our old BMW 7 series saloon I believed what they said. When they told me that they were having great difficulty in finding a replacement tank I believed them. And when

29

they rang me, two hours later, and told me that they'd found one in Germany but that having it flown in would be very expensive I believed them and agreed to pay up. An acquaintance who works in a garage laughed himself silly when I told him how lucky I'd been. Apparently the 'we've managed to locate one in Germany/Japan/America/Swaziland' is the oldest trick in the garage trickster's book.

But this time I knew I was in trouble. First, there were two of them. No reputable central heating company sends two engineers to an evening call. And second, the one who talked, a black guy with a small, neatly clipped moustache, smiled when he saw me and greeted me with a warm handshake. He carried a smart leather briefcase in the other hand. This is not the way things are normally done in France. Heating engineers carry tons of stuff with them but it's packed in metal tool boxes or black nylon holdalls. They don't arrive clutching a banker-style briefcase. On the other hand, the other man, white, smaller, considerably older and dressed appropriately in a boiler suit, did look and behave like a central heating engineer. He carried a small tool box and neither smiled nor shook hands. The one with the little moustache looked as though he had done his apprenticeship selling cheap models of the Eiffel Tower from a blanket spread out on the pavement. His father and his father's father probably worked the 'find the lady trick' from an upturned cardboard box. He didn't need a peg leg, a hook instead of a hand and a parrot for me to spot him as a pirate.

I showed them into the kitchen and pointed out the cold boiler. What else could I do? The small one, the one wearing overalls, messed with the controls as though trying to work out what they did. He then tried to pull the front cover from the boiler. Since it is screwed in place this didn't prove effective and nor did it soothe any of my doubts. I was beginning to wonder if he knew anything at all about boilers. The one with the moustache, who had been busy smiling and shaking hands with Antoinette, asked to see our circuit breakers. I showed him. He looked at them and turned one or two of the switches on and off as if he knew what he was doing.

Eventually, the man in the boiler suit managed to remove the front of the boiler. He stared at the innards as though rather shocked at what he'd found. I'd seen them before and they always look pretty much like the inside of any other boiler to me. He looked confused,

30

as though he had been expecting to find something else. A couple of chickens, a cupboard full of crockery or a well-disguised television set, perhaps. He fiddled around for a couple of minutes and then removed the circuit board. He handed it to his moustachioed colleague, who did that sucking in air and head shaking thing that workmen of all varieties do when they're about to rip you off mercilessly and want you to know that the bill is going to be astronomical.

'Your circuit board is finished, ended,' he told me, in French, with all the gravitas of a doctor dishing out the bad news to a concerned patient. In case I hadn't understood he shook his head and pulled a face.

'Can you repair it?' I asked. I don't know why I asked. I knew the answer.

He shook his head.

'It is impossible to repair and very expensive to replace,' he told me. 'It will be 890 euros for a new circuit board and then we have to charge you more for the fitting. But we can fit you an entirely new boiler for 1790 euros. Plus the labour charges, of course. This is a much better idea. If we replace the circuit board something else on your boiler could break.'

I stared at him, unable to hide the disbelief.

'And it is very difficult to obtain the circuit boards,' he said. 'But we can fit a new boiler for you this evening.'

I stared at him. The boiler was no more than three-years-old. Just old enough to be out of warranty.

'You need to make a decision now,' said the man with the moustache. The chap who had the screwdriver and who had managed to remove the front from the boiler folded his arms and stood staring at me.

'I think we'll leave it,' I told him. 'We can't possibly afford so much money.' I tried hard to look aged, frail and impoverished and I think I managed this quite well.

The man with the moustache stared at me for a while, frowning. Then he repeated the spiel about the circuit board being beyond repair and virtually irreplaceable. He offered again to fit a new boiler that very evening. Once more I declined. Eventually, he shrugged and took out an invoice pad. 'I have to give you a bill for the call out,' he said. I nodded. He put the invoice pad down on our kitchen table and took a calculator out of his briefcase. Two minutes later he gave me the bill. It was for 392 euros. They had been in the flat for less than half an hour. I stared at him and very nearly laughed out loud. He showed me a price list which was quite different to the price list that had been printed on the small card which had been put into our mailbox. 'It is after eight o'clock in the evening,' he explained. 'The hourly rate goes up after eight o'clock.' I looked at the price list I already had and pointed out that although it was stated that there was an extra, extra charge for work done after midnight or on bank holidays there was nothing about an extra, extra charge for calls after eight. The price on the card was 29 euros per hour. The man with the moustache looked at my price list and examined it very carefully. He handed it to the engineer. They both examined it as though it were something I might have printed myself. I asked for it back and put it into my pocket.

'I will pay you 100 euros,' I told them. 'That's it. Not one euro more.' It was a hefty price for nothing but I just wanted to get rid of them. Just then my mobile telephone rang. I answered it. A Scottish woman with an almost impenetrable accent asked if I could spare a few minutes to take part in a marketing survey. It was the third time she'd telephoned that day and on each previous occasion I had told her, quite politely, that since it was almost certain that she was ringing on behalf of an energy supplier I wasn't interested in taking part. 'Bugger off and leave me alone,' I snarled this time, completely out of patience and goodwill to all men. I turned off the telephone. Out of the corner of my eye I could see that Antoinette had picked up a walking stick and had opened one of our windows. I thought I knew why. The man with the moustache shook his head and demanded the 390 euros. I picked up the telephone and rang the police. Neither he nor the man dressed as a plumber looked at all concerned by this. We waited, the four of us, and nothing was said or done for a few moments. I was still waiting for someone to answer the telephone which was still ringing. And then the man with the moustache and the briefcase shrugged, ripped up the bill he'd written out and wrote out a new one for 100 euros. I handed him the cash. He took it. And, after shaking hands, they left. The engineer winked at me. The man with the moustache gave me a number to ring the following morning if I changed my mind. He insisted on shaking hands.

'What were you doing with the stick and the open window?' I asked Antoinette.

'I was going to hit them with the stick if they became violent,' she replied. 'And if that didn't work I was going to climb out of the window, scramble along the ledge and knock on the window to the apartment next door.'

I closed the window and gave her a hug. I told her that there had been no need to worry because I had been preparing to feign a heart attack or, possibly, a fit.

I then checked out the boiler manufacturer's website. The circuit board which the two men had wanted to replace was readily available at a retail price of 130 euros.

26

I woke early, went through the French Yellow Pages and found another central heating company. I picked the one with the least impressive advertisement. They made no promises. I checked them out on the internet. They had been in business for a few decades and their office was only five minutes away. I rang. They said they would send round a man that morning.

Their engineer arrived, alone, by mid-morning. He carried his tools in two plastic bags and, despite this, looked like a man who mended boilers for a living. It took him five minutes to discover that a fuse had gone in the circuit board. He showed me the faulty fuse, replaced it with a new one, worth about 50 centimes, and the boiler started purring again. He told me that I could either pay for the repair or pay for a one year service contract that would include the cost of the repair and guarantee that a man would visit any time we called, including on Saturday up until lunchtime. I asked him how much the service contract would cost. He told me it would be 136.17 euros for the year. I wrote out a cheque. He left.

Ten minutes after he'd gone the con man with the moustache telephoned. He wanted to know if we'd changed our minds and would like him to come round to fit the new boiler. You have to give some people top marks for trying. I told him that we couldn't afford a replacement circuit board or a new boiler because we were impoverished and English. I said we would just have to bathe in cold water and wrap ourselves in blankets. He did not seem in the slightest bit concerned at this, of course, and simply told me to ring him if and when we found the money. I didn't bother telling him that we'd had the fuse replaced and that the boiler was now working happily. I have absolutely no doubt that if we had allowed him to take away our 'useless' boiler he would have repaired it, put it into a box and sold it to some other poor sucker at a premium price. And the replacement boiler we would have received would, of course, have been someone else's 'useless' boiler.

27

I was delighted to see that the authorities in Paris have decided to let the grass grow in public spaces, and to encourage wild flowers to grow too. The aim is to encourage wildlife – particularly birds and butterflies. What an absolutely brilliant idea. Why should all grass be cut short enough for bowls? Not many cities have as much grass, or as many parks, as Paris but it would heartening to see one or two mayors in Britain following this excellent example. They do so many things with aplomb and style in France. I see today that Christine Lagarde, the French boss of the International Monetary Fund has been in court over a little delicate and embarrassing naughtiness involving 403 million euros. I couldn't help comparing this to Britain where politicians find themselves in trouble for claiming expenses for a packet of biscuits and collection plate donations. The French do these things so much better than we do.

We wandered down to the river Seine in the afternoon, intending to catch the Batobus service along to St Germain. But there was a massive queue for the river bus, which has, I regret to say, become much more popular since I mentioned it in my book 'Secrets of Paris'. So we changed our plans and headed across to the Trocadero. As we did so we passed a queue of rickshaws waiting for customers. The rickshaws, now commonplace in Paris, are a real sign of a future without oil. Maybe we will soon have pedal driven trains. The passengers in second class will have to pedal faster than the passengers in first.

In the park just below the Trocadero we noticed the Aquarium Paris. It looks rather run down and at first glance seemed closed. We've passed by several times but never before felt the urge to go inside. Today, however, we decided to see what was inside. It was, quite truly, a revelation. Neither of us has ever seen a more impressive display of fish. There are sharks, moray eels and a whole host of unusual creatures I'd never seen before: a blue spine unicorn fish, a lemon peel angel fish and a foxface rabbit fish! To defend the reputation of the unfortunate shark, the Aquarium has published a list of the creatures which kill most human beings every year. (I rather suspect that dogs really ought to appear on the list. And I'm surprised that crocodiles aren't on it. But it's their list, and here it is.)

1. Mosquito – two million deaths
2. Snake – 100,000 deaths
3. Scorpion – 5,000 deaths
4. Elephant – 600 deaths
5. Bees – 400 deaths
6. Lions – 200 deaths
7. Jellyfish – 100 deaths
8. Shark – 10 deaths

28

Today we decided to visit the mayor's office so that we could arrange to pay our annual property taxes by direct debit. Each arrondissement in Paris considers itself to be a village and has its own mayor. You might think that this would be an easy task but the French, bless their cholesterol clogged hearts, like to make a ceremony out of everything they do and it is simply not possible to be properly ceremonial if you do things over the phone or through the post. After registering at the entrance desk we were given a ticket and showed where to wait. Sitting in official places always tries my patience, which is never strong at the best of times. It has long been a theory of mine that time is the most important currency in the world; the only currency that really matters. I hate wasting a moment of it. At 2.59 p.m. I looked at my watch. After about six hours I looked at it again and it read 3.02 p.m. I suspected that we would be there for days. To my surprise, however, we waited no more than 15 minutes before we found ourselves in a booth sitting opposite a bureaucrat straight out of central casting. If Jacques Tati had still been alive he would have put this guy under long-term contract. He could have played any number of standard French council officials, railway employees and postal clerks with consummate ease. I explained that I wanted to pay both our taxes automatically. The first tax is the Taxe d'Habitation. This is an annual residence tax which is charged on the occupier of every property in France. The idea is that you pay the tax on whatever property you are living in on January 1st of each year. But, since this is a French tax, it is still payable on any property you own and could be living in even if you're not actually resident there on January 1st. This doesn't make a good deal of sense but in France very little does. The second tax is theTaxe Foncière. This is an annual tax which must be paid by the owner of a property, whether or not they are resident in the property on January 1st or, indeed, any other date. You and I may not be able to spot much difference between the two taxes but to the French the Taxe Foncière is completely different to, and entirely separate from, the Taxe d'Habitation which is paid by the occupier of a property on January 1st each year, whether or not they are actually occupying it on January 1st. Naturally, these two taxes are paid separately and involve different forms and bills and, almost certainly, different departments and different bureaucrats. Our bureaucrat of the day was, however, prepared to overlook the regulations and to deal with both taxes all at once and pretty well at the same time, though naturally there were a good many forms to fill in and a good deal of rubber stamping and stapling and photocopying to do and it all had to be done twice. Filing cabinets had to be opened, colleagues needed to be consulted and boxes had to be ticked and signed. If you've ever seen the film *Avanti!*, starring Jack Lemon, you'll know just how much rubber stamping an enthusiastic continental bureaucrat can get through when he puts his mind to it.

In the end we were finished and on our way in just under the hour, which I thought was pretty good going for such a complicated and hazardous procedure as setting up a direct debit. We now live in hope that come the autumn, when the taxes are due, the Mayor's office will succeed in taking the money we owe straight from our bank account (in two separate transactions, of course). If they don't succeed they will doubtless send us two separate bills and we will send them two separate cheques. We will then go back to the Mayor's office and try again. Maybe next time we should go twice.

When we got back to the apartment I found a note from one of the many busy body organisations set up under the auspices of the EU. This one wants to send someone round to check that we know how to turn our gas on and off. I gather there is to be a 15 minute tutorial on the subject. These people write to us every few months and I usually ignore them. This time, however, I have sent them a jolly fax reminding them that English is now the official language of the EU and that if they write to me again they should, therefore, do so in English. I will, of course, also expect my tutorial to be conducted in English though if my hearing deteriorates any further I will need it to be in 'signed' English.

29

In Paris the elderly do not spend their days slumped in plastic armchairs watching awful quiz shows on the television. Instead of heading off to the local nursing home at the first sign of maturity, they remain in their apartments, surrounded by their treasures and memories, and continue to look after themselves. They value their independence, do the Parisians, and even though it might take them a couple of hours to walk two hundred yards to the shops, buy their baguette, cheese and bottle of wine and then totter back home, they do it with dignity and pride. The daily walk to the shops is an important part of their lives. They look after their appearance, too. The residents in British nursing homes always look as though they've just clambered out of bed. Hair is never brushed and women don't wear any make-up. It's a habit, a state of mind and a result of the fact that no one around them gives a damn or encourages them to give a damn. In Paris, there are hairdressers and shops selling cosmetics every few yards and I would guess that many of their best customers are in their seventies and eighties. There are at least half a dozen 'coiffeurs' and 'magasins vendant des produits cosmétiques within a ten minute stroll of our apartment. The elderly dress smartly (women never wear trousers and would rather be in a coffin than wear anything beige or elasticated) and they aren't too proud to use those colourful shopping bags on wheels so that they don't have to carry heavy bags back from the shops. Both our local ironmongery shops reckon that shopping bags on wheels are among their best selling items.

I am completely convinced that it is this independence which keeps the elderly fit in mind and body. Folk who live in British nursing homes are encouraged to live like children. They get up, have breakfast which has been prepared for them, and then slump into an armchair where they spend the day staring at a dozen other sorry souls sitting in armchairs. Occasionally, they are wheeled into the dining room or handed a cup of milky tea. Twice a week an excessively cheerful young woman turns up to conduct an exercise class which consists of a little half-hearted arm waving. And once a week a volunteer conducts a bingo session. Onward and downward. That's no life for anyone; it's barely even living. I much prefer the Parisian way.

In Paris, on my daily trip to the supermarket and the boulangerie I frequently see the same totter of elderly citizens doing their shopping. Most are alone. I suspect that many live alone and shop by themselves because their loved one has gone on ahead to better things; gone to find a nice apartment to rent on a quiet cloud. Or maybe one half of a couple goes to the shops and the other, less agile, stays home and lays the table.

There are, of course, a few old married couples who do their shopping together; hand in hand or arm in arm. And two elderly ladies who live (in separate apartments) in our building go to the shops together every morning simply because they are so frail that they literally need the support. One is in her late eighties and the other is in her early nineties. They walk very slowly, more of a shuffle than a walk, looking around them, chatting, enjoying their daily journey, and they hold tightly on to each other. Two legs are better than one but four legs are better than two. The assistants in the shops always have time for them. No one hurries them if they struggle to pull their purses out of their bags. The assistants help them pack their purchases. Other Parisians smile, say 'good morning' and give them the space they need.

As I walked to the supermarket this morning the two elderly ladies had finished their shopping and were heading back home. Each carried an old leather shopping bag that had done many years' service. Each one had a baguette poking out of the top of her bag. They were holding onto each other. Behind them strolled three British women in their thirties. They were enormously fat, dressed as if for a disco, and pointing at the two old ladies and laughing as if they'd never seen anything so funny in their lives. I suppose it was the fact that the two old women were obviously holding up each other that they found so funny. Or maybe it was the fact that they were shuffling along, creaking knees hardly able to lift their feet up from the pavement. The three British women tried imitating the old ladies. They shuffled their feet and they held on to one another. They thought this was all terrifically funny. Even though they were touching one another they shouted as though they were a street apart. Their nastiness, their malice, appalled me and not for the first time I found myself ashamed to be British. Why, I wonder, do we now lead the world in our ability to mock and to sneer, and in our contempt for the elderly? These are not skills in which we should take pride.

In referring to the elderly I should declare an interest. When I look in the mirror in the morning I often wonder why I am forever shaving the face of an old man I do not recognise. And if I bang a toe my nerve pathways are so worn out and decrepit that it takes ages for the pain message to reach my brain. Long enough for me to have time to choose a suitable expletive for the moment when the pain finally arrives, and time too to put two soluble aspirin tablets into a glass of water. I suspect that if things deteriorate at the present rate there will be soon be time for the aspirin to start working before the pain arrives. A pre-emptive strike I think they call it in the military.'

30

It was an unusually warm and sunny day so we went to the Luxembourg Gardens. The gardens are formal and elegant but we go not for the flowers but for the people. The Luxembourg Gardens seem to be a magnet for really odd folk and every time we go there we are entertained by the passing show. There's usually a couple practising their tai chi, a man going through his aikido moves and a man pretending to be a tree. The last time we were there we watched a man practising his rumba steps with an imaginary, entirely invisible, partner. He seemed to be enjoying himself enormously and as far as we could tell his partner was having a good time too. Today, we sat on a bench beside the tennis courts, had a picnic luncheon which we had brought with us, and watched a couple of blokes playing tennis. This was nothing like the tennis you'd expect to see at Roland Garros or Wimbledon but it was far, far more entertaining. The professional stuff I can take or leave. The ball travels so fast that half the time I can't tell where it is or who is doing what to it. Amateur tennis, particularly low level amateur tennis, is all about the people rather than the ball.

The two men, who both looked to be in their late twenties or early thirties, weren't good at tennis. In fact, they were so bad, so mouth gapingly terrible, that I have a suspicion they may not have played before. The one on our left was wearing a pair of knee length Bermuda shorts that looked as if they were made with material a manufacturer of Hawaiian shirts had discarded as being too loud, and a T-shirt with the message 'Ne regardez pas a lui – me regarder!' On his feet he wore brown brogues with white socks. The player on our right was wearing a pair of luminescent heliotrope swimming trunks that had either shrunk in the wash (which seems unlikely since one might reasonably assume that bathing trunks are made of material which isn't likely to shrink when it has been in contact with water) or were not large enough when they were bought, and one of those tennis shirts which has, for reasons which I have never understood, a reptile on the wearer's left breast. The shirt was mainly white but had blue and yellow stripes. This one wore those plastic clogs that are, for some peculiar reason, popular with those environmentalists who haven't yet realised that plastic comes from oil and the oil is running out. I have described the two players as the 'one on our left' and the 'one on our right' since these two were not sufficiently aware of the niceties of the game to realise that it is customary, every now and then, for the two players to change ends.

For a while the two men played by themselves rather than together. One would hit the ball but it would either go into the net or soar way over the head of the other. After a while the other would then hit the ball but that too would either go into the net or be too high or too wide for the other player to reach. They tried serving but both gave that up when it seemed clear that the chances of their actually hitting the ball were close to non-existent. They then both reverted to bouncing the ball and then hitting it as it came up off the ground. All this took some time since they only had one ball and consequently the player on the other side of the net had to wait until the ball had somehow made its way over or around the obstacle and into his half of the court. Finally, after about a dozen shots each, our two heroes succeeded in having what might perhaps be described as a primitive sort of rally. The player on our left managed to hit the ball over the net and the player on our right succeeded, certainly more by luck than judgement since he had both eyes closed at the time, in hitting the ball back over the net. It actually landed in the doubles tramlines but it did made its way over the net and the opponent, the player on our left, then managed to knock it back again. Was this a rally? The official definition of a rally in tennis is 'an extended exchange of strokes' but in these circumstances I think we could describe three shots as constituting a rally. It wasn't, perhaps, the sort of stuff that would have had a Wimbledon crowd on its feet but Antoinette and I were mightily impressed. We put down our sandwiches and clapped heartily.

At this point the two players started to take themselves seriously. They had, I think, mistaken this serendipitous rally as a sign that they were getting the hang of things.

The player on our left fingered the strings of his racquet and examined them very closely, as though he had found some fault in the tension of the catgut or whatever else it is that they used to string racquets half a century ago (which was, I suspect, about the time when his racquet was made). He called to his opponent, waved his racquet, shouted something we didn't hear, and then disappeared from the court.

While he was gone the other player took off his plastic clogs and examined them closely. I have no idea what he was looking for. When he had done this he took them off and then hobbled, in his socks, to the bag he'd left on one of the chairs within the confines of the court. He put the shoes down on the floor and took a pair of plimsolls out of the bag. The plimsolls were black and reminded me of the sort of footwear which was compulsory when we had gym lessons at school. He then sat down on another chair and slipped the plimsolls onto his feet. I don't think they were his plimsolls because judging by the trouble he had squeezing his feet into them there were at least two sizes too small. He stood up and walked about it, like a customer in a shoe shop trying on a new pair of shoes. He then sat down and waited for his partner to return.

After a delay of five minutes or so, the player who had been on our left returned to the court. He was still carrying the racquet with which he had left with but now he had an additional two racquets in the other hand. He examined all three racquets very carefully, checking to see that there weren't any unexpected holes and testing the tension in the strings, before putting the two new racquets down

41

beside his bag and returning to the court carrying the racquet he'd been using when he'd been playing before.

The two men then played another rally. This time the rally only consisted of two shots but when both players have difficulty in hitting the ball over the net, and even more difficulty in hitting it back again, it seems fair to describe an exchange of shots as a rally.

Exhausted, and perhaps excited, by this repeated success the player on our right decided that it was now his turn to leave the court. With a wave of apology to his companion he hurried off, and disappeared. I have no idea where he went but he reappeared a few minutes later carrying a pair of wrist bands. He made a great show of putting these onto his wrists, adjusting them and making sure that they were satisfactorily positioned for best aesthetic and sporting effect.

And so, properly and comfortably equipped, they continued with what they probably regarded as a game of tennis. Sadly, things did not go terribly well and there were no more rallies. The ball made its way over the net a couple of times but on neither of these occasions did it make its way back again.

All too soon our two players had run out of time. Another pair of players was standing at the entrance of the court, looking at their watches, shaking them ostentatiously, and making it clear that they were in a hurry to get on with things. Our two picked up their bags, their rackets, their spare shoes and their ball and they left.

The two replacements weren't any fun at all. They were both dressed in Wimbledon white. They carried proper tennis bags, replete with racquets and wrist bands and towels and tubes of brand new balls. They knocked the ball around for a while and then started in earnest. They served properly and clearly knew how to play. Watching them was boring and since we had by now finished our picnic we put our rubbish in a nearby bin, put what was left into our shoulder bags, and left.

31

The Eurostar service between Paris and London is excellent. It is far, far easier to travel between the two countries by train than it is to fly. Indeed, I cannot understand why airlines continue to have customers for their flights between the two capitals. There is, inevitably, une mouche dans la soupe. And in this case the mouche is quite definitely the UK Border Force, which has a presence at the Gare du Nord as well as at the English end of the line.

The French have their own border control staff, of course, but for reasons which absolutely no one can understand, the British Government insists on double checking all travellers. The British staff are far more trouble than the French ones and infinitely more offensive and troublesome than the Roma beggars who hang around outside the station hassling travellers. There are never enough passport inspectors (most of the available booths are invariably empty and shut), the ones who are there are usually rude, slow-witted and bored out of their skulls and as a result there are invariably lengthy queues to get through the UK Border Control. The hiring policy at the UK Border Force seems to be to employ the sort of sad, dumb bastards who would be working night time security for a tyre storage depot if they hadn't lucked into civil service jobs. Their prize: a uniform, a pension and a chance to ooze insolence and arrogance. Things aren't helped by the fact that the border clerks always seem to be working to rule and examining passports as though expecting every single one to be a forgery and every traveller to be a high ranking member of Al Queda en route to blow up the Houses of Parliament and throw sticky toffees at the Queen. (In contrast, the French clerks who examine the passports of travellers who are leaving the UK are remarkably lackadaisical. Just for fun, Antoinette and I frequently go through customs using each other's passports. If anyone ever notices we simply laugh and say it was a mistake. But they rarely do spot the difference.)

The authorities claim, of course, that their rudeness, their authoritarian notices and their high handed approach are all a necessary part of the war on terrorism. The plan, presumably, is that terrorists will be put off by the rude reception and will turn round and go back home in a sulk. This is, of course, utter bollocks. Terrorists are stronger and far tougher than the authorities seem to believe. Any hope that the uniformed fools examining passports might spot terrorists and send them back home is also wishful thinking. The idiots manning the UK Border Force booths wouldn't spot a terrorist if a man in a mask wandered through carrying a rocket launcher. ('It is a present for my niece's birthday party. She likes fireworks. This one will make a lovely big bang and send down sparkly stars.') The truth is that Britain's absurd duplication of the passport checks conducted by French officials a few feet away is clearly political rather than practical. No stranger would ever guess that both countries are enthusiastic members of the European Union.

At the increasingly unpleasant and unfriendly Gare du Nord today, we found ourselves facing the usual lengthy queue at the passport desk. (The station has been recently redesigned and I suspect that the 'improvements' were made by bin-men using stuff they'd salvaged from council tips. The new furniture they've installed in place of the old seating may have a function but it isn't providing something for people to sit on.)

Today's problem was largely caused by a bad-tempered looking woman customs officer who was examining every passport offered to her as though it carried a secret blueprint for an invasion. When it was eventually our turn to be officially ignored I asked the woman her name. 'What do you want it for?' she demanded, rather startled. I said nothing but just stared at her and took out a pen and notebook. I then repeated the question. Nervously, she told me. I nodded at her, wrote down her name, showed it to her so that she could confirm I'd spelt it correctly and then put my notebook and pen away. 'What do you want it for?' she asked, looking very uncomfortable and handing me my passport with hardly a glance. I took the passport, gave her the 'dead eye thousand yard' stare, picked up my bag and walked away. My dead eye stare is pretty good. Even goldfish have been known to quail before it.

I find that this simple technique is the best way to alarm officious, pompous servants of the people. Nothing worries an official more than the thought that they might be investigated by their own system. It is, of course, perfectly true that the pen is only mightier than the sword when the other guy doesn't actually have a sword but much in life is dependent upon belief rather than reality. People who work in a bureaucracy know only too well just how unfair and unjust their system really is. Most would rather face a poke in the eye with a dirty loo brush than an internal investigation. I wish more travellers would face up these authoritarians with dignity. I have an awful feeling that most people would strip naked and walk through customs on their hands and knees if told to do so by an idiot in a uniform.

Surprisingly, it wasn't the border guards whose inefficiency and incompetence caused our train to be late. That was the fault of a pair of elderly Americans who turned up with two trolleys piled high with luggage. I lost count of the number of bags they had with them but it took the train staff many minutes to cram the suitcases into the available racks. Only when they had checked the way their bags had been stowed, and had ordered some adjustments, did the two travellers wander along the carriage and take their seats. 'Are you moving over here?' I asked. The man, who was still trying to ease his eighteen month pregnancy into his seat, stared at me as if I were madder than I undoubtedly am. 'We're on our vacation,' he told me, gasping and wheezing with the effort. 'We're seeing Europe.' I nodded and asked him how long their vacation would last. 'We've been here a week and we've got another week to go!' he wheezed.

February

1

Our boiler in the UK has stopped working. It is presumably jealous of all the attention the French boiler has recently received. I telephoned British Gas and they sent round an engineer who discovered that the engineer who had fitted our new towel rail and radiator had not sealed the thing properly. The result has been that water has been leaking, the system has lost pressure and the boiler has shut itself off. The new engineer explained that our brand new radiator doesn't seem to have a valve that is waterproof but is, instead, fitted with a smart looking but leaky chromium plated end piece. 'You can have a nice looking cap or a waterproof one,' he said. We chose the one that didn't leak. What a pity that the people who make these things don't make valve caps which are both waterproof and handsome. Still, I suppose that would be a lot to ask. William Morris will be rotating.

2

I found a little card which had been pushed through our letterbox. It came from a delivery driver for one of the many courier companies which are taking over now that hardly anyone trusts Royal Mail any more (even if they can afford its outrageous prices).

We have a note permanently fixed to our front door asking delivery drivers to leave packets and parcels in a large box, tucked safely into a nearby stone nook. But the driver had refused to do this because the company which had sent the parcel had demanded a signature. This is happening more and more often (presumably because so much stuff is being stolen en route) and is extremely annoying because it means that we always have to remain alert for someone knocking on the front door. And if we are in the garden it is quite impossible to hear a caller, however hard they knock. If the delivery was something valuable I could understand the need for a signature but the parcel contains nothing more valuable than a 10 kilogram bag of sunflower hearts for our bird feeders. Since we live in the middle of nowhere, the sunflower hearts will be at risk only from the squirrels and the birds themselves. And if there is a squirrel or bird alive that can carry away a 10 kilogram bag then we are all in deep, deep trouble.

3

A former Goldman Sachs trader is suing the bank for $16.5 million. His complaint is that his bonus for the year 2010 was smaller than he had expected. The trader, a 35-year-old called Deed Amin Salem, apparently told his mother that he was due a $13 million bonus but was aggrieved when he received a paltry $8.5 million. It seems that Salem, who had previously boasted about how he had successfully 'played' the 2007 mortgage crisis in America, is peeved not so much about the money he hasn't had but about the fact that he'd told his mum that he was getting $13 million and then he had to confess to her that he'd only got $8.5 million.

It's clear from this and from other recent news stories that bankers still don't understand why they are now hated more than estate agents and traffic wardens. The Goldman Sachs philosophy, for example, doesn't appear to have changed at all. The plan is simple. First, you do an outrageously profitable deal that scrapes the barrel of morality but makes $10 billion profit. Second, after five years of legal battles and a wide variety of complaints and accusations you pay $100 million in damages to settle the whatever it is, being careful to make sure that the authorities allow you to continue to deny any wrong doing even though you've settled. This gives you a nice $9.9 billion profit. In a sane, civilised world the entire staff of Goldman Sachs (excluding, of course, the poor souls who sweep the floors and clean out the lavatories) would be hung, drawn and quartered. Bankers have damaged every aspect of our society. So, for example, it is bankers who encourage company executives to buy other companies ('you have to expand, develop a global presence') and then, when things go wrong, to sell them ('slim down and focus'). It's all done for the fees; with no regard for the employees who are, inevitably, made redundant.

4

I read yet another article promoting vaccination. The writer, a journalist, claimed that vaccination has saved millions of lives and that parents who don't have their children vaccinated are unfit to be parents. If you say something is true often enough people will believe you. And so, thanks to articles like this one, it is widely believed that vaccination, vivisection and medical screening are all 'good things'. In reality there isn't a shred of evidence to show that any of these are useful or effective. Indeed, there is loads of evidence proving the exact opposite. Sadly, any doctor who dares to breathe a whisper about this in public is likely to find herself being pilloried by the General Medical Council. As a result medical journalists are able to continue to help propagate these dangerous myths. I'm a little surprised that the GMC hasn't tried to censure me for writing my book *Anyone Who Tells You Vaccines Are Safe and Effective is Lying. Here's the Proof.* I suspect that they've kept quiet because they know that everything in the book is true. The medical establishment would score an own goal if it tried to punish me for writing it. But it isn't like the GMC or the medical establishment to show such good sense.

5

Astonishingly, eight per cent of recent university graduates had at least one parent accompanying them when they went to their first job interview. Nearly half of those had one or both parents sit with them during the interview itself. I wonder how many of them took their parents with them on their honeymoons. I wonder if the parents accompanied their children on their first day at the office? And I wonder if it is politically incorrect to suggest that we have bred a generation of wimps.

6

We opened a joint account with Barclays. I know they're a bunch of crooks but there isn't much choice these days. The words 'banker' and 'crook' are synonymous. And so are the words 'banker' and 'incompetent'. Barclays posted us two plastic cards and two PIN numbers so that we could operate the account. All four items arrived in the same post on the same day together with a note warning us: 'Do not keep your card and PIN number together'. I wrote to Mr Barclay suggesting that it might be a good idea to consider posting the PIN numbers a couple of days apart from the plastic cards. I very much doubt if they will take any notice.

7

WHO research has shown that up to 25% of the $4.1 trillion of public money spent on health care is lost to corruption. I am surprised that they seem surprised by this. I proved long ago that an even greater percentage of NHS money is lost, wasted or stolen by scoundrels and thieves. The WHO has also predicted that the incidence of cancer will double over the next twenty years. They seem surprised by this too, though it has for years been patently clear to anyone with functioning cerebral tissue that since the number and potency of carcinogenic chemicals in our air, water and food is rising, the incidence of cancer must inevitably continue to rise.

8

Japan has eight million people over the age of 80 and nursing and rest home beds for just 300,000 people. The other 7,700,000 must live at home, wander the streets or get themselves arrested and put in prison. The problem is that the modern Japanese don't seem to like old people very much. This is probably the only thing that we as a nation have in common with the Japanese. I read this morning that Japanese girls who are still single are now renting boyfriends to take home to show their mums. They are apparently doing this so that their mothers do not think they have been left on the shelf. The average rental fee for a boyfriend is 300 yen a day. Most rented boyfriends will hold hands and hug without any extra charge and will kiss for a small extra fee but there is, apparently, a standard charge of 30 yen for talking to old people. I have decided that in future I will charge 300 yen to speak to anyone from Japan, or to attempt any sort of conversation with anyone under the age of 25.

9

I have reached an age when I spend much of my life spring cleaning. This morning I spent a couple of hours sorting through my book shelves and DVD collection and putting the ones I won't ever read or watch again into plastic bags to take to a charity shop. 'You're getting rid of stuff but I'm still collecting,' said Antoinette, who is much younger than I am. But, inspired by my clear out, she spent this afternoon doing her own spring cleaning. 'I've changed my mind,' she said. 'I too have reached the throwing out stage.'

10

I called into Lloyds Bank in Cheltenham, took out my cheque book and asked the teller to give me £1,000 worth of euros. He leant across the counter, so that no one would hear him. 'Our rate is 1.15,' he said. 'You can get 1.18 at Moneyshop just down the road.' So I went there, where I saved myself the cost of a few glasses of vin chaud and a couple of expressos. Not bad for a three minute detour. Plus, there is the added bonus that it makes a pleasant change to stuff a bank rather than be stuffed by one. It is hardly surprising that Lloyds Bank staff are no longer loyal to their bank. I feel sorry for counter staff at banks. They are frequently berated for the sins of their absurdly dishonest and overpaid bosses and to be honest it isn't difficult to see why. I discovered a couple of days ago that, on top of all its other sins, Lloyds Bank has now been fined £218 million for manipulating interest rates. The vastly overpaid traders at the bank even fiddled the special rate that the bank was paying to the Bank of England when Lloyds was toying with bankruptcy. (I found this particularly astonishing. Crooks at the bank were deliberately cheating the authorities who were helping it survive!)

While I was in the bank I tried to change some commemorative £5 coins I had found at the back of a drawer. (I am always amazed at the stuff which finds its way to the back of my drawers.) The coins are supposed to be legal tender but the bank wouldn't touch them. Later on I tried the Post Office. They wouldn't change them either. So I dropped them off at a branch of the Blue Cross charity in the hope that someone there would know of a way to turn them into real money. Or maybe they could just sell them as curios. I find it appalling that the Government flogs us commemorative coins which have a face value printed on them but then turn out to be absolutely worthless.

Antoinette and I had parted to do some shopping and when we met she looked embarrassed. She was carrying a large inflatable cat. She started to explain, though no explanation was needed. It looked to be a very smart, inflatable cat. 'Don't worry,' I told her. 'I've bought you a talking rabbit.'

11

We are told that it will take 14 years to build HS2, an upgrade to the main railway line which connects the north of England to the south.

Any project which takes that long will cause enormous disruption and will, inevitably, cost ten times as much as the original estimate. I'm not surprised by this news. It took contractors years to put up a few speed camera gantries on the motorways near Bristol. While they were doing this the Government must have made a fortune in fines because the whole area was littered with speed cameras. Now that they've finished it has become clear that the whole idea of a 'managed motorway' is to create as many long queues as possible. Whenever the traffic is running smoothly the computer, programmed by the Russians, the Chinese or quite possibly a bunch of malicious Martians, clicks into action and puts up a sign telling motorists that the speed limit is now 60mph. Or maybe the software was written by a 12-year-old who simply wants to create the world's largest traffic jams. What happens is that the 60 mph limit inevitably, and predictably, produces the beginnings of a traffic jam the computer clicks in again and puts up a sign reducing the speed limit to 40mph. Brilliant! This produces huge queues, totally screws up the motorway and costs the country billions in wasted fuel and lost working hours. (Occasionally, when this happens, it will be possible to spot a vehicle safely parked on the hard shoulder. The authorities responsible for reducing the speed limits don't seem to have worked out that the hard shoulder is there for precisely this purpose.) The silver lining is, of course, that the associated speed cameras produce vast quantities of ever welcome moolah for the constabulary and so in future all Policemen's Balls will be bigger and brighter than ever.

The HS2 upgrade will take forever because there must be many meetings where dull people in suits can sit around considering every possible eventuality. There will be planning considerations to examine, and health and safety considerations galore. Whole forests will have to be cut down so that reports and memoranda can be written and circulated widely. The Chinese, of course, would have done the motorway work in a weekend and the railway upgrade would have taken about the same length of time.

We used to be able to complete huge engineering works as quickly as the Chinese, of course. In May 1892 the Great Western Railway converted the entire London to Penzance railway line (a distance of 300 miles) from seven foot wide broad gauge to standard four foot ten inch gauge in 31 hours. They did it quickly in order to avoid disrupting travellers. Workmen had to lift the rails, move them and reattach them to railway sleepers and they had to do all this without the aid of cranes or health and safety experts in smart suits.

The railway company was, of course, left with a good deal of rolling stock which no longer fitted the rails. They held an auction in Gloucester and tried to sell seven first class carriages, six second class carriages, six third class carriages, three horse boxes, one passenger engine, one goods engine, twenty nine high sided wagons, eight low sided timber wagons and a number of carriages and wagons. Sadly, there were absolutely no bidders at the sale.

12

A local man who wanders the streets with a placard forecasting the end of the world has changed the date of Armageddon. Previously, his poster and leaflets suggested that all would end last December 31st. He is now predicting that the end will come in five years' time. I told him that I was pleased to see we are now safe for a while longer. He told me that the delay was entirely a result of his prayers and shook a tin at me for a contribution. I believe that all eccentrics need to be encouraged (before the EU has them all locked up) and so I popped a couple of quid into his collecting box. I can't remember when or where but I am certain this isn't the first pundit who has been forced to change his end-of-the-world-forecast.

13

A few weeks ago Antoinette went into a charity shop in Barnstaple, bought a skirt she liked and, because she wasn't in a hurry and the shop was quiet, spent some time chatting to the volunteer shop assistant, a woman in her 80s. It turned out that the assistant had read a few of my books and enjoyed them and so the next time Antoinette visited the shop she took her a bag of my books as a gift. The two then started to exchange emails.

While this was going on Antoinette was still trying to persuade me to allow my books to be turned into e-Books. Massive Royal Mail price increases for parcels finished off our mail order business, though massively increased prices for advertisements (and many bans) didn't help, and it has for many months looked as if our publishing business is over. At the height of my self-publishing business I employed 17 people and had a turnover approaching £1 million a year. Now Antoinette and I were putting the books in jiffy bags ourselves; and making a loss. With no other hard or paperback publisher in the UK it also looked as if my books would only be available to British readers who managed to find second-hand copies in bookshops or on the internet. I am still selling foreign rights to publishers abroad but I refuse to offer my books to British publishers or agents who are, generally speaking, arrogant, patronising and decidedly snooty about anything which has been self-published. (Actually, some years ago I started to describe myself as 'an independent publisher' in the same way that people who make their own films call themselves 'independent film-makers' and I am pleased to see that this smarter sounding nomenclature has now been fairly widely accepted.) I have a fine collection of dismissive letters from 19-year-old editorial assistants working for agents and publishers. 'If you ever want to have your book published you should buy a copy of *Writers and Artists Yearbook*, wrote one neophyte publisher, ignoring the fact that the book I'd sent for consideration for their paperback list had sold nearly 70,000 hardback copies in the UK alone. 'We see no market at all for these old-fashioned books,' said another sniffily, returning one of my Bilbury books after a long delay. Publishers deserve to go bust. And I have no doubt that they, along with literary agents, will soon disappear from our world. Much real estate in the environs of Bloomsbury will suddenly become available. It has for some time been clear that no author needs an agent or a publisher to help them produce an e-Book. What will all those utterly talentless and pointless Fionas, Deborahs and Felicitys do for a living? In the last year, 98 British publishers have gone bust – that's a 42% rise on the year before. The industry leaders usually blame the recession for this and hardly ever mention the true cause: e-Books. The truth is that e-Books have liberated self-publishers and will destroy publishers, agents, bookshops, wholesalers and libraries. Today no one knows, or cares, if a book is self-published. All they care about is whether they want to read it and what it's going to cost. There is no conceivable reason for authors to continue to use publishers – except for the fact that publishers do help to ensure that new books are instantly greeted with a raft of five star reviews from staff and 'friendly' reviewers.

I had a choice. Sit and sulk and do nothing or abandon myself to e-Books.

I contacted a large company which specialised in producing e-Books but the experience was deeply dispiriting. I sent them a total of 29 emails but we were still no closer to seeing any books being converted. They seemed more interested in creating emails than in creating e-Books. I was also worried about the fact that in addition to wanting big upfront fees they also wanted substantial royalty payments on the books they were converting. I could see the process dragging on for years and ending up with me earning little or nothing from my books. In the end I abandoned the whole thing and, with great sadness, told Antoinette that my books would have to die.

And then it turned out that R, the octogenarian Antoinette had met in Barnstaple, was a world-class computer wizard. Antoinette asked her if she knew anything about e-Books. She said that she didn't but kindly offered to find out what was required.

That was a few weeks ago. And now the first electronic versions of my books are beginning to appear on Amazon. Since Amazon now sells around 90% of all the e-Books sold, and since their Kindle device is the clear market leader around the world, it made sense to start by publishing our e-Books exclusively on Amazon. And, although I don't specialise in doing things that make sense, that is what we're doing. I have opened a publishing account with Amazon, and Antoinette and her octogenarian friend are learning fast about how to convert traditional books into e-Books, how to create covers and so on. I have no idea what is going to happen but I have to admit that it's exciting.

14

A Japanese company is now making a doll which ages. Over a period of twelve months the doll slowly acquires wrinkles and skin blemishes which can be removed with special creams and injections. The company is apparently also planning to produce a doll which can be enhanced with 'cosmetic surgery operations'. I'm sure it will be very successful.

15

A bloke I know who produces e-Books has shown me some research which proves pretty conclusively that most of the really bad reviews which are given to e-Books come from readers who obtained their books free of charge. (The bad news for authors and publishers is that the vast majority of readers never pay for the books they read. They only download books which are being made available free of charge – usually as a promotion for the author.) This really isn't much of a surprise, of course, since most people tend not to value highly anything which they obtained free of charge. There is, I suspect, an optimum price for appreciating a book. If you pay too much then your expectations will be too high and you will be easily disappointed. If you pay too little you will have little or no respect for the author or the book. What is perhaps surprising is the vehemence with which many of the one star reviews are written. Readers, who often admit that they haven't finished the book they are reviewing, and who frequently boast about the fact that they didn't pay a penny for it will, in addition to damning a book with a one star rating, attack both the author and the book in the most vitriolic of terms. My pal has also discovered that the majority of really nasty reviews (the ones which can kill a book's sales dead overnight) are written by a very small number of women who will apparently stick in the knife, the stiletto heel and whatever else comes to hand, with enormous enthusiasm. In a way this isn't particularly surprising. My chum points out that it has been known for years that most of the really horrid newspaper profiles are written by female journalists.

16

I planned to sit in the bower in the garden today and to do a little quiet reading but all the neighbours for miles around seem to have set up a rota for mowing, strimming and cutting hedges. As soon as one whiny piece of machinery stopped another started and so on, hour after hour. Wouldn't it be nice if everyone agreed to mow their lawn and do their strimming and hedge trimming on the same half day or the same evening. I'd be quite happy to put up with a cacophony for a few hours if I knew that it wouldn't happen again for another week.

17

Most people tend to think of psychopaths as being exceptional individuals – slobbering at the mouth and rushing around cutting people up and eating their livers. In fact a fifth of the population are psychopaths. If you know five people then the chances are good that one will be a psychopath. If you know 20 people then you will know four psychos. It isn't difficult to identify them and I have listed the salient signs and symptoms several times in other books (such as '2020'). Psychopaths are exceptionally selfish, constant liars, manipulative, callous, grandiose and parasitic. They bully, they are never anxious, and they are invariably likeable. They seem strong, calm and confident but they lack personal insight. They never learn from experience and they never show remorse. The problem today is that our society is well suited to psychopaths – who can, and often do, easily rise to the top in politics and business. Most of our Ministers and company directors are psychopaths. They get to the top because they don't care about people in the way that sensitive folk care. And that, inevitably, gives them an enormous advantage – a killer edge. It's interesting too that lie detector machines don't usually catch psychopaths – they are just too good at lying to be caught by a machine.

18

I went into a small shop today and stopped dead in my tracks. A huge and nasty looking Doberman was sprawled just inside the doorway and I really didn't like the look of him. In order to get into the shop I would have had to step over him. He could have easily posed for pictures as the Beast of Bodmin Moor. Or he could have definitely taken the lead in the Hound of the Baskervilles. He was drooling and when he eyed me up I definitely got the feeling that the saliva was there so that he could digest a couple of my limbs more readily. 'Is that your dog?' I asked the man behind the counter. He grunted something which sounded like an affirmation in Neanderthal.

'He looks pretty fierce,' I said.

'Guard dog,' said the shopkeeper.

'He looks as if he might bite.' I said.

'Wouldn't be much good as a guard dog if he didn't would he?'

This seemed logical but it wasn't much comfort, so I left.

I wonder how long it will be before the shop goes bust.

19

We were sitting in a café and Antoinette had a form to fill in. In our wonderful paperless world it is, of course, almost impossible to get through a day without filling in a form or two. She asked if she could borrow a pen. I handed her one of mine (I rarely leave the house without at least half a dozen assorted pens and pencils though I am relieved to say that these are never arrayed in my breast pocket) and asked her idly if she needed a new refill for the pen she'd been using earlier. (I'm afraid I usually carry a few spare, assorted refills too.) She said something which I didn't quite catch. I asked her to repeat it. She looked a little embarrassed and then told me that earlier in the day she'd gone into a church to pray for a friend. The church has a table on which there is always a pile of small cards and a pen so that visitors can write out a prayer and leave it in the church. There was no pen. Someone had taken the pen that should have been there. And so when she had written out her message, Antoinette had left her own pen on the table. It wasn't just any old pen; it was a favourite pen, favoured not because it was expensive but because of the pictures of cats which were painted on the side of it. I'd given it to her a few months earlier.

'I had to leave it,' she explained. I nodded. I understood. And then I rummaged around in my shoulder bag, took out an identical pen and handed it to her.

'It was like this?' I asked.

'Exactly like this!' she said, holding the pen and beaming with delight. 'Where did you get it from?'

'I bought a spare,' I told her.

20

Every week the landlords in 31 British public houses cry 'Time, gentlemen please!' for the very last time. Sometimes, it happens more than 31 times and sometimes rather less. But it's 31 on average. There are now fewer pubs in Britain than at any time in the last century – around 57,000 at the last count. Some of those who worry about the incidence of alcoholism will doubtless be cheering at this news, but they're making a huge mistake. Britons aren't drinking less alcohol than before – they're just buying it from supermarkets and drinking it at home or in the street. And when booze is bought in a shop it is invariably cheaper than when it is bought in a pub. As a result people drink more of the stuff. And so the incidence of alcoholism (and the huge range of physical and mental disorders associated with heavy drinking) is soaring. When we lived in Weston-super-Mare the number of empty beer and lager cans thrown into our front garden steadily rose. When a new supermarket opened nearby the number of empty cans rocketed.

21

For a couple of decades now my toenails have been infected with the athletes' foot fungus. I suspect I picked it up at a public swimming pool. I've tried everything to cure the problem but I've refused to take anti-fungal tablets because I don't like the side effects. They really are nasty. If I'm going to wreck my liver I'd much rather do it with a good malt whisky. The creams and varnishes I've tried have been utterly useless and my toenails have gradually become increasingly discoloured and disfigured. They have become so bad that for some time I have felt confident that if I found myself threatened by muggers I would only need to take off my shoes and socks to scare them away. And then a few weeks ago Antoinette had a brainwave.

'The athletes' foot fungus doesn't like sunlight, does it?'

I agreed that most fungi don't like sunshine. They grow best in dark, moist places.

'That's probably why the fungus affects toe nails, and hardly ever affects fingernails?'

'Yes.'

'So why not give your toes some sunlight?'

I agreed that the idea sounded worth a try.

And then Antoinette, who is a creative genius, had another brainwave. She dug around on the internet and discovered the details of an ultraviolet light device designed for drying painted fingernails. I bought one. And for a week or two I've been putting my toes into the machine. It seems to be working. The fungus really seems to be retreating and my toes no longer look as if they belong in a horror museum. Moreover, my toes now have a nice sun tan too. Incidentally, I don't suggest that anyone else try this at home (or in the car or anywhere else for that matter). It is undoubtedly dangerous, illegal, politically incorrect, unreasonably harmful to fungi and likely to lead to an increase in money laundering and tax avoidance.

22

I telephoned Lloyds bank hoping to be able to move some money from one account to another. This is never easy to do and I often wonder just whose money it is. Today was no exception. 'Why do you want to move the money?' asked the woman to whom I spoke. 'What are you going to use it for?' I thought for a moment. 'What size bra do you wear?' I asked. I could hear her bristle. There was the sound of breath being drawn in sharply. 'That's a very impertinent question!' she said. 'And has nothing to do with you!' I could sense her already preparing her official complaint. 'Absolutely,' I agreed. 'One impertinent, irrelevant question deserves another.'

23

Our DVD player has developed a fault which means that every thirty minutes or so it stops working. The only way to make it start again is to hit it quite hard. (I have found over the years that much electrical equipment responds well to a good thump.) I went into the living room this evening to find that Antoinette had moved her chair forwards and had equipped herself with a broom handle.

'What on earth is that for?' I asked her, pointing to the broom handle.

'It's the new remote control for the DVD player,' she explained. 'It means I can give it a bang without having to get up out of my chair.'

I have always said that my wife is a genius and here is yet more proof. I was going to buy a replacement DVD player but now there is no need.

24

I am pleased to see that the argument for either the decriminalisation or the legalisation of drugs such as heroin is gathering support. It's about time. It has been clear for decades that the law does nothing to prevent drug use but merely turns drug users into criminals, helps keep the price of illegal drugs unreasonably high and supports the gangs who import and sell drugs. Thirty odd years ago I wrote a series of articles and leaflets (and even a couple of books) explaining precisely why criminalising drug use was harmful. I was, inevitably and predictably, widely attacked by many of the same people who are now advocating a change in the law.

25

I'm not an envious person. Up until now I don't think I've ever seen anything and said or thought 'I want that!' But all that has changed. I've seen the most amazing miniature silver railway. There is a vast expanse of track, a train and a number of wagons. The train was made by Armstrong Whitworth and Co for the Jai Vilas at Gwalior and it was built to carry port and cigars around the dining table. If a guest reached out for a refill or a fresh cigar the train would stop automatically. How utterly, totally brilliant. Far, far better even than the silver-encrusted bed designed for the Nawab of Bawalphur. The bed had full sized naked female statues at the four corners. And the statues were designed to fan the Nawab while he lay in bed. The bed might appeal to some but I don't think it is a patch on the silver train set which may well be gloriously indulgent (OK, it obviously is) but it would have satisfied William Morris's demands in that it is both beautiful and useful. I want it. Though since the track is about the length of a cricket pitch we might need an extension to the dining table and, indeed, to the house.

26

Sorting out some old papers I've just found this sad letter which my Dad wrote. It was sent to the charity, the NSPCC, which had written to him asking for money. This is what it said: 'Please forgive me not responding to your appeal for support. My wife died earlier this year after a long illness ending for 18 months in a nursing home. The total cost of care which the great, British NHS could not afford to pay, amounted to £50,000. Please remove my name and address from your files. I am 87 years of age and unlikely to accumulate enough funds to be able to contribute to yours.'

27

This morning, I found another piece of paper from my Dad's old files. This one shows that his car failed its MOT test at Pollits Devon Diahatsu Centre in Exeter. The garage failed the car (causing massive inconvenience to my father) because: 'Offside lower windscreen has a sticker or other obstruction encroaching into the swept area by more than 40mm outside zone A.' The refusal form was signed by someone called P.J.Spencer. The 'sticker or other obstruction' was actually my Dad's cardboard disability parking badge, which he had left visible, propped up against the windscreen. Unfortunately, I didn't know about this until my father had died. But it still makes me angrier than I can put into words.

28

I found this wonderful Author's Note at the end of *The Last Juror* by John Grisham.

'I took great liberty with a few of the laws that existed in Mississippi in the 1970s. The ones I mistreated in this book have now been amended and improved. I misused them to move my story along. I do this all the time and never feel guilty about it, since I can always disclaim things on this page. If you spot these mistakes, please don't write me a letter. I acknowledge my mistakes. They were intentional.'

Wonderful. Love it.

March

1

We were had to go to London for the day and I'm afraid I now find it a depressing, dirty, tawdry and rather frightening place. I used to enjoy visiting the capital but I suspect that today even Dr Johnson would find himself eager to be somewhere else. Buildings everywhere look shabby and run down and cafés are dirty inside and outside. I knew and loved London in the fading years of its glory, when it was still a proud city, steeped in culture and history. Today it looks like a scruffy transit camp for indigents. Successive mayors and governments have simply destroyed it as a city. One of the saddest aspects of London today is the absence of trees and birds. There are lots of trees in the big parks, of course, but few in the streets, where leaves might fall onto the ground and make a mess. Only a few hardy pigeons and sparrows have managed to survive the war against birds which has been fought by successive mayors. (The end of civilisation began when an old lady was arrested for feeding the pigeons in Trafalgar Square. The end was completed when the authorities at Lord's Cricket Ground allowed advertising people to paint slogans on the grass. Nothing has been the same since then.) Today, only the Chinese and Japanese tourists now feed the few remaining birds for the British know that throwing a scrap of food to a sparrow is likely to result in an arrest, a fine and, quite possibly, a term of imprisonment. The city stinks, the air is filthy and clogged with fumes and the noise is infinitely worse than in any other city I can think of. The city's emergency service vehicles don't seem to go anywhere without using sirens. The drivers probably put their sirens on when going home for tea. And the noise of these sirens, considerably greater today than it used to be, is so intense and urgent that it seems designed not as a warning to move aside but to cause the maximum amount of stress and panic. I wonder how many people die because of these constantly screaming sirens. I wonder how many lives are shortened. And I wonder how many accidents occur because motorists and pedestrians simply don't know which way to move or whether to move at all. Whatever the answers to those questions might be, the end result is that the city vibrates with the noise and everyone is in a constant state of fear.

As an elderly, white Englishman I confess that I felt out of place and unwelcome in a city I used to love. Multiculturalism has not added to our culture but has detracted from it. We went into a shop to buy drinks and I overheard an Asian shelf filler talking to two colleagues about a forthcoming England football match. 'I hope England lose!' he cried with a laugh. His two colleagues immediately agreed with his blatantly racist sentiment. (It is, of course, perfectly acceptable for visitors and immigrants to say derogatory things about the English without any fear of being officially accused of racism. It was long ago decided that England no longer officially exists and so the English have absolutely no rights.)

On the way back to the railway station we listened in mounting horror as our taxi driver conducted an increasingly emotional telephone conversation with someone at Nat West bank. The bank had apparently made an error which had resulted in his credit rating being adversely affected and the driver, who was trying to get a mortgage to buy a new house, was explaining that unless the bank corrected the error, and removed the stain from his credit rating, he would either be unable to continue with the purchase or would have to pay a much higher rate of interest resulting, as he pointed out, in an eventual cost running into many thousands of pounds. He was told that it would take three weeks to correct the error on the computer. (A task which, I suspect, would require no more than one or two key strokes.) This conversation, clearly enormously distressing to the driver, continued as he drove through busy London traffic with tears in his eyes. As the call ended the driver, half turned and spoke to Antoinette and myself in the back of his cab. 'I'm sorry about all that,' he said. We told him we understood and sympathised and I suggested that he telephone the chairman of the infamous Royal Bank of Scotland (which owns Nat West) and make a complaint to the top of the organisation. I explained that complaints which filter down always seem to be resolved more speedily than complaints which have to work their way, slowly, up through a reluctant bureaucracy. We both felt so sorry for this poor cab driver. I wonder how many thousands of people have similar conversations every day. Banks, utility companies and other giant organisations care little or nothing for the welfare of their customers and when they make mistakes, which they do with astonishing frequency, they often cause unending misery, stress and, in the end, ill health by refusing to take responsibility for, and to correct, their errors. The arrogance and incompetence of the people who run these organisations never fail to astonish me and I am frequently appalled at the indifference of call centre staff who are clearly devoid of humanity and empathy. The irony, of course, is that in their own lives these individuals are, of course, as vulnerable as everyone else. The uncaring gas company employee suffers at the hands of the indifferent hospital employee who suffers at the hands of the indifferent telephone company employee. Are these people, I wonder, all taking revenge when they use their own power to ignore mayhem in their customers' lives? As we left the cab, sorry for the driver's plight, I couldn't help thinking that allowing drivers to use hands free telephones is crazy. The unfortunate sod driving our vehicle had been so distracted by his conversation that it was a miracle we hadn't hit anything. Maybe the cab, after a few hundred thousand miles of experience had, looked after itself.

Our rail journey home was delayed and our guard explained that the problem was sudden and unexpected congestion at Reading. How do the lines at a railway station become congested? Did trains suddenly converge on Reading and get in the way of one another? I understand only how too well how congestion can develop on the roads. But I thought trains always followed well-thought out time tables. One train has to be in Manchester at 7.16 p.m. and another needs to chug into Bristol at 7.17 p.m. It is rather alarming to think that trains can wander about willy nilly, converging unexpectedly on the hapless Reading, and creating congestion for weary travellers. Is it only Reading which suffers in this way, or are all stations similarly affected by marauding trains?

When we eventually arrived back in Stroud we discovered that in order to reach our car, which had been parked in a small car park outside the front of the railway station, we had to cross a footbridge. We could find no alternative. No lift. No escalator. Just a steep flight of steps going up, a bridge across and a steep flight of steps going down to ground level on the other side of the tracks. A frail and elderly couple struggled to cross with their heavy suitcases. A young woman dragged her pram up the steps. Travellers helped one another as much as they could. I've had a faulty knee for a month now, and it had been improving slowly, but clambering up and down the steep stairs of that bridge brought back all the pain. I suspect my knee (long past its sell-by-date and undoubtedly well out of warranty) will, as a result, be bad for another month or more. I've had tennis elbow, golfer's shoulder and swimmer's ear and now I've got runner's knee. I'm going to use a walking stick. If I carry a stick I can hit people with it when they annoy me, which many doubtless will. Who is going to complain? 'A pensioner hit me with his stick' always sounds so pathetic. They'll get laughed at and I'll get all the sympathy. It is only when we are temporarily disabled in some way that we really understand the plight of those who are permanently disabled. We always say we do understand, of course, and in our hearts we undoubtedly think we do. But there's nothing like a real chance to share the inconvenience or distress that others suffer on a long-term basis to arouse our natural feelings of outrage. How do people in wheelchairs cross from one side of the Stroud station to the other? Well, it appears that in the absence of a handy helicopter and hoist they must wheel themselves the best part of a mile around the town, crossing over a road bridge and then wheeling themselves up the hill to the other side of the station. Those who merely have bad arthritis or other disabilities can choose between this long trek and dragging themselves up and over the footbridge steps. How can this be allowed? If the railway station at Stroud was a sweet shop or a hairdressing salon the council would have forced them to provide access for disabled customers or to close their premises and stop taking any customers at all. Councils frequently close their own public lavatories on the grounds that they are not accessible to disabled users and, therefore, should not be available to able bodied ones. I wish someone would start a campaign to persuade the council to close Stroud railway station until the responsible railway companies do the decent thing and install a pair of passenger lifts or a pair of escalators. Faced with a massive loss of income and screams from hordes of angry commuters the problem would doubtless be solved in days. The Chinese would sort it in a day and have time for a firework celebration in the afternoon.

I sent an email of complaint to Stroud Council and received a reply from Ashley Nicholson, the Senior Community Safety Officer who wrote: 'Stroud District Council have no responsibility for the railway station and therefore are unable to comment on the provision provided relating to access for disabled users'. I wrote back expressing surprise at this abdication of responsibilities and asking if the council would take such a laid back attitude if a cafe, shop or theatre failed to provide any access for the disabled. 'I realise you don't own the station,' I wrote. 'But surely the Council has a responsibility to protect the welfare of citizens. If not then what is the Council for?' I received no reply.

2

The empty headed lunatics who are constantly screaming about the hazards of man-made climate change are now claiming that the planet is short of water because of climate change. This is arrant nonsense and there is no evidence whatsoever for this politically and economically convenient assertion. There is a global water shortage and there are two very good reasons for it.

First, the number of people eating meat has rocketed in recent years. What's that got to do with it, I can hear people crying. Well, it takes 924 gallons of water to produce one burger. All that water is needed to grow the feed to give to the cow who will become the burgers. Most of the planet's water is used by farmers who pay very little for it. And most of the water is used by farmers producing meat.

Second, more and more of the planet's rivers, streams, springs and lakes have been so polluted that the water in them is unusable. Water bills for household consumers are soaring in developed countries, and in many parts of the world water is a scarce commodity and unaffordable by ordinary folk.

The answer is awfully simple (as these things often are): every person on the planet should have access to cheap or free water for drinking, cooking and washing but should pay through the nose if they want to wash their cars or fill their swimming pools. And farmers and industries have to pay more for the water they use – then, maybe, they will stop wasting it and stop polluting it. The main trouble with the world is that someone put the grown-ups in charge. And most of them don't have the common sense of a six-year-old.

3

I rang our car insurers, to tell them that our address had changed. They charged £12.72 to change the registered address for our truck and £11.66 to change the address for our BMW. I am beyond complaining about these absurdities. There just isn't enough life to protest about all the bad stuff. No other company with which we do business has ever charged us to change an address. It would, of course, have to be an insurance company which found another way to gouge money out of its long suffering customers.

4

We've now distributed all the printed copies of my new book on the EU. Reviewers won't look at any of my books (partly because I am known to be a self-publisher and partly because my other books attacking the EU sold a lot of copies, proved extremely popular and so annoyed the EU's supporters) and so I published this one under a pseudonym. Actually, I used two names, just to confuse reviewers. How many people would imagine that one author would use two pseudonyms for the same book?

I called the book *The EU: The Truth About The Fourth Reich* and subtitled it *How Adolf Hitler Won The Second World War*. The authors on the cover are listed as Daniel J Beddowes and Flavio Cipollini.

Believing that the EU is by far the greatest enemy we have, we sent copies to MPs, to every public figure we could think of and every publication in the land. In view of the fact that the book shows the direct link between Hitler and the EU I took care to send it to every Jewish publication I could find, too. (To my enormous surprise none of them seemed much interested in the fact that the book shows conclusively that the modern EU was created by Hitler and other 1940s Nazis.) I don't think anyone actually bought a copy of the book but we have distributed the entire print run and the book has been given a considerable amount of coverage – especially on the internet where it has aroused interest in quite a variety of different languages. Nothing has happened though. And nothing will. The EU simply has too much power and too much money.

The basic theme of the book is that the EU has systematically and purposefully suppressed democracy and accountability, vigorously and ruthlessly separated authority from responsibility, authorised official bullying and introduced a seemingly endless variety of blatantly fascist policies. The amount of power any organisation has depends entirely upon what the leaders of the organisation are prepared to do to expand and protect that power. And the leaders of the EU are, like all good Nazis, prepared to do whatever it takes.

Hitler was the man who gave bones to the dreams first expressed by Charlemagne and Napoleon, but he finishing touches to the EU as we know it were put in place during World War II by a man called Walther Funk, who was President of the Reichsbank and a director of the Bank for International Settlements (BIS). It was Funk who predicted the coming of European economic unity. Funk was also Adolf Hitler's economics minister and his key economics advisor. The European Union was designed by Nazis and it has been carefully created according to the original design. It is not a 'group' or an 'association'. It was always a union. And in a union the members are not affiliated, they are joined. 'What good fortune for governments that the people do not think,' Adolf Hitler once said.

The EU's fans like to pretend that the fine points of the organisation were planned in the 1980s and 1990s. But that's not true; it was Hitler and Funk who designed the EU precisely as it exists today. The Nazis wanted to get rid of the clutter of small nations which made up Europe and their plan was quite simple. The EU was Hitler's dream but it was Funk who outlined the practical work which needed to be done. In my book (or, rather, in the book by Beddowes and Cipollini) I described, in detail, precisely how Hitler and Funk et al planned the EU and the euro.

In 1940, Funk prepared a lengthy memo called *Economic Reorganisation of Europe* which was passed to the President of the BIS (who was an American called Thomas McKittrick) on July 26th 1940. 'The new European economy will result from close economic collaboration between German and European countries,' wrote Funk. It is important to note that even then the EU was seen as a union between Germany, on the one hand, and the rest of Europe, on the other. There was never any doubt which nation would be in charge of the new United States of Europe. (The phrase United States of Europe was devised by Adolf Hitler himself). There are commentators and economists today who note Germany's control of today's EU with surprise, and who seem puzzled by the fact that Germany is booming and has by far the largest and most dominant economy in the EU. No one should be surprised because the EU was always planned that way. Germany is benefitting enormously from the euro crisis but Funk knew that would be the case. Back in 1940, Funk had the idea for the euro but warned that even after monetary union it would be impossible to have one standard of living throughout Europe. He knew that the euro would be flawed but he also knew that Germany would come out on top. He would not be in the slightest bit surprised by the fact that modern Germany is by far the largest and most dominant economy in the European Union. That was always the Plan.

In reality the euro was bound to cause chaos and massive unemployment throughout many parts of the European Union because of policies which German politicians set in process after the unification of West and East Germany and before the foundation of the euro. The policies, which were designed to enable a unified Germany to control the EU, involved Germany entering the euro at an advantageously low exchange rate, thereby giving it a huge competitive advantage over other euro countries. The aim was that Germany would get richer while other countries got poorer and that is exactly what is happening. (The French chose to join the euro with a strong franc because they felt it made them look 'big' and because it meant that they could enjoy cheap holidays in the rest of Europe.) The result is that because the euro is undervalued relative to the German economy, Germany exports far more than it imports and grows ever richer and stronger at the expense of its other euro 'partners'. Germany currently runs the world's biggest trade surplus – and has been running big surpluses for a decade. German politicians have refused to spend the money they have been accumulating and so other countries in Europe, struggling to cope with a euro artificially strengthened by a rich Germany, have slumped further and further into depression and their unemployment rates have soared.

The Germans are fighting hard to protect and preserve the euro, and will continue to pay money to preserve the status quo, because if the European currency breaks up two things will happen. First, Hitler's plan for a German dominated United States of Europe will be in tatters and second, the Germany mark will be as strong as the Swiss franc and cars and refrigerators made in Germany will be priced out of many markets. If the Germans can keep the euro alive then in due course, the inevitable will happen: Germany will have complete control of the European Union and Hitler will have a posthumous victory.

Economists, who tend to have a limited understanding of the world, are constantly producing articles expressing surprise at the fact that the euro was created at all and dismay that, despite all the evidence showing that it has caused enormous damage to countries and individuals, it is being kept alive. If they understood how and why the European Union was created (and who created it) they would, perhaps, have a better understanding of why it exists and why those who support it will fight to the death to preserve it.

Today, the EU spends billions every year on keeping its supporters happy. The BBC, a renowned supporter of the European Union, and an organisation which has confessed to being biased in the EU's favour, has received millions of pounds from the EU. The money is invariably described as being given as a 'grant' but the word 'bribe' might be more appropriate. The BBC repays this financial support by defending unpopular EU policies (such as those on immigration), by insisting that all measurements referred to in its programmes are in EU friendly metric units rather than proper British imperial measurements and by taking every opportunity to disparage England and the English. Joseph Goebbels, the Minister of Propaganda in the Third Reich, would have been proud of the BBC which is now an essential part of the Fourth Reich. Goebbels would have probably also been proud of the fact that scores of British universities have professors funded by the EU. The professors are paid to teach students the value of European integration. And, naturally, the EU has, over the years, spent many large fortunes producing literature and teaching aids for teachers to use in European schools. On the rare occasions when voters in European countries have been invited to vote on EU issues the EU has been the main contributor to 'Vote Yes' campaigns. In 1975, when Britons were last given the opportunity to air their views on the EU, the EU helped fund the 'Vote Yes' campaign.

It was back in 1941, when he was still planning the new European Union, that Walther Funk launched the Europaische Wirtschafts Gemeinschaft (the European Economic Community) to integrate the European economy into a single market and to establish his idea for a single European currency. It was almost entirely Funk who helped plan the European Union Community although when it was finally established he was still labelled a war criminal and still a resident of Spandau Prison in Berlin. It wasn't considered a terribly good idea to give him medals or to organise a thank you 'roast'. All subsequent suggestions that Funk be recognised as the founding father of the European Union have been rejected on the grounds that it is too soon to put up a statue to the man to whom Hitler handed the responsibility of ensuring the good health of the Fourth Reich.

Funk planned the EU in precise detail. It was even Funk who proposed a Europe free of trade and currency restrictions. In June 1942, German officials produced a document entitled *Basic Elements of a Plan for the New Europe* which called, among other things, for a European clearing centre to stabilise currency rates. The aim was to secure European monetary union and 'the harmonisation of labour conditions and social welfare'.

Hitler and the rest of the Nazi leadership welcomed Funk's plans and in 1942 the German Foreign Ministry made detailed plans for a European confederation to be dominated by Germany. In the same year a group of German businessmen held a conference in Berlin entitled *European Economic Community*. (The phrase 'European Economic Community had been first used by Hermann Goering in 1940.) In 1942, Reinhard Heydrich, who was head of the Reich Security Central Office and renowned for his ruthlessness against enemies of the State, published *The Reich Plan for the Domination of Europe* – a document which is notable for its remarkable similarity to the EU's Treaty of Rome. In March 1943, 13 countries (including France and Italy) were invited to join a new European federation which would be under German military control.

When the Nazis realised that they were losing the war they knew that they had to make a deal in order to preserve German domination in Europe. Thomas McKittrick, the president of the BIS, acted as go between and helped set up the negotiations. The underlying plan was to ensure that Germany dominated post-war Europe. Funk and his colleagues decided to talk about European spirit, liberty, equality, fraternity and worldwide cooperation as the basis for their planned European Union. They decided to agree to share power, and even to allow other countries to take charge for a while. The Nazis knew that all they needed to do was retain men in power in crucial posts. And this they succeeded in doing. In 1944 a secret conference was held in Berlin entitled *How Will Germany Dominate The Peace When It*

Loses The War. Rich and powerful Germans decided to move a huge amount of money out of Germany and to take it to America. (The money stayed there until after the Nuremberg Trials when it came back to Europe.) In August 1944, the heads of the Nazi Government and a group of leading German industrialists, met at a hotel in Strasbourg and decided to hide more large sums of money in order to pay for the fight for a German dominated Europe to continue if their country lost the war. The Nazis realised that their back-up plan for European domination would take years to reach fruition but they believed that if their military tactics failed then their subtle economic and political tactics would prove successful.

In 1961, President Kennedy told British Prime Minister Harold Macmillan that the White House would only support Britain's application to join the Common Market if Britain accepted that the true goal of the Common Market was political integration – Hitler's famous United States of Europe. In 1966, American President Johnson encouraged Britain's membership of the developing European Economic Community and Foreign Office civil servants in London decided that the 'special relationship' with the USA would be enhanced if Britain joined the Common Market. In 1968, the Foreign Office warned that 'if we fail to become part of a more united Europe, Britain's links with the USA will not be enough to prevent us becoming increasingly peripheral to USA concerns'.

It is also important to remember that the European Central Bank (ECB), (which today has so much power over European citizens) was designed and set up by the German Bundesbank, which was Germany's post war central bank. And the Bundesbank was the son of the Reichsbank which was the name of Germany's central bank before and during World War II. The President of the Reichsbank before and during World War II was, of course, Walther Funk. The ECB would probably have a Walther Funk Founder's Day if they thought they could get away with it and the only surprise is that Funk hasn't yet found himself portrayed on euro coins and notes. He has more of a right to appear on them than anyone else because they were his idea.

Today, thanks to the Maastricht Treaty, each EU member's gold reserves belong to the EU and are effectively controlled by the ECB. As planned, the ECB (grandson of Hitler's Reichsbank) is not democratically accountable to anyone. It is actually prohibited from taking advice from Eurozone Governments and the European Parliament has no authority over it. No one knows how the ECB makes decisions because everything is done in great secrecy.

There are some supporters of the EU who claim that the absence of democracy within the organisation was never the original attention. They are wrong. The EU was always designed to be an undemocratic organisation. It is the Anti-Democracy. Way back in 1950, Clement Attlee, Britain's Labour Prime Minister recognised the problems associated with the planned European unity. He said, when responding to the Schuman plan for the European Coal and Steel Community (the initial version of the EU): 'It (is) impossible for Britain to accept the principle that the economic forces of this country should be handed over to an authority that is utterly undemocratic and is responsible to nobody.' Churchill, too, was vehemently opposed to the plans for a united Europe.

The unwritten, unspoken aims of the European Union are to regulate every activity and to ensure that everything which every citizen does will be controlled by the State. The plan is to eliminate small businesses, small hospitals and small everything else. As far as the EU is concerned 'small is bad'. It is much easier for the State to control production and tax gathering if it only has to deal with large international companies. (It is hardly surprising that the executives of large companies are among the most vocal of the EU's supporters. In the UK, for example, they will often threaten to close down factories if citizens vote to leave the EU.) By licensing every occupation, and insisting that individuals pay annual licensing fees, the EU can control citizens and take in more taxes. Individuals who speak out or protest can be controlled by having their licenses withdrawn.

Back in 1945, Hitler's Masterplan was captured by the Allies. The Plan included details of his scheme to create an economic integration of Europe and to found a European Union on a federal basis. The Nazi plan for a federal Europe was based on Lenin's belief that 'federation is a transitional form towards complete union of all nations'. It is impossible to find any difference between Hitler's plan for a new United States of Europe, dominated by Germany, and the European Union we have.

Today, the tragedy is that we are being oppressed not by an evil Great Dictator (a Hitler) or even an obsessive revolutionary (a

Lenin) but by a relatively small army of nonentities sitting in offices in Brussels; nonentities who are led into battle by a cluster of professional bureaucrats who are (irony of ironies) paid by us to take away every ounce of freedom.

The eurocrats, who believe that procedures are everything and outcomes are nothing, have won and things will stay the way they are until the people of Europe find their voice, discover a real leader, and crush the most fascist, anti-democratic organisation ever created.

The EU has made us all poorer in every way.

I'm proud of the little book which we have published. But I doubt if many people will ever read it. Still, it's now available as an e-Book. (Still under the names Beddowes and Cipollini.)

5

Newspapers, television and radio are full of a story claiming that vegetarians are less likely to die early because the vegetables they eat make them healthier. There is some truth in this but, as usual, the nation's medical correspondents have missed the main truth. Vegetarians are less likely to develop cancer or have heart attacks not because they eat lots of vegetables but because they don't eat meat. The evidence proving that meat causes cancer, for example, is so exhaustive that in my book *Food for Thought* I was able to publish summaries of 26 relevant scientific papers which showed a direct link between meat and cancer. Sadly, this truth is only rarely aired in public. Advertisements for *Food for Thought* were 'banned' by the Advertising Standards Authority after complaints from the meat industry (which didn't like the truth being made available) and when I wrote a newspaper column drawing attention to the link, the Press Complaints Commission responded to a complaint from the meat industry by censoring me and the newspaper which had published the column. Neither body seemed interested in the facts or in the public's right to the truth. The incidence of cancer will continue to soar as more and more people around the world start eating meat. The incidence of cancer in Japan has already gone up for this reason and the same thing will happen in China.

6

A local police station reports that it now has a new 'custody suite'. And I read, separately, that the council scrapyard for unwanted motor cars is officially known as the *End of Life Vehicle Centre*. George Orwell would not have dared make up such nonsense. This bizarre news reminds me that it's about time we bought a new car. There's nothing wrong with the ones we have (and I love the Ford truck) but something new and exotic might be fun. The trouble is that just about all the cars on sale these days look the same. When I was a kid I could identify scores of different motor cars. These days they all look as if they've been designed according to some wretched EU template; which, of course, they have. I'm tempted to buy an old classic but there are one or two problems with this. The first is that I know absolutely nothing about cars. Whenever the AA man has to come I fail miserably at the first hurdle, feeling a complete fool when he asks me to open the bonnet and I have to dig out the instruction manual to find out how to do it. The only two technical words I know are radiator and carburettor and although I could probably answer rudimentary questions on radiators I don't have the foggiest idea what the second of these does or looks like. My last classic car was a 1956 Bentley S1 and that was fun but it would be a pointless purchase these days. I used to take it into a local garage and have a cup of tea in a nearby café while I left it connected to a hose through which heavily leaded petrol poured into the tank. A tankful of fuel would just about take me to the next garage. These days a motorway trip would be impossible because there are frequently gaps of over 50 miles between filling stations and a beautiful Bentley S1 would never make that sort of distance without refuelling. There must be something out there with a bit of pazazz.

7

I have been putting off calling the sweep because I have to ring him and he will doubtless be out, sweeping chimneys, and I will have to leave a message and he will ring back and we will fix a date and I will have to remember to be in and to listen for the knock on the door because the previous owners of our home took the doorbell with them and we haven't got round to getting a man in to fix a new one, and the sweep will get lost on the way here and I will have to spend ten minutes reassuring him that although there is a sign at the top of our lane saying 'unsuitable for motor vehicles' it doesn't really mean what it says and then he will ring again thirty seconds later and tell me that he's come across a sign repeating the warning and he will want to know if there is anywhere to turn around I will tell him there isn't and that there are 3,700 delivery vans dumped in a huge pit opposite our home because there is nowhere to turn round and he will laugh nervously and then he will be cut off because mobile telephones don't work very well down here and a minute later he will ring back because he's managed to climb a tree and get a signal and he will tell me that he is lost even though he is only a minute away from where we live and eventually I will talk him down the hill and then he will want to know where to park his van and I know that wherever he puts it a tractor will want to get past in five minutes time and when he's eventually parked he will come in and we will chat of this and that, including the weather, and Antoinette will make him a nice mug of tea and put some chocolate biscuits on a tray and he will want the loo and then he will go back out to his van to fetch his brushes and stuff (though why he didn't bring them in with him in the first place I will never know because sweeping the chimney is what he came for, after all) and then he will come back in and ask me to show him where the chimneys are and then he'll put a small dust sheet down in front of the fireplace and I will worry about whether I should wait and watch or go into my study and pretend to work but really just fret about what he's doing and how long he will take and how I will know that he has finished and whether he likes to be paid cash or by cheque because some workmen are offended if you offer cash because they think you are suggesting that they fiddle their taxes and some dislike cheques because the bank charges a fortune to cash them and then eventually he will finish and we will work out a way for me to pay him and we will chat a bit more and then he will go and I will discover that he has left his mobile phone behind and I won't be able to ring him to tell him this because he won't have a phone with him and I don't have a landline number for him and so I will have to wait for him for him to find a telephone box and ring and see if he left his mobile phone with us and then he will have to drive back to pick it up and all things considered that's why I've been putting off ringing the sweep.

That is the longest sentence I've ever written. It is probably the longest sentence anyone has ever written. But by cutting out full stops I have saved electricity and done my little bit to save the planet. Praise, in the form of a five star review, will be gladly accepted.

8

I have no idea why but I picked up a book by John Locke this afternoon. Locke said that the law is a contract between the people and the government. It occurred to me that the trouble these days is that the contract isn't worth the vast amount of paper it's written on because it's written to benefit one side only and so it isn't a contract, it's a command. If you or I break the contract we will be thrown into prison. But if the government breaks the contract they will simply change the contract so that they haven't broken it. That's not a healthy, sane or rational basis for society.

9

In London today the air was so thick that enterprising traders were chopping it into little cubes, sticking a flag on top of the cubes and flogging the resulting souvenirs to tourists. Air pollution is one of the many great unmentioned scandals of our time and Oxford Street has recently been shown to be the most polluted place on the planet – worse, far worse, than anything Beijing has to offer. Nitrogen dioxide levels, from vehicle pollution, are ten times the limit recommended by the European Union. We, wrongly, assume that legislation, notably the Clean Air Act of 1956, has banished forever the sort of smog that would from time to time blanket London and make it impossible to see your hand in front of your face. Politicians never discuss air pollution and the Government never does anything about it but today air pollution kills ten times as many people as die in road traffic accidents. Nitrogen oxide and the fine dust particles thrown out by exhaust pipes and boilers have been linked to cancer and circulatory disease. I wonder how many people realise that more people die as a result of breathing in our polluted air than die from alcoholism and obesity combined. How many know that the health costs of air pollution are considerably greater than the health costs of smoking. Most of the pollution comes from cars and lorries, of course, though a good chunk of it is industrial and aeroplanes play their part too. Winds ensure that pollution that started out on mainland Europe ends up damaging lungs in the English countryside. It could all be sorted out fairly easily, of course. We need to ensure that owners and drivers of vehicles which pollute are punished. The EU, ever eager to produce new legislation, could insist that the existing rules are obeyed and that instead of worrying about motorists travelling at 31mph, or parking outside the pharmacy for three minutes, the police are encouraged to do something about lorries belching out killer fumes. Sadly, my bet is that the EU will do nothing. Lobbyists for the transport trade are far too powerful and effective to allow anyone to interfere with their profits.

10

A motor racing spokesman said today that Formula I is helping car manufacturers move forward with new developments which will enable motor manufacturers to make great improvements to the family motor car. So we will soon all have tyres that wear out after 50 miles and engines which have to be thrown away when they've done 500 miles. The good news, I guess, is that the man from the AA will be able to change a flat tyre in 2.3 seconds.

11

I was standing next to some plants in a local garden centre when an elderly woman approached me. 'How high do those grow?' she asked, pointing to something I was not able to identify. 'I'm afraid I don't have the foggiest idea,' I replied. She looked disappointed. 'You look like a man who would know!' she insisted firmly, reluctant to admit to having chosen an unsuitable adviser. 'They grow to six foot four inches,' I told her confidently. 'Thank you,' she said. 'That's better. Why couldn't you tell me that in the first place?' She stalked off muttering something about needing a plant that would not grow so high. After she'd gone a few yards she turned back and spoke to me again. 'I'm 93,' she said. 'I'm rather frail for my age.'

12

It seems that our bankers are still stealing and cheating. Barclays Bank has been fined a modest £26 million after an employee fixed the gold price so that the bank would make more money. The same bank was recently fined £290 million for fixing interest rates so the fines seem to be coming down, and Barclays probably paid this one out of the loose change they keep in the top drawer. Heaven only knows how many individuals lost money as a result of this piece of brazen chicanery. What surprises me is that whenever a bank is found to have stolen or cheated it is fined (meaning that the shareholders lose money) but no one goes to prison. The bank pays a fine of a tiny part of the profit they've made and the thieves get to keep the loot they've stolen. On the other hand, if a little old lady feeds the pigeons in the park she'll go to prison. And if an old man can't afford to pay his television licence he'll go to prison too. Bankers, modern shylocks and shysters, are it seems, immune to all the usual laws of the land as well as the laws of morality. And in a way I'm not surprised, for the one group of people who are making money out of the thieving and cheating bankers are the lawyers. Firms of solicitors in London are making millions of pounds defending crooked bankers, and making sure that instead of the guilty individuals being punished it is bank shareholders who pay the price when the banks themselves are fined. The shareholders, of course, are largely pension funds looking after the savings of ordinary working folk. No one seems too bothered about the fact that the enormous fines being levied on banks – particularly by the American Government – will almost certainly result in at least one major bank going bust in the near future.

As an aside, we received two communications from Barclays this week. One tells us that they are reducing the interest they pay, and will now hand over just 0.25% on sums of £10,000. The other offers Antoinette a Barclaycard and tells her that she will have to pay just 34.9% interest on the cost of her purchases or on any cash she takes out.

13

My new Acer laptop broke. A message appeared on the screen telling me that it was on strike and would not be accepting any more words from me. I did everything I could to persuade it to cooperate but nothing worked. In the end I fetched a hammer and hit it very hard. I then put the wreckage onto the bonfire. I hate computers and wish fervently that Babbage, the damned idiot who invented them, had invented something useful instead. Everything computers do is complicated, time consuming and clunky. I cannot be the only person to have noticed, for example, that library book catalogues were far easier and quicker to use than modern, computerised systems. And the old-fashioned card catalogues never broke down either.

There is something rather strangely satisfying about watching a laptop disintegrate, melt and slowly disappear in the middle of a good bonfire. Afterwards, when I raked over the ashes, there was very little left of the damned thing.

14

One of the problems in Europe is that there are now powerful social, cultural, economic and political forces generating and sustaining mediocrity and suppressing originality and creativity. It is, inevitably, the European Union which must be blamed for this sad state of affairs. The result will be the continuing decline of Europe in contrast to the rest of the world. Thanks to computers, the collecting and sorting of information is vastly faster now than it was just a decade ago and bureaucrats, who can now quickly spot bizarre and possibly exceptional incidents, are quick to cover their backs by introducing regulations designed to prevent such incidents occurring again. The trouble is, of course, that the new laws suppress all sorts of honest, innocent activity. Everything is made considerably worse by the mass of lawyers ready, willing and able to encourage complainants and to represent individuals who believe that their rights have been infringed in some way. We live in a world designed by eurocrats for the profit of bankers and lawyers.

15

I dug out the lawn mower today to see if it would start. It never does, of course. No lawn mower I have ever owned has worked after the winter respite. While staring at it and wondering just how big a hole I would need to dig in order to bury it out of sight I remembered the instruction manual. I'm no great fan of manuals which seem, on the whole, to have been written by semi-literate Japanese octogenarians with long memories and hearts filled with hatred for English speakers, but sometimes there is no alternative. My Briggs and Stratton operator's manual frightened the life out of me. Here are some extracts from the first few pages:
* Fuel and its vapours are extremely flammable and explosive. Fire or explosion can cause severe burns or death.
* The engine exhaust from this product contains chemicals known to the State of California to cause cancer, birth defects or other reproductive harm.

* Starting engine creates sparking. Sparking can ignite nearby flammable gases. Explosion and fire could result.

* Engines give off carbon monoxide, an odourless, colourless poison gas. Breathing carbon monoxide can cause nausea, fainting or death.

* Rapid retraction of starter cord (kickback) will pull hand and arm towards engine faster than you can let go. Broken bones, fractures, bruises or sprains could result.

* Rotating parts can contact or entangle hands, feet, hair, clothing or accessories. Traumatic amputation or severe laceration can result.

* Running engines produce heat. Engine parts, especially muffler, become extremely hot. Severe thermal burns can occur on contact. Combustible debris, such as leaves, grass, brush etc can catch fire.

By this time I had reached page 5 of 88 and to be honest I was relieved that I hadn't been able to start the damned thing. I very gingerly wheeled the killer mower back into the shed and went indoors to make a cup of tea, being careful not to burn myself with the kettle. Antoinette and I have decided that the 'wild garden' look is definitely 'in' this year. The Ministry of Defence should stop buying jet planes and tanks and, instead, spend its entire budget on lawn mowers. The enemy wouldn't stand a chance.

16

I now have a new Toshiba laptop to replace my broken Acer. It's only been on my desk for half an hour and already I hate it. The keyboard is, of course, absolutely terrible. This, however, doesn't matter very much because I always plug in a proper keyboard so that I can have my laptop sitting on a pile of books and perched at eyelevel. The keyboard I'm using cost me £5 and is a million times better than the really crappy keyboard fitted to the Toshiba. I also hate the fact that pop-ups appear all over the screen every time I try to do something. Promotional rectangles for the blasted McAfee (which I loathe with a vengeance and which I swear I will never use) pop up with annoying regularity. I want a laptop to be as simple to use as a toaster, or even a dishwasher, but there doesn't seem much chance of that. I bought a copy of Microsoft Office to go with the new Toshiba (because otherwise the Toshiba is about as useful to me as a buggy whip) but the machine won't accept it. Either the laptop is the wrong model or the software is the wrong model. One will have to go back. So for now it's out with the notebook and pencil.

17

I am old enough to remember when cricket was played on graffiti free green grass; when sightscreens were made of wood and painted white, and when umpires wore coats without advertising slogans. The only cricketer to have a sponsor was Denis Compton, the Brylcream boy, and even county championship matches attracted vast crowds of enthusiastic spectators (largely male) who wore hats which they could throw into the air when things went well enough. I can remember when cricketers could play all season without whingeing, when teams could play for a whole hour without needing a tea break and when bowlers could bowl for two days in succession without complaining of exhaustion. I am well aware that we all tend to look back through the rose tinted retrospectoscope but in cricket it seems to me that everything has changed for the worse. Cricket played a massive part in my life until about 20 years ago. As a boy I used to follow cricket avidly. My birthday present each year was a day at one of that year's Test Matches. When I became a professional author I used to go to Edgbaston, Worcester, Lord's or Taunton whenever there was a game. I would take a notebook and write bits of my latest book during the luncheon and tea intervals; or while Bob Willis was trudging back to start his run up. I used to go to the cricket with my sandwiches in a bag, a book or two to read at dull moments and a notebook and a few pens. I carried a golf umbrella for protection during the inevitable showers. I never much minded when it rained. There are few more relaxing things in life than sitting on a wooden bench, eating sandwiches and reading a good book while sheltering under a decent umbrella.

But a few years ago I lost interest in the modern game. The last match I attended was at Taunton where Somerset was playing. I could put up with the fact that none of the players seemed desperately interested in what they were doing, to me they seemed to be as enthusiastic about their work as motorway road workmen, but I could not cope with the fact that two youths sitting in the seats in front of me spent the day blowing their air horns every time a run was scored, a wicket was taken, a ball was fielded or the pavilion clock ticked. I could put up with an occasional cry of 'Well played, sir!' or a jolly piece of barracking but where's the fun in sitting a couple of feet away from a couple of air horns? When they're blasting out the decibels they're deafening and when they're not you're waiting for them to do so. I did manage to hit the operator of one air horn on the back of the head with the cork from a champagne bottle, but I fear that this might prove to be a hazardous habit. Instead of going to cricket matches I started to buy old copies of *The Cricketer* magazine to feed my enthusiasm. I enjoyed reading about promising newcomers such as Laker and Lock. I doubt if I'm the only cricket fan who is still in love with cricket but who has fallen out of love with the modern game. It's not nostalgia. My enthusiasm for the cricket of Tyson, Trueman and Wardle is inspired simply by the unarguable fact that the game then was, in almost every imaginable way, far superior to the game as it is played today.

I can remember when players were selected for England because they already knew how to play. It was acknowledged that some players might not do things according to the coaching manual, but that since they had proved successful enough to be picked it would be wise to leave them alone. No one told Denis Compton that he was doing everything wrong. When cricket was run from a cupboard at Lord's (instead of smart offices in Dubai) the idea of anyone telling Brian Statham that he had to spend his mornings running around St John's Wood would have seemed bizarre. Can you imagine someone introducing Ted Dexter to his new batting coach? I've got a photo of the Reverend David Shepherd taking batting practice with a bunch of scruffy schoolboys. The wickets were chalked on a nearby wall. Players who were selected improved their skills by watching and talking to their contemporaries. They were not above learning from watching and talking to their opponents too. These days players are, it seems, regarded as little more than raw material. Squads of highly paid coaches fall over themselves to explain precisely how eggs should be sucked. When the English cricket team goes on tour they take with them an army of advisors. The bloke in charge of the baggage has reported that the team now travels with between 120 and 180 suitcases and bags. With so many people offering instructions it's hardly surprising that players become confused and forget how to do what they used to find quite natural.

Cricket is, today, all about the money. There are battalions of administrators and interfering busy bodies with fingers stuck into the pie; all constantly pulling out plums. That's why there is so much need to make gazillions out of the game. The gate at an average sort of Test Match would more than cover the costs of paying the players and umpires. Add on the profits that can be made from selling TV rights, scorecards, sponsored pies and sponsored fizzy drinks and you're talking banker bonus money. Why, then, do they have to sell advertising on the grass, the sightscreen, the players, the umpires and the stumps? It's to pay for the vast army of support staff who are, it seems, now essential for any international side. The money isn't the means to an end, it is the end.

In the bad old days, when spectators often had good reason to throw their hats into the air, a touring side would consist of 16 players, a manager, a scorer and, possibly, a bloke to look after the baggage. These days the England team takes a bigger force than the Eighth Army. There are facilitators, advisors, psychologists, video analysts and coaches to give instruction on how best to tie shoe laces. It is the cost of all these hangers-on which explains why spectators must have their sandwiches confiscated if the ingredients aren't on the approved list of sponsors, why the grass at the average Test Ground carries so much painted advertising that it looks like a Jackson Pollock groundsheet and why there is so much unbridled enthusiasm for 20-20, a new version of the game which seems to me to be a bastard child of biff-bat and French cricket designed for those who like their films and books without plots or characters and their music without rhyme or melody.

Modern cricketers are molly coddled and have started taking themselves far too seriously. During preparations for a recent disastrous tour of Australia it was revealed that the team had given the Australians an 82 page dietary document, prepared by the team's official nutritionist, listing the team's requirements. This bore a remarkable resemblance to the sort of diva driven nonsense issued by rock bands to prospective promoters. The Australians were given a list of 194 approved dishes including such traditional English delights as piri-piri breaded tofu, mung bean curry with spinach and quinoa, cranberry and feta salad. The fact that two players came home mid-tour rather suggests to me that fish, chips and cucumber sandwiches might have proved more efficacious. And since the remaining players did worse than terrible the experiment seems to have proved that a diet which consists largely of cheese sandwiches, ice cream and pints of beer is more likely to produce impressive performances on the field. Sadly, I suspect that the authorities will respond to failure by ensuring that the team hires another two nutritionists and issue a list of dietary demands which will take up more space than Britain's tax regulations. I seem to remember Lord Boycott once reporting that he'd survived a tour of India on a diet of boiled eggs and bananas.

Nor am I impressed by all the rubbish talked about England players suffering from stress. Young folk these days are so cocooned by our health and safety world, and our politically correct busy bodies, that they are protected from real world anxieties. Coaches and administrators talk about the stresses cricketers have to endure as though no one else knows what stress means. Bollocks. Today's international cricketers haven't been battle hardened by life. There are no medals to be won at the school sports day because when there are winners there must be losers and we can't have that. Everyone must pass all the exams they take so that no one feels like a failure.

All sports professionals constantly claim that they are under stress. Even snooker players witter on about the enormous stress they suffer earning a living banging balls about when they could be having far more fun shelf stacking at Tesco. None of these molly coddled prima donnas knows anything at all about stress. A doctor working in a casualty department or doing night calls knows what stress tastes like. A soldier defending himself and his colleagues can certainly claim to be acquainted with stress. But a cricketer? A snooker player? Please.

And if I hear again the excuse 'they're just boys' I will scream. Hannibal was crossing the Alps at 25 and the average house surgeon, making life and death decisions, is younger than that. Our molly coddled cricketers don't know what stress feels like. Back in the 1950s, Yorkshire players who came out of the pits knew they'd chosen the easy path through life. Modern players need two years of psychotherapy if someone criticises them (and four years if the criticism came from Shane Warne).

I think I will continue to live in the past, thank you. Cricket was always important because we could pretend it mattered but know, deep, deep down, that it really didn't matter a damn. It seems to me that to today's players and support staff, cricket matters a great deal because it's the best paid job any of them could possibly hope for. Today, it's all about the money. And that's what has spoilt it.

18

Our UK boiler maintenance man came yesterday. There was nothing wrong with the boiler but we have a service contract and the company with which we have the contract had sent us three reminders and although I suspected that their eagerness to service the boiler was probably allied to a desire to sell us a new sludge cleaner, an iPhone app or a new boiler I succumbed and made an appointment.

An hour after the engineer had gone we discovered that we had no hot water. We had plenty of lukewarm water (the sort you might be prepared to bathe in on a sunny day) and endless supplies of cold water, but absolutely no hot water at all. Since I had spent much of the afternoon in the garden and had been looking forward to a hot, relaxing bath I was not well pleased. This isn't the first time this has happened and I am now certain that boiler servicing is as likely to produce problems as car servicing. (I long ago discovered that I am always more likely to have problems with a car if I have it serviced than I am if I leave everything alone. Men with spanners have an innate tendency to bugger things up and when they check the oil they somehow manage to stop the windscreen wipers working properly.)

This morning another engineer turned up to find out what had gone wrong. He discovered that his colleague, the guy who had done the maintenance work, had turned down the hot water thermostat. None of us had the faintest idea why he had done this. Maybe it was as part of a test – and he'd forgotten to turn the thermostat back up again – or maybe it was part of a plan to save energy and preserve the planet by forcing us to take lukewarm baths. Or maybe he didn't like the biscuits we provided. Anyway, we now have hot water again. What peeved me more than anything was that the second visit wasted another half a day of my time and I really don't feel that I have half days I can squander in this way. It isn't the ringing up that wastes time, or the actually visit itself, it's the waiting. Antoinette and I are alike in this. Neither of us feels that we can do anything much when we're waiting for a workman to arrive. It's worse than waiting for a train. I can't work because I fear that there will be a bang on the door when I'm half way through a tricky sentence. I can't go out into the garden because if I do I won't hear the knock on the door at all. I can't make telephone calls in case the workman who is coming gets lost (as he almost certainly will) and needs to telephone us for directions. Still, I have made another, rather belated New Year's resolution. In future I will not allow the maintenance company to service our boiler. We'll wait until the boiler has broken down before we let them into the house.

When the boiler man had gone, I decided to a little tidying up and found an old Manfred Mann album. It had fallen down the back of a bookcase. (I always find far more interesting things behind bookcases than underneath sofa cushions.) Sight of the album reminded me that when I was a teenager I attended a live television show at the Cavern in Liverpool. I was in Liverpool working as a Community Service Volunteer for a year and since my income from CSV was, I think, just thirty bob a week, I was trying to earn a little extra money working as a freelance writer. I'd somehow managed to persuade the *Daily Mirror* to commission me to write about the show and, even more miraculously, I'd managed to persuade the doorman at The Cavern to let me in without a press pass of any kind. The bill for the show was pretty impressive and included Gene Vincent and the Redcaps, Sandie Shaw, Gerry and the Pacemakers, Petula Clarke and Manfred Mann. After the show I wandered into Manfred's dressing room (as you do when you're 18 and it's the 1960s) and talked to him, lead singer Paul Jones and the rest of the band. None of this is of any significance except for the fact that I remember Manfred talking about the fact that he was going to stop making single records because he could not cope with the stress of waiting to see whether his latest record was going to get into the charts, how high it would go and how long it would stay there. I seem to remember him telling me that the chart positions were released on Tuesdays and that his whole life seemed to revolve around that day of the week. He was one of the biggest stars of the 1960s and I had never before realised just how stressful it must be to stay at the top of a profession. When I filed my story for the *Daily Mirror* I didn't mention any of this. I remember thinking that what he'd told me was too personal to be used in an article. I did, however, remember what he told me and I was pleased for him when he stopped making singles and started a successful second career making albums rather than singles.

19

I have for years written about the dangers of chemotherapy, which is often prescribed without logic or common sense. My book *How to Stop Your Doctor Killing You* contains a good deal on the subject and was, inevitably, widely attacked by drug industry hacks when the first edition appeared in the 1990s. Neither doctors nor drug companies like to be reminded of the faults and frailties of chemotherapy; a vastly overrated but enormously profitable form of treatment. I read today that 27% of people who die within a month of receiving chemotherapy are killed not by the disease but by the treatment they have received. And 19% of the people who died shouldn't have been given chemotherapy at all. It really is time for a proper, independent evaluation of chemotherapy and radiotherapy. But big industries are involved so it will never happen, of course. The medical profession was bought many years ago, lock, stock and syringe, by the ruthless pharmaceutical industry which now makes billions out of drugs which, as a breed, do far more harm than good.

20

Politicians are again claiming that we have to encourage immigration because we are all living longer and will need immigrant children to look after us when we are old. (Amazingly, one in ten children under four in Britain is Muslim.) This is, apparently, official policy for Britain's main political parties and for the Liberal Democrats too. It seems to me a rather devious reason for encouraging people to come and join us on our overcrowded and soon to start sinking island, but it's also wrong because it is based on one of the most popular myths of our times. The myth is that life expectancy is far greater now than it was a century ago. As I have explained in several of my medical books this is a nonsense. Not for nothing did the Bible talk of three score years and ten. The truth is that our apparent increase in life expectancy is due almost entirely to the fall in infant mortality rates. In the early 1900s the infant mortality rate was 127.6 per 1000. In other words over 12% of babies never grew old enough to walk, say Mama or blow out birthday candles. Today, thanks to better living conditions and clean drinking water (and nothing to do with better medicine and better medical care), the infant mortality rate in the UK is 4.5 per 1000 (this isn't anything to gloat about, by the way, it just gets us into the top 40 countries in the world) and clearly this means that the vast majority of babies now live long enough to go to school, drive cars, have their obligatory tattoos inked into place and claim their benefits.

(Tattooing is especially fashionable now, of course, but even when I was a GP, during the years immediately following the Boer War, I remember seeing a number of patients who had tattoos. One male homosexual had 'This way up' tattooed at the base of his spine and several women had stuff tattooed on their breasts. One particularly well-endowed woman, I remember, had a pair of eyes tattooed onto her breasts. She explained that during the summer months, when she wore low cut frocks, men always looked at her breasts before they looked at her face and so she'd had the eyes tattooed there to stare back at them. It did occur to me that she could have simply worn a more modest dress but I was young and embarrassed and didn't like to say anything. Another woman had the names Diana and Barbara tattooed on her breasts. When I asked why this was so she told me that these were the names her husband had given to her breasts. She did not know why. She told me that a friend of hers had been so impressed that she had asked her own husband if he wanted her to have her breasts labelled. He had rather spoilt the moment, however, by suggesting that she had them tattooed with the words 'left' and 'right'. I knew him, for he too was a patient of mine, and I had always thought him a very prosaic individual. He didn't have an ounce of romance in his soul.)

When the infant mortality rate was high the average life expectancy was low. Now that the infant mortality rate is low the average life expectancy is, inevitably, considerably higher. It isn't difficult to work this out. If the average adult lives to be 80 and one child in ten dies before their first birthday then the average life expectancy is 72 but if the average adult lives to be 80 and virtually none dies before their first birthday the average life expectancy is just under 80.

If our politicians were honest (an unlikely event I grant you) they would admit that there are more old people in Britain because our population has grown rapidly and our population has, of course, grown rapidly because of massive immigration. So the official solution to our problem is, in reality, the cause of it.

I have a strong suspicion that the only people who are really enthusiastic about our sticking to the EU's immigration policies are the bosses of large international companies (who delight in the availability of cheap foreign labour) and cabinet ministers and newspaper editors who enjoy having a constant supply of cheap nannies, gardeners, chauffeurs and housekeepers.

21

Around six months ago, I laughed while eating and some food found its way up into my nasal cavity (as happens to most of us from time to time). I have for some time felt that there was still something in there and a few days ago I surprised myself by coughing up a piece of beetroot which had slid down into my throat. It had, without any doubt, been hiding in my nasal cavity for all that time. I felt concerned enough about this to visit our GP and to ask for an appointment with an Ear Nose Throat surgeon so that he could check and make sure that there wasn't any more food hiding in there. The kindly GP arranged this but I could tell that the young ENT surgeon who put a camera up my nose thought he was wasting his time. I really don't think he believed that a piece of food could stay hidden for so long. To my relief his searches with the camera proved that there was nothing else uninvited in my nasal cavity but I found that scepticism and disbelief disturbing. I've been a qualified doctor for nearly half a century and I long ago learned that, in medicine, virtually nothing is impossible and that just because something isn't listed in the textbooks, that doesn't mean that it can't happen. The problem with the truth is that it is often stranger than fiction, and therefore, far less believable. Fiction has to make sense; life and the truth do not.

22

We drove to Cheltenham today and, as usual, our route took us through Painswick. We both like Painswick, which is a rather beautiful village, though it always manages to seem terribly posh even if you're just driving through. In the old days people from nearby Stroud would never eat in Painswick because they believed that the people who lived there ate 'bow wow' pie – a local delicacy made from stray dogs. These days the locals are all dressed by Christian, Alexander, Stella, Tommy and Ralph. The man who signs his shirts with a crocodile is nowhere to be seen. Nor is the man who signs his shoes with the ticky swoosh thing. We passed St Mary's church which has an amazing collection of shaped yew trees in the graveyard. There are 99 of these trees and they are all cut and shaped by skilful topiarists. Most of the clipped trees were planted in the year 1800 and attempts to take the total up to around 100 have always failed. Every time a new one is planted, one of the old ones will die and have to be dug out. Local superstition has it that this is the work of the devil but Laurie Lee, the author of *Cider with Rosie*, who lived in the nearby village of Slad, claimed that it was because whenever the Painswick folk planted a 100th tree the locals from Slad, who regarded Painswick folk as terribly stuck up and quite above themselves, would always kill one of the old ones just to piss them off.

We were delighted to find that since there was no Festival in progress we could park the car and potter around the shops fairly easily. Cheltenham has more festivals than anywhere else I know. There is the horse racing festival, of course, which has been a feature of the town for longer than anyone can remember. In the second half of the 19th century, Dean Francis Close wrote a review which seems rather savage even by today's Amazon standards. 'Every species of profligacy – adultery, fornication, uncleanliness, lasciviousness, hatred, violence , emulations, wrath, strife, envying, drunkenness, revellings and such like are promoted by race week. If you wish your child to plunge into the world's vain pleasures, to acquire the taste for dissipation, send him to Cheltenham races.' Come to think of it, the Dean's bad review probably did the races a good deal of good and was undoubtedly regarded by many as a reason to make the journey there.

Inevitably, Cheltenham also has a literature festival. Literature festivals are probably the fastest growing industry in Britain today and it is, it seems, compulsory for all towns and villages which want to be taken seriously to have at least one every year. They don't have anything to do with literature or books, of course. Most of the speakers are politicians, cooks, gardeners, topless models and newsreaders who have appeared on the television and had (usually heavily illustrated) books written for them who are, therefore, regarded in the 'literary festival' business as 'literary figures'. Their appearances usually involve a good deal of posing for photographs and a great deal of book signing.

Cheltenham does not content itself with horse racing and 'literature', however. The town has a jazz festival, a music festival, a science festival, a folk festival, a poetry festival, a festival of performing arts, a cricket festival, a food festival, a food and wine festival, a beer festival, a beer and food festival, a beer and cider festival and a beer and wine festival. There is probably a Cheltenham Cleaning Your Teeth Festival and if there isn't a Cheltenham Composting Festival I have no doubt that there soon will be. I suspect that these endless festivals are, like quangos, simply a good excuse for people to have a damned good time at someone else's expense. It occurs to me that if my books stop selling and times get hard I could probably make a few bob by founding the Cheltenham Festival for Festival Organisers.

In the town I called in to one of my favourite bookshops. The old man who runs it had put up a huge notice advertising the fact that he is selling all his books at half price. I picked out an armful of old Penguin paperbacks and half a dozen old books on animals and gardening that I thought Antoinette would like. I always buy as many books as I can from him. I have long suspected that he struggles to make a living. We get on well now, though our first meeting was something of a trial. As he walked around the shop I couldn't help noticing that he rolled from side to side.

'Were you at sea before you opened the bookshop?' I asked him.

He looked at me quizzically.

'The roll,' I said, mimicking the way he walked. 'The way you walk.'

'I've got bad feet,' he snapped. 'If you had my feet you'd walk funny.'

I apologised and tried to explain that I hadn't meant to be rude. Eventually, I managed to smooth things over by buying £40 worth of books.

'You're my first customer of the day,' he told me, sadly. I looked at my watch. It was three o'clock in the afternoon; nearer the end of the day than the beginning. He told me that he was going to close the shop in three months' time. I told him how sorry I was and asked him whether he thought he'd been finished off by the internet, the council's car parking policy or the charity shops. He told me, without hesitation, that it was the charity shops. 'There are three or four charity run bookshops in the town,' he told me. 'Plus all the ordinary charity shops with their unending shelves full of cheap books.'

I used to be a fan of charity shops and I still visit some of them. Antoinette and I donate an enormous amount of stuff to them too. But I do worry that they've got out of control. It is charity shops which have forced many of our small, independently run shops to close. How can someone trying to make a living possibly compete with shops which pay nothing for their stock, nothing in wages and little or nothing in rates and rent? It seems wrong that charity shops are now forcing honest, hard-working shop keepers out of business. And I wonder if I am the only person to have noticed that as charity shops have taken a stronger hold in the High Street, and got rid of much of the competition, so they have put up their prices? Charity shops are no longer a source of cheap clothing and in some I suspect that the best stuff is cherry picked by staff or by outside 'experts' brought in to value the donated stock. It is now difficult to argue that charity shops are of any value to the communities in which they are situated. I am told that it is perfectly possible to buy new clothing from chain stores such as Primark at a lower price than the charity shops charge for their stock. Oxfam book shops are certainly not cheap; often charging the best part of £3 for a tattered old paperback. Charities have turned their shops into ruthless businesses, leeching on local communities and taking more than they give. They are extremely professional and run by highly paid executives who cream off much of the takings in salaries, pensions, expenses and bonuses. How much longer, I wonder, are councils going to subsidise these charities which, it is possible to argue, may now be doing more harm than good? (Many of these charities, we should not forget, already receive huge amounts of taxpayers' money through massive Government grants.)

However, I realise that not many people share this point of view. The other day I received a rather sanctimonious letter from a reader telling me that he was supporting authors and 'proper' publishers by buying books from charity shops. He suggested that I should encourage people to do likewise. What he clearly doesn't understand is that the people who buy books from charity shops are in reality doing irreparable harm not just to local bookshops but also to authors and to publishers. The charity shops, which between them sell vast quantities of books, have helped the internet destroy 'back list' sales – the sales of an author's earlier books. It has always been back list sales which have kept authors and publishers alive. Neither authors nor publishers receive any royalties when books are sold in charity shops but every time a book is sold in a charity shop the reader doesn't buy that book from a proper shop, and so the author loses out. To my own surprise I realised that e-Books are the author's only way to fight back against this problem. (The income of the average professional author is in steep decline. It was £15,540 in 2005 but is now around £11,000 a year.)

I deposited the books I'd bought in the car boot and carried on into the town. Cheltenham has a slightly upmarket reputation but that, I fear, is largely false. The truth is that Cheltenham has always been a rather seedy town. Cudgel matches used to be staged in the High Street on long summer evenings. The matches had much in common with the Irish sport of hurling. Men with heavy clubs would knock each other senseless for no very good reason. The man who broke the most heads would receive a good hat and a guinea. New hats were popular prizes in those days. Bull baiting and cock fighting were also enormously popular in the town.

Today, things are probably worse and there are as many tattoos, overhanging naked bellies and drunken youths as there are in Birmingham. The city centre was, as it always seems to be, full of beggars. Some have dogs, some sit waiting for their wax cups to be filled up, some lie on the pavement or in a doorway. Antoinette always gives them money; not infrequently emptying her purse and then going to one of the hole in the wall cash machines for more money. She's not alone in her kindness, of course.

An organisation based in Cheltenham, has published a thin book about a beggar called Alan who lives and 'works' in Cheltenham. The author wrote: 'Alan is an entrepreneur. He works the street seven days a week and earns £50-£70 a day. He knows where to find the money, the most profitable places to go and what days he will earn more. On Saturdays he can earn over £100. Alan can spot a good customer a mile off. He's shrewd. He's on the ball.'

I object strenuously to this language. Alan, who looks like a man trying to look like a tramp and who has long, matted hair, a long dirty beard, filthy clothes and nails which look as if they were last clipped and cleaned in 1972, is in my view a confidence trickster not an entrepreneur. He doesn't 'work' and he doesn't 'earn'. And he doesn't have 'customers'. He scams kind, sensitive, hard-working people and takes money from them because he plays on their good nature. I saw him take £15 from one kind-hearted passer-by and it was 'taking' just as much as if he'd pointed a knife at her throat. No tax, no national insurance. All cash, of course. No cheques or credit cards. You'd have to earn well above the national average wage to make that sort of money. What a bizarre world it is when a lazy bastard can sit on his bum on the pavement all week and end up with more cash in his pocket than some poor, honest sod working a gruelling 40 hours for minimum wage in a burger bar. It seems to me that Adamson has glorified this self-pitying beggar and his selected life-style; he has made him into both a victim and an anti-hero. The rarely spoken truth is that begging has become a career and life-style choice for the lazy who prefer to sit on their bums in the sunshine rather than labour for their daily bread. Many of those who choose to live like Alan, working the street and conning and scamming the innocent, also claim benefits so taxpayers pay twice. The ones who are drug addicts find themselves swamped with support from social workers who probably believe they are all behaving like Florence Nightingale but who are, in reality, all more a part of the problem than the solution. I don't think Florence would have had much time for heroin addicts or their social workers. She'd have told them all to grow up a bit and take responsibility for their own lives.

At night the young addicts go back to their hostels, invariably subsidised, where they can plan the next day's begging. The plain medical fact is that cocaine and heroin addiction are easier to kick than tobacco, alcohol or benzodiazepine addiction. Illegal drugs such as heroin and cocaine are far less addictive than tobacco and far, far less addictive than prescription drugs such as the benzodiazepine tranquillisers. Every drug addiction expert in the world will confirm that it is relatively easy to 'kick' cocaine and heroin. In Vietnam, tens of thousands of American soldiers became addicted to heroin. But within two years of returning home their rate of addiction was no greater than that of soldiers who'd never been to Vietnam because the war had ended. Huge numbers of addicts give up without any help whatsoever. And it takes quite a lot of effort to become addicted in the first place. For example, heroin addicts take the drug for about 18 months before they are hooked on it. Thomas de Quincey, probably the most famous literary addict, took laudanum for a decade before he became addicted. The bald truth is that people take heroin for social reasons (the people around them take it) and people deal in it for money. In the end heroin users become beggars or criminals in order to obtain the money to buy their drug of choice.

Addiction to street drugs is not an illness; it is a lifestyle choice. And it is an increasingly popular and fashionable one. (Alarmingly, an independent survey recently found that over a third of young, well-educated middle class Britons said that they had taken cocaine in the previous twelve months.)

I have, and always have had, enormous respect for real tramps. I have written, many times, about how such individuals find themselves on the street. The older ones are often there because they have, through ill-fortune of some kind, lost their homes, their families and their jobs. No one will employ them because they are too old.

But I have nothing but contempt for the young breed of professional beggars like Alan. He's 40-years-old and has been a leech for much of that time.

Many of these young beggars are, in my view, manipulative, indolent, self-pitying parasites. Alan says he's a drug addict and the naïve probably assume that his addiction has been his downfall. But if he wanted to stop using drugs, and become a decent, productive member of society he could probably do so without much difficulty. The problem is that those who pity him, and encourage his self-indulgent lifestyle, are simply making the problem worse. Alan, and those like him, needs a kick up the bum – not sympathy, and certainly not money.

I watched in horror as an old lady in her eighties, shabby coat, down at heel shoes, stopped beside another young beggar, and took money from her purse to give to him. He took it from her, of course. I felt an almost uncontrollable urge to snatch the money out of his greedy, grasping hands, run after the old lady and give it back to her.

23

We bought our home in the country because it promised to be quiet and private – the two most luxurious commodities in the world these days. But our normally quiet lane was full of walkers yesterday. Most wore hiking boots and shorts and had rucksacks on their backs. They looked very professional and were, I was told, taking part in a charity walk. I couldn't help noticing that none of them seemed the slightest bit interested in the world around them. They were far too busy talking (very loudly) and playing music on their leaky digital players to see or hear anything very much. What a pity. Most will, I suspect, regard themselves as country lovers but they might just as well have been marching along a motorway hard shoulder.

A day before the main party started plodding past our front gate an advance group painted large white arrows on the road and on our wall. No one asked us if we minded. Today, after the walkers had passed by, I spent the best part of an hour collecting beer cans, cola bottles and crisp packets which had been thrown into the hedge or simply dropped on the lane. Our peaceful piece of England looked as though we'd hosted an outdoor rock concert. Those amateur country-folk were clearly professional townies; unable to shake off the strange comfort of noise and litter.

24

I received an angry letter from a reader who complained that although my book *Diary of a Disgruntled Man* frequently made him laugh out loud it contained a good many angry entries. I confess that I had thought that the word 'Disgruntled' in the title might have given a clue as to the direction of the contents.

25

I have long thought that the best way to get to know somewhere is to get lost there. In Paris I have spent long, glorious days wandering around trying to get lost. The map in my pocket was to be used only in extremis. I used to wander wherever my fancy took me; always taking the most interesting looking street, wherever it was heading.

But we got lost trying to drive through Gloucester the other day and it wasn't much fun at all. There seemed to be very few signs and the ones which we saw didn't seem relevant to our requirements. We got fairly close to the cathedral on three separate occasions. As we drove close to it for the third time, Antoinette told me that a man called John Stafford Smith was christened in Gloucester cathedral in around 1750. It was Mr Smith who composed the tune to the 'Stars and Stripes', which was later adopted by the United States of America as the country's national anthem. Antoinette, who knows just about as many odd things as anyone I've ever met, told me that Smith died in 1836 when a grape pip got lodged in his throat. Just why anyone should die because they had a grape pip in their throat is beyond me but I believe her because she is undoubtedly absolutely right.

After our unhappy experience in Gloucester, I gave in and bought a satellite navigation system. I purchased one made by Garmin who sponsor a cycling team in the Tour de France. The team never seems to do terribly well and so I thought the company deserved all the support I can give. Antoinette, it should be said, has been encouraging me to buy one of these things for years but my powerful distrust of devices which rely on electricity has prevented me from doing so until now. Up to the time when councils stopped putting up decent road signs I always seemed to manage quite well with a pair of eyes and an old AA atlas (so elderly that the M25 was still a dotted line marking a road under construction) but our experiences in Gloucester have cured me of that delusion.

Now that we've got our new toy I am delighted with it. It's an endless source of amusement. It sometimes (but not always) says 'go left' when it obviously means 'go right' and the computer's attempts to pronounce ordinary British names are hysterical. It beeps and shouts and tells us that we're in a 50 mph zone when we clearly aren't and it often tries to take us down lanes that would be a bit of a close fit for a thin person riding a bicycle. The gadget came with a little lead which should have enabled us to update the information it contains but we tried that and failed miserably. I really don't mind at all. I'm frightened that if we update the software it might stop pronouncing Swindon as 'Swinedon'.

26

I'm sure it is ageist, and therefore illegal, to say this but I am convinced that each new generation is more stupid and more ignorant than the last one. The appallingly low standard of modern teaching is partly to be blamed, of course, but the reliance on gadgets of one sort of another must also be responsible. Children who grew up using calculators to perform simple, basic arithmetical tasks are quite unable to add two to two without scratching their heads and ringing mum for advice. Today's generation, reliant entirely on mobile telephones and the internet are vulnerable because the little knowledge they have has been culled almost exclusively from 'bent' websites, which serve up conveniently correct news in conveniently palatable chunks, and their reliance on others to provide them with opinions mean that they are largely unable to think for themselves. Give them a real, old-fashioned book and they spend thirty minutes looking for somewhere to fit the batteries before tossing it aside in disgust. Moreover, most seem to spend much of their waking day updating their Facebook profiles and twittering about their unexceptional achievements. The real thinkers and leaders of the future will come from the small band of treasured young people who eschew social media sites and recognise that digital living is no substitute for real life.

27

We visited Weston-super-Mare today. What a sad, depressing place it has become; it must surely be the worst run town in the country. A romantic pier and an outdoor pool have been derelict for so many years that local inhabitants no longer even hope for their restoration. It used to be widely accepted that every village in the country would have an idiot. For one reason or another, the God who doles out idiots has been extraordinarily generous to Weston which now has far more than its fair share – with many of them serving on the local council. Weston, once a pleasant and welcoming seaside resort, seems to have gone downhill faster than anywhere I can think of. The place is now full of hostels for former criminals and drug addicts and the streets are full of people who are clearly drunk or unemployed or both. Not surprisingly, property prices have defied national averages and now seem to have more in common with those of Northern Ireland than the rest of the West Country. Only the amusement arcades seem to be thriving. I suspect that the unemployed happily spend their days and their benefit money in these places and so some business owners are undoubtedly doing good trade.

Weston-super-Mare reminds me of Blackpool but without quite so much glamour. And it would come high up in the top ten towns in the country for its potholes, some of which are so deep that cavers have probably been lost in them. The Chinese could build a power station in the time the local council takes to mend a pothole.

I sometimes wonder if councils are now using potholes instead of speed bumps. They save money twice. The traffic calming nonsenses now defacing our roads (the pointless and dangerous chicanes; the sleeping policemen which wreck cars, cause agony for back sufferers and force ambulances to drive miles round (endangering lives) and the roundabouts which have no apparent purpose other than to increase fuel consumption) can all be abandoned when the potholes have become big enough.

(As a postscript I saw a sign today which said: 'Uneven road surface'. It made me smile. Councils throughout the country would save money by putting one of these signs at Land's End, facing north, and another at John o'Groats, facing south.)

28

We had our bird splattered BMW cleaned today by a posse of a dozen men armed with hoses, sponges and soap dispensers. They worked as a team. The first guys squirted on the soap, the second set of men operated the pressure hoses and the final group did the polishing. Only one of the army seemed to speak English but the rest made do very effectively with signs ('move forward', 'lift the bonnet' and so on). They charged £9 which was close enough to the £7 on their notice and the £10 note I handed over. But it was well worth it. They worked hard and quickly. I can't think of anywhere in Britain where it would be possible to find such hard working individuals able and willing to work as a team except, perhaps, in an army barracks.

While we sat in the car Antoinette and I tried to think up silly book titles – the sort likely to end up on the shelves of a shop specialising in remaindered books.

These were our favourites:
1. Collecting Used Sticking Plasters
2. How to Photograph Deckchairs
3. My Many Interesting Experiences on Buses in Northamptonshire
4. How I Reconciled My Beliefs as a Jehovah's Witness with my Work as a Long Haul Stewardess
5. Drawer Liners Through the Ages

6. The Boy's History of Mothballs

29

I'm still waiting to read research proving that mobile telephones cause brain cancer. I first realised that mobile phones could be dangerous in the 1980s when I noticed that after using mine for more than a few minutes my ear felt very hot. The telephone itself wasn't particularly hot. But my ear felt as if it were boiling. I cut down my mobile phone usage and wrote articles suggesting that some research be done to find out whether or not there was a link. Naturally, my suggestions were dismissed as absurd scaremongering by lobbyists for the joint forces of the medical establishment and the mobile phone industry. Today every child over the age of two has at least one mobile phone and most of them spend longer talking on the phone than they spend talking to real, live people. (I read today that the average Briton spends between eight and nine hours a day on their mobile phones, tablets and laptops: texting, emailing, surfing, blogging, reviewing, shopping and twittering.) How many will get brain cancer? I have no idea. I can't prove that mobile phones can be dangerous. But no one else can prove they are safe. Thanks to lobbyists, the general rule these days is that new devices should be rolled out and used by millions before the snags are discovered and the goose stops laying golden eggs.

It is lobbyists (supported by dishonest academics who allow themselves to be bought for thirty pieces of silver) who are responsible for the propagation of many of today's most outrageous myths (such as those concerning climate change and vaccination) and I have no doubt whatsoever that it would be perfectly possible to put together a panel of convincing academics ready, willing and able to argue that the earth is flat and that if we sail too close to the edge we will fall off and disappear into oblivion.

30

A friend's mother has been told that she has just twelve months to live. This is complete nonsense, of course. Unless you are lying in a pool of your own blood, with your blood pressure 60 over 40, your heart in ventricular fibrillation and the nearest hospital six hours away the only honest answer to 'How long will I live?' is 'I haven't got the foggiest idea.'

Doctors who try to give themselves professional airs and graces by making specific predictions, and apparently accurate prognoses, are setting themselves up to look the fools they undoubtedly are and they are not doing their patients any favours. General predictions about life are usually fairly reliable (things will get worse and cost more) but specific predictions about human life are invariably faulty. The human body is an eternally variable organism and human beings vary enormously in the way they react to illness – whatever that illness may be. I have known patients who have been warned to prepare for the end to survive for years and I have known patients to die suddenly when doctors had told them that they had been cured. I have known patients who have been abandoned by their doctors to survive and I have known patients who have been 'cured' to die days later. And, of course, I have known patients who have been thoroughly examined and given a clean bill of health to drop down dead the next day. Predicting human longevity is an even more inexact science than predicting the weather. (Despite their alleged reliance on 'science', today's weather forecasters are so incompetent that they are really only any good when offering retrospective advice. 'It was showery yesterday so you should have taken a mac or an umbrella with you.') A doctor who tells a patient that he or she has a year to live is as daft as a weather forecaster who tries to forecast the weather in a year's time. Insurance companies which demand prognoses when patients want to travel abroad are showing a surprising level of ignorance.

My main objection to the enthusiasm for making firm and precise forecasts of this nature is not, however, the fact that such forecasts are impossible to make with any accuracy but the fact that there is a chance that a forecast will come true simply because the patient believes the doctor. Witch doctors can kill people simply by telling them that they are going to die. The power of the mind is so great that when a stern and powerful looking individual tells a susceptible individual that he is going to die then there is a good chance that he will die. The same is true for us. We may not be quite so susceptible to the ravings of wild men wearing chicken feathers and grass skirts but we are susceptible to the ravings of men and women wearing white coats and having stethoscopes hanging around their necks.

There are times, of course, when the wise man or woman will want to make some plans for their demise. A patient who is about to undergo serious surgery, for example, may want to tidy up loose ends and 'put their affairs in order'.

But patients and relatives would be wise to ignore the pontificating doctor (or nurse) who claims to have the power to foretell the date when someone will die.

31

I had to telephone the piano tuner today.

'When can you come?' I asked.

I could hear pages being turned in what sounded like a large, old-fashioned notebook. 'I just need to check my diary,' he said.

'OK,' I said. I waited. It was clearly going to be a few weeks before he tottered round.

The pages were flicked back and forth. I continued to wait. It sounded as if we would be lucky if we got fitted in within the next twelve months.

'I could come tomorrow,' he said at last.

'Fine. What time?'

'What time would suit you?'

'In the afternoon? About three?'

'Three o'clock tomorrow then,' he said.

April

1

Antoinette asked me this morning if I knew that the EU had introduced the new 'Fair Right of Purchase Legislation' to cover the sale of residential property. She explained that under the new legislation, sellers of houses would have to undertake to give a refund to house buyers if the value of the house they had purchased fell below its selling price during the first five years after completion. I told her that I had been waiting for such a law to be brought in and that I wasn't in the slightest bit surprised. I then asked her if she knew that the manufacturers of flat pack furniture had, for years been fitting cameras and microphones into the fasteners which purchasers use when putting their furniture together. I told her that the cameras and microphones feed images and sound to GCHQ in Cheltenham via the broadband system and that, in their never-ending search for signs of insurgency and terrorism, the Americans use keyword and image recognition software to sort through the mass of information obtained in this way. We then both agreed that it is now almost impossible to create April Fool jokes which are not believable.

2

Every communication we receive these days seems to be either threatening or frightening or both. Utility companies and government departments all send letters full of capital letters, exclamation marks and printing in bold. There is much underlining and red ink. These are the sort of letters lunatics write, except that they use copious amounts of green ink too. This morning we had a letter with the word URGENT on the envelope, together with a message telling us that it had to be opened immediately and dealt with post haste. I tore open the envelope to find a letter instructing us to arrange an annual, routine service appointment for a household appliance which seems to be working perfectly well without having an engineer's grubby and expensive fingers rummaging around inside it.

Around 20 years ago I wrote a book called *Toxic Stress* in which I argued that much of the stress which makes us ill is inescapable because it is part of modern life. I suspect that I am not the only individual who constantly feels bullied, abused, threatened as well as treated without respect. It sometimes seems to me that the only emotion people in power understand is fear. (Most of the time they use it to bully us but, of course, even the bully has hidden fears of his own.) Today there are no moral certainties in our lives and no honourable leaders. It is not surprising that most people go through their lives bewildered and confused; lost in a jungle of uncertainties and cruelties. Just about everyone working for the EU, the Government and the local council is a fully paid up bully. Even most NHS employees are bullies. (Even if you are not a bully at heart, you are a bully if you behave like one.)

Whatever happened to compassion, integrity and old-fashioned good-manners? Well, I suspect that the milk of human kindness has curdled and it will be a hell of a job to uncurdle it.

3

Royal Mail has sent us a leaflet telling us that we can no longer send nuclear waste or human remains through the mail. Since they are now bothering to tell us that we cannot do this I can only assume that it was, until recently, perfectly possible to pop nuclear waste and bits of Aunt Edna into an envelope, drop them into a red post box and expect them to travel comfortably through the mail. Another missed opportunity.

4

While sorting through some old paperwork I discovered an insurance policy for a laptop I bought in 1998. It was a fairly standard laptop at the time (and today would be considered slow, clunky and primitive in every respect) but what amazes me is the price. I paid £2,616.33 for it. Price deflation in electronic goods is as startling as performance inflation.

My first website was put up when men had tails, lived in trees and carved software with chisels on solid lumps of granite. My first fax machine cost about £3,000 (back in the 1980s) and apart from publishers I knew only one other person who had one. My pal Tony Sharrock, now sitting on a cloud with a bottle of gin that never empties, had a fax machine and we used to fax each other just because we could. My first fax machine used rolls of paper and long faxes would come out of the machine looking like a piece of wallpaper. It was, I remember, quite fun cutting the paper up into pages – like slitting open the pages of an uncut book.

5

HMRC, like the NHS, is now considering selling taxpayers' financial information to any companies which want to buy it. I don't suppose this will make much difference. They have, after all, been losing confidential information with such regularity that I cannot see that this will change anything. These days privacy is regarded as a sin and it is popularly acknowledged that only those who are guilty of something can possibly want to protect their lives from public intrusion. (My position on privacy is a simple one: individuals are entitled to it, institutions are not.)

And so we must now all assume that everyone tells everybody everything. Anyone who works for the government or local council can already access your medical records and, probably, your tax return. There is no privacy these days. If you contract a sexually transmitted disease, become depressed or develop dementia any of your neighbours who have jobs as civil service employees (even quite low grade ones) will probably know about it.

All those who have chanted the mantra 'If you have nothing to hide, you have nothing to worry about' will presumably be happy about this state of affairs.

6

At Ebbsfleet railway station today, waiting for the train to Paris, I amused myself by spotting and counting the surveillance cameras. I counted ten in the relatively small waiting room alone. There are probably more. But, curiously, there are no waste bins. The whole place would have given Jacques Tati nightmares. Why so many cameras? Why do the British have such enthusiasm for watching one another? The French, who are supposed to be voyeuristic perverts, have put only 326 CCTV cameras in Paris but the English, who are supposed to be straight laced, have 7,431 CCTV cameras in London. I wonder what the authorities expect to happen here in this miserable, unfriendly station? The place is hardly likely to be a magnet for terrorists. Why would anyone want to blow up Ebbsfleet railway station? Maybe the absence of litter bins is a clue. Maybe they are hoping that they'll spot someone dropping a piece of litter and will be able to call in tanks, helicopters and the SAS. We were, of course, stopped on our way through customs and subjected to the usual pointless search. I am always stopped at customs posts and I suspect that the guards have been told that the standard modern terrorist is an elderly gentlemen wearing an embroidered waistcoat, pince nez and an MCC tie. The last time my bags were emptied the half-wit doing the searching completely missed two large zip pockets. Since the profiling of travellers is not allowed (it would be politically incorrect to stop and examine all suspicious looking dusky skinned men and so the customs idiots stop examining all swarthy men with sticks of dynamite strapped around their chests, and with ticking rucksacks on their backs, when they've reached their annual quota) an old lady with a Zimmer frame was also lucky enough to win a ticket in the lottery of the absurd and to be subjected to a search. She was about ninety and very patient and brave during the deliberate and pointless humiliation that is what travel means these days. Naturally, no one thought to look inside the tubes of the Zimmer frame to see whether they were stuffed with Semtex. The whole pointless process of security at railway stations is designed by the stupid and put into practice by the rude and brainless. Security rules designed by the politically correct mean that the guards pick out as many little old ladies as they do swarthy, bearded men with rucksacks and alarm clocks strapped to their waists. There was one sweet moment during the whole pointless process. I had a rag doll in my suitcase and when the young woman examining my belongings reached the doll she saw that its skirt had accidentally been pulled upwards. With great and surprising tenderness she smoothed down the skirt and gently placed the rag doll to one side. She didn't check it to see what had been stuffed inside it head and body. Everyone in the world except the people working at these border controls knows damned well that the examinations are utterly pointless and never, ever catch any real terrorists. The absurd, time wasting and impertinent measures introduced since September 2001 would not, of course, have stopped what happened in September 2001. There's irony for you. The checks are done to keep us all in our place and remind us of our impertinence in believing that we are entitled to

107

travel freely around the world. Travel used to be leisurely, full of anticipation; today it's an angry business full of anticipated disappointment. Arrival is also, generally, a disappointment: offering the sort of feeling which follow the pulling of a Christmas cracker and finding inside it a shoe horn, metal egg cup or nail clipper. Angst is the new zeitgeist.

Eurostar has stopped serving champagne these days and they serve diet cola in tiny little tins which would make suitable props for a child's toy shop. For reasons best known to themselves they hand out squarish drinking glasses. People have been using drinking glasses for centuries and they have always been round. I wonder why Eurostar's designer of plastic crockery decided to break new ground by making square glasses. When you try to drink from them some of the liquid always trickles down onto your chin and shirt.

When we got to our apartment we found that the boiler had been leaking. I really don't think boilers like us very much. It wasn't much of a leak. Just a steady drip drip. But over a period of weeks a steady drip can produce a hell of a mess. The water had dissolved a fresh packet of ground Arabica coffee so the whole kitchen was covered in wet, cold coffee. Still, if we hadn't spent an hour or so clearing up the mess I expect we'd have just wasted the time sitting down listening to music, reading good books and sipping fresh coffee. The Griswolds never had as much fun.

When we'd finished I rang the boiler service company and left a message for someone to call round and fix the leak.

I realised today that my French vocabulary has changed a good deal over the years. I used to know how to order things in restaurants. But here are the seven phrases I now seem to use most frequently:

1. Nous avons une fuite
2. Notre chaudière ne fonctionne pas
3. Il est trop cher
4. Vous etes fou
5. Je suis un pauve Anglais
6. Nous n'avons pas de gaz a nouveau
7. Il y a une discotheque dans l'appartement ci-dessous

7

We had only been in Paris for a few hours when Antoinette developed the symptoms of a nasty bout of influenza. I'm sure she caught it in a café last week. A member of the serving staff was sneezing and coughing all the time we were in there and although we fled as soon as we had gulped down our drinks we should have left sooner. Now that there are millions of people taking immunosuppressive drugs there will, I have no doubt, be many people who are killed by bugs they catch in this way. We had huge plans for the week but I think that the wise move would be for us to stay in the apartment and take things easy. This is not a bad thing. We are both exhausted and a few days rest will do us both good. We have several thousand music CDs and books here so we will not be unable to amuse ourselves. When I eventually got round to opening the mail I discovered one from the gas company telling me that in future we must keep all our gas bills, and the mass of associated paperwork, for at least five years. I threw the letter away.

8

We were both woken at about four in the morning by a terrible noise. At first I forgot where we were and assumed that I was hearing a vixen protecting her cubs. When I remembered that we were in the centre of Paris I decided that someone was being murdered. Or maybe a woman was in labour. I opened the window and looked out. All up and down the street tousled heads were visible. We weren't the only ones who had been woken up. Lights were on in dozens of apartments and in the Embassy across the road. The noise continued for about thirty minutes and then, eventually, reached an unmistakeable finale. The quiet which followed was greeted with rapturous applause. And then a rather proud looking man and a sheepish looking woman appeared in a window a few buildings away from ours. The man waved and beamed. The woman blushed and waved rather apologetically. It had been a very impressive performance. They both looked to be in their seventies.

9

I discovered today that it is now possible to obtain prescriptions online with remarkably little fuss. Since GPs have largely abandoned their responsibilities this can only be regarded as a 'good thing'.

10

I lost my reading spectacles this morning. It took me twenty minutes to find that they were in the toothbrush holder in the bathroom. I still haven't found my toothbrush but I've no doubt I put it somewhere safe. Antoinette is worried that I am showing early signs of Alzheimer's Disease. I told her that if I start becoming noticeably potty I will join the Liberal Democrats so that no one will notice.

11

In French cafés the eating and the drinking are largely incidental activities; they are an excuse; the price of admission. People go to cafés to be seen, to see, to start a romance or have an assignation, to read a book, to have a business meeting, to sketch or to snooze.

The English invented coffee houses but somewhere along the way we lost sight of the point and for decades cafes became places where tired shoppers went for a cup of weak tea, a slice of dry fruit cake and a chance to rest their feet. Patrons were expected to sit down, eat and drink and then get up and go. Loitering was strictly against the rules. Once the tea had been drunk and the cake crumbled on the plate so that it looked as if it had been eaten, they were expected to leave.

Now, I'm delighted to say, things are changing a little in England. There are now plenty of cafés which serve excellent coffee and edible cakes and no one seems to mind how long you sit there. It's not uncommon to see two or three patrons pecking away at laptops as they write their books and inch their way towards fame and wealth a la Rowling.

12

Something called the UK Biobank is carrying out a large study of over half a million people. The theory is that by searching through masses of information they will be able to find clues about disease patterns. Oh dear. They're wasting their time. As I pointed out in my second book, *Paper Doctors*, in 1977, we already have enough quality information to help us improve lives dramatically. The problem is that lobbyists ensure that no one takes any notice. So, for example, the evidence proving that meat causes cancer is indisputable. But most people still eat meat because the meat industry's powerful lobby helps to suppress the truth and ensure that people keep eating their carcinogenic products.

13

Why aren't mobile phone makers told to standardise their chargers? Today I threw out a dozen old chargers which no longer fit any of the telephones we have. If I keep them, in the vain hope that one of them will be useful in the future, I will doubtless mix them up with the leads which are relevant and then spend hours sorting them all out again. Standardising phone chargers would save time, money and vast amounts of our rapidly decreasing oil supplies. Sadly, however, all those goody-goody politicians who talk endless drivel about global warming and climate change do not really give a fig about the way we are trashing our planet and using up our valuable natural resources in this way. Politicians do endless bad things for the greater good only of themselves. When politicians talk about the need to do things for a better planet, a more secure economy or a happier society you can be damned sure that they thinking either of the next election and their majority or the lucrative jobs they will be given once their political career is over.

14

Coutts Bank has admitted that it has been giving bad advice to customers since 1957. They say that they will offer compensation. How can any organisation not notice that it has been behaving badly for decades? I used to have an account with Coutts. A man in a frock coat gave me a very handsome leather cheque book holder and an equally handsome leather wallet with the bank's logo stamped on it in gold. But the bank proved so incompetent that I closed the account and moved the money elsewhere. Since Coutts is owned by the Royal Bank of Scotland (the world's worst bank) which is largely owned by British taxpayers it will be taxpayers who will have to pick up the bill for Coutts' serial incompetence. We would all be so much better off if Gordon the Moron had simply closed RBS and fired all the staff. Incidentally, it does not seem to be widely known that Alex Salmond, the deeply unpleasant and dangerously rabid Scottish nationalist whose personal definition of the word 'truth' seems to be rather different from mine and whose grasp of history might, I suggest, be described by some Englishmen as prejudiced if not challenged, worked for the world's worst bank, the Royal Bank of Scotland, as an economist. I suspect that the end result of his political career will be much the same as that of the bank: humiliation and disaster. Assumption and complacency are always the mother and father of disaster.

15

We put up a new squirrel proof feeder today. Within fifteen minutes a squirrel had unscrewed the bottom of the feeder so that all the sunflower seeds which were inside fell to the ground. But that wasn't all. He carried the bottom piece of the feeder away so that I couldn't screw it back on. I suspect that our squirrels are considerably more intelligent than the people who make what they claim to be squirrel proof feeders. We are quite proud of them, really.

16

For several months now I have been attempting to persuade Royal Mail to stop stuffing unaddressed junk mail through our letterbox. Today, I've given up. I have filled in forms, sent emails, written letters and made telephone calls. I've spoken to the local postman. I've communicated endlessly with two personal assistants in the Moya Greene's office. Ms Greene is the Chief Executive and you might imagine that an instruction from her office might produce results. 'Would you please stop stuffing our letter box with advertisements for pizza houses and local politicians,' I begged. But although I have received many assurances the junk mail still keeps coming.

'How do you know that we're responsible?' demanded one Royal Mail employee.

'Because I've seen the postman get out of his van and push the junk through our letterbox,' I replied.

'Ah, but how do you define junk mail?' the employee demanded.

'It's mail I didn't ask for and which doesn't have my name or address on it.'

'But some of it might have important information for you.'

'I don't want it.'

At this point the person with whom I'm communicating always tells me to contact someone else. The bloke at the head office tells me that I need to tell the local office to stop delivering the stuff. The bloke at the local office tells me that they can't do anything unless an instruction comes from the head office. The problem, of course, is that everyone at Royal Mail makes money out of delivering unwanted, unaddressed junk mail. I discovered today that even the postman on his rounds receive a bonus for delivering the stuff.

So now I've given up. And the junk the Royal Mail insists on stuffing through my letterbox goes straight onto the bonfire. I suppose it must help the environment in some strange way.

17

We changed our address some time ago and we have been trying to persuade Lloyds Bank to send statements and other correspondence to the new address for several months. I've written four times and telephoned three times without success. I have long had a suspicion that Lloyds is largely managed by people who have something better to do. The only full-time employee seems to be the compliance officer, who is always thinking up new and exciting ways to prevent customers doing anything with their own money. (Actually, there are probably more than one. The American bank J.P.Morgan reckons it needs 13,000 new compliance officers by the end of 2014.) The only good thing about all these cock ups is that we usually receive a chunk of compensation. Indeed, for the last year or so I suspect that the compensation from Lloyds Bank has been coming in so regularly that it is my main source of reliable income and I really ought to regard myself as employed in the banking sector. Maybe I can apply for a bonus or one of those splendid pensions they hand out to executives. After my last telephone call complaining about our mail still going to our old address we were offered £150 in compensation and £21 in costs (to cover the telephone calls I've made). They couldn't even get this right, however. They paid us the £150 compensation twice and had to take one of them back.

Lloyds now has a television advertising campaign in which people whom I do not recognise but assume must be celebrities moan about the fact that they want more time to do things they want to do. My first thought on seeing the advertisement was that the mini celebrities would have the time they craved if they didn't waste their lives making stupid advertisements for an incompetent bank. My second thought was that if Lloyds has money to spare I wish they would use it on making their service more efficient. Their general incompetence results in my wasting huge chunks of my life.

18

Our extended family now includes one deer, three badgers, a fox, five squirrels (there may well be more but we have only seen five at a time), a very aristocratic cock pheasant, a nervous hen pheasant and an enormous variety and number of wild birds. Feeding all these creatures requires a constant supply of hazelnuts, peanuts, sunflower seeds and so on and our supplies now arrive in large hernia-ready sacks rather than the neat little packets sold in garden centres and pet food shops. It really is a joy and a privilege to have all these visitors dining at our home though I realised this morning that it now takes me half an hour every morning just to fill up the feeders. Our squirrels seem particularly insatiable and they seem to believe that hazelnuts grow on trees. We take care not to encourage any of these creatures to be too friendly lest they are shot or otherwise attacked by any of the many folk living in Gloucestershire who seem to regard all other members of the animal kingdom as unwelcome interlopers. It is, incidentally, worth noting that most mass murderers started off their evil careers by killing birds and small animals.

19

Now that English has become the unofficial language of Europe (just as it is the unofficial language of the rest of the world), the French and the Germans frequently boast about their skills in speaking the language of 'les rosbifs'. We, being polite, tend to congratulate them on their language skills even though they invariably sneer whenever we try to get our tongues around their languages. What we don't usually tell foreigners is that their English is awful. We don't like to disappoint them and so we tell them they speak English like a native when what we mean is that they speak English like a native carrying a spear in one hand and a shield in the other. Their grammar is appalling, and often comical, and their accents are straight out of 1950s black and white movies starring Maurice Chevalier. Over 90% of EU staff draft new legislation in English rather than French (which was originally the EU's official language) but the trouble is that their English is rarely as good as they think it is and great confusion often ensues as a result. Those who work for the EU are, inevitably, particularly arrogant and particularly incompetent and likely to be foreign (in the way that anyone such as Boris Johnson who was not born in England must inevitably be foreign) and the main problem is that these semi-literate foreigners frequently use words in a way that would not have been approved by Dr Johnson or any of his lexicological descendants. Many probably think that David Copperfield was a magician and Shakespeare was a sister. And so, as a result of their ignorance of our language, EU law writers frequently use words without any regard for their proper meaning. They use the word 'control' as if it means 'check' or 'verify' instead of 'exercise power over' and they use the word 'assist' as though it means 'be present' rather than 'help'. The word 'guideline' means one thing to the English (to whose language it properly belongs) and another to the eurocrats (who have hi-jacked it) who use it to mean 'directive'. The result of this tower of Babel problem is that when eurocrats speak to the English they speak in a language we do not recognise and when they speak to those of other countries their resulting words, translated by EU translators and mixed up with a few idioms and figures of speech, are even more jumbled. It was long ago obvious that the fact that the EU has 24 official languages would lead to chaos, confusion and disaster and that is exactly what is happening. The worst part of the problem is, of course, that all this confusion ends up in legislation and we end up having to obey laws which sound as if they came straight out of a Marx Brothers script. The courts which have to interpret the laws then get into an unenviable tangle, with dire consequences for everyone. The EU is creating laws which make even less sense than most of us thought possible. It all rather reminds me of Lewis Carroll. 'When I use a word,' Humpty Dumpty said in a rather scornful tone, 'it means just what I choose it to mean – neither more nor less.' 'The question is,' said Alice, 'whether you can make words mean so many different things.' 'The question is,' said Humpty Dumpty, 'which is to be master – that's all.' And we all know who our masters are. Still, it can all be rather fun. A pompous Frenchman told us today that he spoke perfect English and when I congratulated him on this he told us that he was 'beside his shoes with pleasure'. I have no idea whether this was derived from a French idiom or one borrowed from one of euroland's other 24 languages but it is certainly one which I shall be introducing into my own personal repertoire of favourite English idioms. I can't wait to try it out on people when we get back to England. 'I am beside my shoes with pleasure!' I shall announce as often as I possibly can.

20

I doubt if there has been a worse company than Npower in the history of the planet. We recently gave up with them and moved to another supplier. (It says something that we moved to British Gas to get better service.) I read today that in the last year 1.4 million customers complained about Npower, making it top of the most loathed companies list. Even leaving the damned company proved difficult, time consuming and expensive. And getting back the money they owed us was so difficult that I almost gave up. Almost. Npower has earned its place on the world's most 'evil companies list', alongside Goldman Sachs, Monsanto, Google and Microsoft. Why is such an appalling company allowed to sell gas and electricity? Why aren't the executives all spending their days sitting in the stocks so that customers can hurl rotten vegetables at them? The people who work on the shop floor aren't any better. I can just imagine the job interviews. 'Do you find it easy to be rude to people? Can you ignore what people tell you? Do you find it easy to ignore customers who cry on the telephone?' The people who run Npower aren't fit to live in a civilised society; they are the sort of folk who would be bewildered by the idea of indoor plumbing and they should be banished to live on a shrinking ice floe. We'll send the loathsome Nick Clegg with them as their leader. (It really is about time someone put Clegg out of our misery. He's a perfect example of why politicians are different to all other human beings. They have no backbone. He should become a verb. 'To clegg' meaning 'to betray and disappoint'. Just how he became Britain's Deputy Prime Minister will always be a mystery to me.)

I wonder how many people in this modern world are proud of what they do for a living and, the corollary, I wonder how many are ashamed of how they earn their daily bread. I would hazard a guess that there aren't many Npower employees who go home at night feeling a glow of satisfaction. Most, I would imagine, sneak home in the shadows and, if they are asked what they do for a living, probably prefer to say that they are estate agents or, perhaps, that they work for Her Majesty's Revenue and Customs.

21

Antoinette bought a memory card game to help delay the onset of my Alzheimer's. Today she suggested that we play it. We would have done so but, unfortunately, we couldn't find the game anywhere. We had both forgotten where we put it. Another good intention mislaid.

22

An acquaintance from London arrived to discuss something or other. (I really couldn't work out what he wanted but I really don't think it was anything of any benefit to us in particular or to mankind in general.) He runs a bookstore which specialises in unpopular political tracts, lives in a house which looks as if it receives daily deliveries from the local garbage man and once boasted to us that he gets most of his food out of dumpsters. We couldn't bear the thought of inviting him to a meal at the house (he would probably never leave) so we took him to a café near to the railway station so that we could get rid of him as soon as we had fed him.

'Have you got green meat?' he demanded of the waitress, who looked at him as if he were as barking as he undoubtedly is.

'Green meat?' she asked. 'You mean rancid meat?'

'No, no,' he explained. 'I mean organic meat. Grown locally.'

'I don't know,' she said.

He insisted that she fetch the manager.

'Our meat is local,' the manager told him. 'We buy it from the butcher just up the road. You could walk there, but we fetch it in the van.'

'But where are the animals reared?'

'I don't have the foggiest. I suppose the butcher would know.'

'Would you ask them, please?'

Antoinette and I were cringing and trying to disappear into the woodwork.

The manager went away and came back seven or eight minutes later. 'I spoke to someone,' he said, though if he had any sense he was probably lying. 'Their pork comes from a farm in Wiltshire. And the lamb is from somewhere here in Gloucestershire.'

'You don't know precisely how far? Is it more than 20 miles?'

'I don't know.'

'What about the eggs?'

'They're from free range chickens.'

'Proper free range birds? Happy chickens?'

'I would think so.'

Our acquaintance thought for a while. 'I'll have a fried egg and a double helping of chips.'

Antoinette ordered a peppermint tea and I had a coffee. We couldn't wait to get rid of him. Fortunately, there was a fast train due in thirty minutes. We managed to stuff him on that.

23

People in every trade like to play jokes on neophytes. Every new engineering apprentice will be sent to the stores to fetch a bubble for a spirit level. Apprentice bankers in Switzerland are sent down to the vaults to polish the gold bars. And farmers in the Cotswolds deliver two buckets of food to new restaurateurs. One bucket is filled with ram's balls and the other is filled with their tails. It is, I think, supposed to be a joke but the joke backfired when a food writer and restaurateur called Prue Leith received her two buckets. She cooked the testicles, which she claimed were 'unbelievably delicious' and after boiling off the wool she marinated and griddled the tails which were, she said, 'the most wonderful crunchy little things, rather like pork scratchings, which the children adored'. Score one to Ms Leith and nil to the farmer.

24

I spent an hour talking to an old man who delivered some logs. He is, it seems, quite an authority on the area. He told me that five hundred years ago a couple who ended up in court accused of cohabiting ended up having to spend the night on their hands and knees. They had to wear hair shirts and pray all night. Then the local bishop ordered that as an additional punishment they be stripped naked, strapped to a cart and paraded through their village on a Saturday so that as many people as possible could see them. I said I thought it sounded a bit like one of the things they make contestants do on one of those reality television programmes. He also told me that in the late 18th century it was the custom in a village near to Stroud for newly elected mayors to be placed in an armchair and then dumped unceremoniously in the middle of the village pond. Everyone would then gather round and sing a very sombre song. I said I thought that this was a custom which should be revived. What fun it would be if all elected politicians were to be treated in this way. It might remind one or two of them who is in charge.

25

There is much excitement in the village and the villages around. A nearby smallholding, consisting of a modest and rather ugly little farmhouse and nine acres of scrubland, has been sold and there is much talk about the identity of the new owner. Some say that the owner of this small estate, who bought it for the proverbial song from a bank which had foolishly lent the previous owners far too much money, is a well-known pop singer looking for a Cotswold retreat. Others say that this story is rubbish and that the house has been bought by a London gangster who plans to hide his stolen loot in the barn and bury his gangland killing victims in one of the fields. Naturally, Antoinette and I are determined to remain aloof from all this idle speculation. We have started a rumour that the new owner is an alien and that his people (from an unnamed planet) are planning to settle on earth because their own planet has been overrun by an uncontrollable infestation of estate agents. The house has been purchased, we are telling anyone who will listen, as a first step towards colonisation of the entire Cotswolds. Within weeks the land will be covered with strange plastic cocoons inhabited by small purple men with very long ears and no feet. You wouldn't think anyone would believe this rubbish but I only started the rumour a day ago and today it was repeated to me by a woman in a shop in Stroud. Even allowing for the fact that there are a lot of New Age hippies living in that town this does seem rather remarkable and I hope the locals don't start arming themselves with flaming torches and marching on the aliens' headquarters, determined to repel the invasion before it becomes too well established.

26

We were all wrong. The new owner of what was previously, and unimaginatively, known simply as The Barn turns out to be a peer and a mighty industrialist whose first action has been to be rename his purchase 'The Manor House' and to erect a smartly painted and suitably lettered sign at the gated entrance to his driveway. This seems to be a rather ambitious name for a modest dwelling which has two bedrooms and a toilet which was glued onto the side of the house in the 1950s, and not enough land to merit being described as a small holding. (More of a tiny holding.) The new owner of The Manor House, whom I saw clambering out of a gold coloured Rolls Royce, is a diminutive fellow with a head full of jet black hair, some of it, notably the stuff in his ears, probably his own. His people have set up a special website and he has announced that he is holding a special meeting in the church hall. He intends to introduce himself and his family and to describe his development plans for the area. Even at some distance it seemed clear that it wasn't just the hair which was bought. His teeth were wobbling about in a rather unnatural way, suggesting that they too had been provided by man rather than God, and I couldn't help hoping that whatever else might have been tacked on had been fastened rather more securely. Naturally, his impending news, and the word 'development', have caused considerable anxiety and I have no doubt at all that if it now turned out that my rumoured aliens had arrived they would be welcomed warmly. If there is one thing that country folk hate more than taxes, caravans and planning people it is change. Sadly, I never go to meetings of any kind on the sensible grounds that they are a waste of time and serve only to allow egos to be taken out, given a thoroughly good airing, displayed for admiration and polished before being put away. Still, there is no doubt that we will be regaled with extensive accounts of the meeting. We have already heard that our new neighbour has been boasting on what is, I believe, called 'social media' that he is enjoying being Lord of all he surveys. Since his new house has a relatively modest acreage attached to it (of which approximately three acres is a small lake known locally as Meg's Mere in memory of a local witch who is reputed to have been drowned there in the days when ducking was an inexact science) one assumes that he has one eye closed and is squinting through the other when he does his surveying. In the Cotswolds an estate of nine acres is usually regarded as being something between a large garden and 'somewhere for the kids to play'.

27

It turns out that his Lordship, our new and imperious neighbour is not quite as grand as had previously been thought. It seems that he made most of his money through dealing in second hand vans, for which there is, apparently, an insatiable demand in the area of England enclosed by the M25, and that he added to the fortune thus obtained through an investment in a company which manufactures brand new antiques. This is, apparently, quite a lucrative trade which is welcomed by antique dealers since it helps to ensure that supply matches the ever growing demand. He is also a director of two additional companies. One makes special grenades which are attractive to small children. When a child picks up the grenade the device explodes but with only enough force to maim – usually blowing off a limb or two. The principle behind this brilliant idea is, apparently, that these grenades cause great distress and result in the enemy having to spend more time and money dealing with the injured children than would be taken up with simply burying them. The other company he is involved with manufactures a variety of remarkably profitable but carcinogenic chemicals which are, apparently, especially popular on the export market.

It also appears that his Lordship's title is not quite what it had originally seemed. It was, so we were reliably informed by a friend who works in what is left of the Street of Shame, purchased in conjunction with a small property in the Home Counties. Our neighbour is therefore the Lord of the Manor in a village somewhere south of the M4. He has, nevertheless, arbitrarily decided that this entitles him to be addressed as though he were a true peer of the realm, and had purchased his title in the more traditional modern way (by bunging one of the political parties a few hundred thousand quid for 'election expenses'). Antoinette and I have decided that we are deeply impressed by his enthusiasm and that if we meet him or discuss him with other local inhabitants we will refer to him as the Duke of Gloucestershire (never to be confused with the Duke of Gloucester, an aristocrat of an entirely different hue).

28

Our new, titled farming neighbour has wasted no time in publicising his plans. He has announced that a former assistant manager of one of his second-hand van establishments has been appointed estate manager and general farm manager. There is no mention of this man having had any experience of anything other than selling white vans but I have no doubt that all concerned are confident that this will be of absolutely no hindrance. I have met him and I confess it did occur to me that if a thought popped into his head while he was out walking he would probably have to sit down since coping with the two things at once would probably be one thing too many. The new estate manager (my, how grand that sounds) will be helped by a full-time staff of six who will be supplemented, as and when the need arises, with extra staff hired in from neighbouring villages. The estate manager's first job will be, he announces on the farm's constantly updated website, to get rid of all the wooden trees and scruffy hedges and to replace them with a good deal of fresh and shiny barbed wire which will blend in well with the neat, metal posts they intend to erect.

'We can get £40 a truck load for the logs,' the new manager told me proudly. 'I reckon we can fill ten trucks – so that's, what, er, quite a lot of money!'

I wondered if he'd worked out that they could use the same truck ten times or if he would buy ten separate trucks.

He pulled out his mobile phone, turned on the calculator facility and pressed a few keys. '£4,000!' he announced.

'£400, I think,' I suggested politely.

All this felling and clearing will, so he tells us all, open up the area, allow the light to get in and enable everyone in the vicinity to see much more. And what he says is, of course, perfectly true, though these days more and more farmers are actually planting trees and hedgerows, because they understand that they provide shelter and shade for their animals, and very few seem to be cutting them down indiscriminately. By chopping down the trees which are closest we will all have a much better view of the trees which are some distance away. These trees will, of course, be smaller, because they will be further away, but we will be able to see more of them and I have no doubt at all that there is a piece of EU legislation somewhere which makes it clear that lots of small trees in the distance are better for the soul than a smaller number of big ones closer up.

The estate manager, having created an area of suburbanised countryside, has also published on the Web a list of the equipment he is buying. The collection will apparently include a selection of bulldozers, diggers, dumper trucks, four wheel drive vehicles, trailers, trucks of several assorted sizes and, of course, an assortment of white vans in different shapes and sizes. There has been some talk locally that parking this huge number and variety of vehicles and machinery will not leave much room left for any actual farming. I reckon the expenditure on vehicles and machines must be somewhere in the region of £250,000 to £300,000. Still, they have £400 coming in from the sale of the chopped up trees. Or £4,000, if only they can manage to persuade the man writing the cheque to use the calculator on the estate manager's phone. And in another 25 years' time there will be another £400 (or £4,000) worth of logs to harvest. Still, even to my untrained mind, this did not look like a business plan destined for success.

29

I returned my useless Windows Office software to Amazon but I will not receive a refund because it didn't arrive. It was stolen en route. (I'm fed up with describing postal items as 'lost' when it's as clear as day that they have been stolen.) And that serves me right for entrusting it to Royal Mail. I should have hired Securicor and a van full of heavily armed guards. As an aside, I hate Windows almost as much as I hate Royal Mail. The damned software appears to me to have been designed by people desperately keen to show how clever they are. It seems to me that they make the stuff absurdly complicated simply because they can – and with no thought whatsoever of the practical needs of the people who will use it. And why, I wonder, do they put the 'send to' instruction right next to the 'shredder' instruction? I suppose it was some 16-year-old software writer's idea of a little joke.

30

The NHS is a gloomy mess. Thousands of people are now dying every week so that a socialist dream of state-run medicine can survive – even though the dream is a proven failure. (My definition of a socialist is someone who wants to spend more money than they earn.) Patients wait two weeks for X-ray results, two weeks for basic blood test results and a month to find out whether or not their lump is cancerous. All these tests should be available within hours but NHS bureaucracy means dangerous delays. Vets provide a far better service for animal patients. Small hospitals and single-handed GP surgeries are closed because they are considered old-fashioned (even though patients like them and they provide an excellent and important service). There are fewer available beds in Britain than anywhere else in the so-called developed world – largely because most of the money spent on the NHS is given to administrators who think only of themselves. The NHS is like every large organisation in that bureaucracies exist to prevent things happening and to support and protect the people employed within the bureaucracy. The interests of patients are of no significance since in the NHS they don't pay overtly for what they consume. The NHS bureaucracy would only be really satisfied if patients were banished from the system.

Moreover, the science went out of medicine decades ago. Today, medicine is a lethal mixture of bad habits and black magic built on a rickety platform of poor logic, bad science and poor ethics. Research papers are written to please drug companies rather than to tell the truth. The basic principles of good medicine have been forgotten or ignored. Hardly anyone working in the NHS has any idea of the basic principles of good hygiene. The other day I watched in horror as a surgeon on a real life TV documentary operated without a mask so that he could talk to the interviewer and be better seen by the cameras. (I have long believed that doctors and nurses who take part in television programmes are endangering the lives of those they are paid to look after. Incidents such as this confirm my belief.)

And if anyone complains about anything in the NHS, the first thing that happens is that all the relevant paperwork mysteriously disappears.

The worst thing of all is the officially sanctioned end of life experience known as the Liverpool Care Pathway, an Orwellian style policy which means that old people who look as if they will live too long, and block hospital beds, are killed off by being starved to death. If the Chinese or the Koreans allowed their old people to die of thirst or starvation thousands would demonstrate in Trafalgar Square and there would be much wringing of hands by left wing commentators. If private hospitals systemically killed patients to save money, questions would be asked in the Commons. But starving old people to death (or denying them water) is a Government approved standard NHS policy which doesn't seem to have bothered anyone at the British Medical Association, the Royal College of Nursing or the General Medical Council. It would be kinder to hit old people over the head with a brick and I daresay that will be the next kind-hearted proposal the enthusiastic supporters of State-run health care will dream up.

To be honest it would not surprise me in the slightest if the Liberal Democrats, those self-proclaimed saviours of the planet, concluded that it would be best if we ate our old people instead of simply burning or burying them. The BBC would immediately invite our favourite television cooks to show us ways to prepare tasty octogenarians for Sunday lunch.

May

1

I spent much of the day working on my annual accounts. Every year I wonder why the manufacturers of calculators always make them with a built-in fault. Give me a calculator, any calculator, and a row of figures and if I add them up six times I will get six different answers. If I added them up twelve times I would doubtless get twelve different answers. As usual, however, I get around the calculator fault by adding everything up three times, adding the three sums together and dividing by three. That is then the figure I put on the form. If the taxman wants to do it all again he's welcome to my box of accounts. And he can borrow my calculator if he wants.

2

According to the *Financial Times*, which takes these things very seriously, a fellow called Christopher Bailey, who is chief executive of Burberry, the store which sells trench coats to gentlemen and scarves and silly hats to minor television celebrities and footballers' wives, has a £440,000 annual clothes allowance. He also receives a huge discount on whatever clothes he buys from Burberry. Just how does a man spend that much on clothes? A fellow can buy a damned decent suit and accessories for £2,000. And hats from Jermyn Street don't cost more than £200 to £300. A really good tie will set him back £150. So, even if Mr Bailey doesn't much like his own company's products (and qualify for the massive discount), it is difficult to see how he gets through £440,000 unless, of course, he buys himself a lot of expensive frocks and gowns in which case he'd probably have to scrimp and save to make that £440,000 last a month. However, in addition to this extraordinary frock allowance Mr Bailey receives £20 million a year in what is sweetly called 'compensation'. The shareholders found this as obscenely greedy as I do and most of them voted against his pay deal when they had a chance to do so. I cannot imagine who thought that £20 million a year was a reasonable wage for someone running a company flogging macs, hats, scarves and so on. Nevertheless, despite the fact that the owners of the company had voted against Mr Bailey's absurd wages the directors decided to give the £20 million to him anyway. I really find that a puzzle. Who on earth gave directors the right to chuck away money belonging to other people?

3

The General Medical Council is a curious organisation which is half charity, half quango, half government department and half protection racket. It used to consist of a little more than a file clerk, who kept the register of doctors who were qualified to practice medicine, and a committee of rather pompous individuals who sat in judgement when erring doctors were accused of bonking their patients on the consulting room couch. The filing clerk kept a mailing list of doctors and presumably stored the list in a couple of filing tablets. No one at the old-style GMC gave a damn whether or not doctors knew anything at all about medicine. The GMC ignored the damage done by doctors who hadn't heard of penicillin and who thought that purging patients was a pretty damned good example of high tech medicine. Today, in contrast, the GMC is a vast organisation with a huge budget and a seemingly insatiable yearning for power. It employs a host of pontificating file clerks with ideas well above their station, though I suspect that most have little or no experience of medicine in practice. And so, for example, the GMC (which is headed by a former journalist and staffed by about a million and a half of the most arrogant and aggressive people outside the HMRC offices) has decided that it no longer approves of the Hippocratic Oath, which it considers rather old-fashioned, and it has happily overseen the disappearance of the principle of medical confidentiality.

Today, the new GMC does a lot of huffing and puffing and a good deal of collecting of money but I fear that it still takes no real interest in patient welfare and I suspect that it now probably kills more people than influenza. In my view it is no stretch to say that the GMC is such a threat to the nation that it should be classified as a terrorist organisation. The GMC does nothing about dirty hospitals, about the overprescribing of antibiotics, about the unavailability of doctors at night and at weekends and about the fact that hospital doctors now routinely murder elderly patients who are blocking beds. The GMC does nothing about the overprescribing of tranquillisers and antidepressants and takes no interest in the fact that doctor-induced disease is, alongside cancer and circulatory disease, now one of the three main causes of death in Britain. The GMC does nothing about the fact that the medical establishment (which is pretty well owned by the pharmaceutical industry) suppresses discussion about controversial issues such as vaccination and seems to find it perfectly acceptable that great chunks of medical education are paid for by drug companies. It is thanks to the GMC (and also the European Union) that patients now often have to wait two weeks to see their GP (or, quite likely, a stand-in practice nurse). It is the GMC's fault that their doctor will be too busy filling forms (to keep his licence) to have time to waste on people. Today, the average patient must be satisfied with just enough time to describe one brief symptom and accept a prescription. It is also thanks to the GMC (and the EU) that patients are unable to call a doctor at night, at weekends or on bank holidays and must, instead, spend eight or nine hours queuing in the casualty department of a hospital 30 miles from their home. (Written down this seems absurd but it is, if anything, an understatement and not an exaggeration. In Northern Ireland, for example, the waiting time target is for patients to be seen within 12 hours but even this appalling target is regularly breached. I wonder how many senior politicians have to sit and wait, bleeding and in pain, for more than 12 hours before they are seen by a nurse or a doctor. In practice, things are often worse even than that, with patients forced to lie in an ambulance, parked outside the hospital, for up to eight hours before room can be found for them in the accident and emergency department. There can be no doubt that patients who might otherwise have been saved have died waiting for treatment.)

The reason for the GMC's new power is simple. After the Dr Harold Shipman scandal it was decided in high places that 'something' had to be done to protect the public from dangerous doctors. Shipman, a general practitioner, had spent years methodically slaughtering his patients and Ministers were embarrassed. When a doctor murders over 200 of his patients, as Shipman did, it does rather stand out and there were calls for 'something to be done'. It was decreed, presumably by people who had no idea what they were doing, that some form of regular testing should be introduced so that doctors in practice could be assessed. The plans for doctors to have competence tests every five years, with annual appraisals in between, were drawn up in 2008 by Professor Sir Liam Donaldson, the Government's chief medical officer at the time. Donaldson was instructed to do something by Ministers who wanted to weed out rogue practitioners and make sure that there would not be another Shipman embarrassment. (Donaldson is famous for having recommended that if patients requested that their personal medical data not be uploaded to the ill-fated, centralised NHS database then the GPs receiving the requests should forward the letters to the Health Secretary. He did not say whether patients who wanted to protect their privacy should be denied treatment, summarily executed or merely placed on a list of troublesome patients.)

The idea behind the 'competence tests' was to weed out the dangerous doctors, to take them off the front line and, presumably to keep them out of the way by giving them jobs at the Department of Health or in the medical school department one of the redbrick universities. Everyone forgets, conveniently, that Shipman had been reported to the authorities many times. Other local doctors had noticed that an unusually large number of his patients seemed to be dying before their time. However, the people with the power to do something (namely the GMC) did bugger all.

Today, of course, everyone in authority claims that the Shipman fiasco had nothing to do with the GMC's brand new revalidation programme. This is silly. The record shows that the revalidation programme is a direct result of the Shipman affair. Politicians were jumping up and down as Shipman's kill total soared above 200 and the General Medical Council, the official body in charge of protecting patients and getting rid of dangerous doctors, was given the job of finding a new way of assessing medical practitioners.

What the GMC did, of course, was to design a system which would vastly increase its own power and its own income – apparently ignoring the fact (or ignorant of it) that if Shipman were still alive and practising he would sail through the new system with flying colours. The GMC's revalidation programme would suit him down to the ground and he would have had absolutely no difficulty in finding patients or colleagues to vouch for him. On the other hand the GMC's power and money grab has been enormously successful. Back in 1973 the GMC's total income from all sources was £662,579. In 2013 the GMC had an income of £95,400,000. (Just to put this in perspective the average annual salary in 1973 was £2,126 and in 2013 the average annual salary was £26,500. The average salary is just over ten times the 1973 level but the GMC's income is well over 100 times what it was 40 years ago. The GMC must be one of the most financially successful organisations on the planet.)

There were two odd things about the Government suddenly asking the GMC to 'do' something.

First, the GMC was the body which was in charge when Shipman killed roughly 10% of his patients. In any sensible run society the GMC would have been roundly bollocked and disbanded, with the responsible officials sent off to cold climates to count penguins. But Britain doesn't work like that. Official bodies which screw up are routinely given extra power and more money. And so the GMC was given the task of stopping another Shipman disaster, even though it is arguable that it was the GMC which was partly responsible for him getting away with it.

The second odd thing was that no one had previously thought of setting up a scheme to re-licence doctors in the same way that airline pilots are assessed every few years to make sure that they still know what all the knobs do. Shortly after I qualified (in 1971) I remember writing articles suggesting that doctors should be required to take an examination of some kind every ten years or so. Even to a neophyte it seemed absurd that doctors were allowed to practice for fifty years or more on the basis of knowledge gained when penicillin was still unheard of.

But no Government ever abandons an idea just because it's a bad one. Once given the go ahead the pen pushers at the GMC set about designing a scheme which everyone with half a brain should have known would never have a hope in hell of preventing another Shipman from killing taxpayers but was, worse still, designed in such a way that it was guaranteed to result in far more deaths than Shipman had managed in several years of medical mayhem. In medical terms the ineptly designed 'treatment' (known as revalidation) was destined to kill the patient.

The bozos at the GMC did, however, make sure that they designed a scheme which brought them in more money; loads of money. Doctors now have to pay the GMC a hefty fee to be registered and another hefty fee for a licence. Any doctor who wants to practice has to pay the GMC both fees. (Selling people licences to do what they're trained to do is a splendid new scam. Everyone seems to be getting in on the act. Today everyone gets marked, rated, tested, reviewed, regulated and assessed. Everyone, that is, except the people with the real power over our lives: the eurocrats, MEPS and civil servants. They can be as lazy and as incompetent as they like, as venal and as criminal as they fancy, and no one ever marks, reviews or assesses them.)

The GMC's revalidation system is an absolute nightmare for anyone who doesn't have six ballpoint pens tucked neatly in their breast pocket. Doctors are expected to collect endless pieces of paper from patients and colleagues confirming that they are 'good eggs'. It is not surprising that doctors are now as unhappy about their work as teachers and dentists.

(I've met about two dozen teachers in my life. They all wanted to be and do something else for a living. A good half of them wanted to be rock stars or famous painters but couldn't since they were not blessed with any talent or, indeed, any enthusiasm for work or for doing anything except lounge around all day dreaming about what might have been if they had been blessed with talent and enthusiasm. It's always been the same with dentists. I've met a number of them and never yet met one who ever really wanted to be a dentist. Most of them drifted into dentistry because the entry requirements for dental school were, at the time, lower than the entry requirements for medical school. They were inspired not by vocation but by the knowledge that no one has ever met a poor dentist. But as soon as they got over the excitement of buying their first new car, the thrill of peering into an endless parade of mouths soon wore off. And they decided that they would have more fun, and probably make even more money, if they took advantage of their natural talent for playing golf or racing motor cars. Over the years this feeling grew, probably helped along by the fact that older dentists tend to earn less than young ones because they simply don't have the mental and physical strength to yank teeth at the same blistering speed. I have known at least four dentists who believed they could quite definitely have won the Open golf championship and three who knew for a certain fact that they could have been world champion Grand Prix drivers. Doctors used to be different. The ones I knew when I was young were enthusiastic about their work. But, sadly, tragically, things have changed. The doctors I meet these days all want to be something else. Their only joy is in the money and their only dream is of the day when they can stop being doctors and be someone else. And that's not just sad, it's bloody dangerous.)

The GMC's new method of assessing medical practitioners will make more doctors hate their professional lives and it will do absolutely nothing to protect patients. It won't stop doctors with murder in their hearts. And it will do absolutely nothing to weed out corrupt or incompetent doctors. The scheme is, indeed, designed to protect the establishment. Doctors who have sold their souls (and their patients) to drug companies will do fine, thank you very much. Most of the Government's medical advisers are, or have been, paid advisers to the drug industry and the GMC is very comfortable with that. None of the overpaid file clerks working there seem to feel that there is anything dodgy about allowing doctors who have taken money from drug companies to decide which drugs the NHS is allowed to buy or what the rules about vaccination should be. The revalidation programme requires doctors to be approved by other doctors and so original, creative and controversial doctors will probably find themselves forced out of the profession. I doubt if Dr John Snow, Dr Ignaz Semmelweiss or Dr Joseph Lister would have managed to get through the GMC's revalidation process. They, and their vital breakthroughs, would have been lost to medicine if the current revalidation programme had been in situ a century ago. Most great medical discoveries come as a result of research or observations made by dedicated but often eccentric individuals. There isn't one truly great advance in medicine that didn't cause a furore when it was first offered to the profession. If something is new it will upset vested interests and establishment lobbyists will soon start sharpening their spears. Medicine is already governed and dominated by tradition. The GMC's revalidation programme seems specifically designed to eradicate original thinking and to suppress creative individuals. And, almost by the by, it will actually help ensure that future Shipmans are not spotted early on. Harold Shipman would have sailed through the revalidation process without a blink. The revalidation scheme is perfectly suited to the dishonest, the cheat, the silver tongued and the rogue. Revalidation will result in a massive deterioration in the quality of medical care and a dramatic increase in the number of patients killed by the actions or unavailability of doctors.

I am not alone in wondering why doctors have allowed the GMC to introduce an absurd, unhelpful and excessively bureaucratic system which makes life unbelievably difficult for practising doctors and almost impossible for locum doctors, ships' doctors and the many physicians who don't fit neatly into the sort of world inhabited by GMC administrators.

A survey of GPs for a medical magazine showed that 78% of GPs thought that the GMC's revalidation programme was a waste of money. (I suspect that the other 22% of doctors were either making a few quid out of it as advisers, consultants and so on or else didn't speak enough English to know what was going on). A doctor from Kent remarked that 'the costs are high and the benefits pure speculation'. He went on to say: 'Yet again, the focus on the measurable encourages the bean-counters, will create a false sense of reassurance and will devalue aspects of being a doctor that are difficult to measure. Those at the coalface have to put up with ever-increasing tasks to conform to the norm and prove their competence. As quality falls, perhaps it will dawn on those in authority that quality is a degree of excellence, not a set of laboriously measured events.'

A doctor from Glasgow, who described revalidation as 'a farce' and 'a joke', wrote: 'GPs should refuse revalidation until there is proper funding for education. I'm fed up with collecting my thank–you cards, reviewing random articles and doing pointless audits to show to some random part-time GP who comes to appraise me. '

4

A lot of very poor or very stupid people live in the Cotswolds because it is customary to build walls without going to the expense of slipping mortar in between the stones. Instead of gluing the walls together, as sensible people do, the people making walls in the Cotswolds (and indeed in Derbyshire) do so by cleverly resting one stone on top of another until the wall has reached the desired height. This is exceedingly clever and takes an inordinately long time to do, but it means that if anything leans on a wall (a walker, a sheep or a well-fed butterfly for example) the wall will fall down and have to be rebuilt. For the people who make these dry stone walls this is excellent news. There is always more than enough work for them and if business does start to slacken they can always pop out with a pea shooter in hand and knock down a few dozen miles of wall while driving along in their limousines.

5

The Duke of Gloucestershire and his talented team have wasted no time in laying waste to their new estate. They are doing this with such enthusiasm that I am convinced there must be an EU grant available for the chopping down of trees and bushes and the general despoiling of the land. For several days now the air has been thick with black smoke as they have burnt the trees and bushes they've been cutting down. There has been much coughing and wheezing as locals have been forced to breathe in air that would have been rejected as unfit for purpose if it had been found floating around in central London. The local vicar, whose church stands next to the burnt area, has had to cancel a christening and a midweek service. The Duke's staff have all been equipped with chainsaws (but not with safety equipment such as goggles or ear defenders) and though they have clearly not been trained in their use (several were seen using them as though they were scythes) they have been extremely effective in clearing away unwanted trees and untidy bushes. The whole area, with burnt ground and smoke filled air would have made a splendid set for a remake of *Apocalypse Now*, though there is probably far too much barbed wire on display. Vandalism is not confined to young people in towns and cities. Our village vandals, armed with chainsaws and matches, have done more damage than a dozen youths armed with cans of spray paint. Moreover, whereas the youths would be arrested, charged, convicted and shamed the Duke of Gloucestershire will doubtless be rewarded with a large EU grant and some sort of medal from the National Farmers Union. There was some distress in the village when one of the more enthusiastic digger drivers succeeded in making a large hole in a main sewer pipe (he was apparently looking for the CD player when he inadvertently found the lever which operated the digger bucket at the front of the vehicle) but we have been reassured, via the social media, that this will be repaired very shortly or at least not long after very shortly. In addition to looking like a site for a disaster movie the area now smells worse than the London Underground.

Once upon a time, long, long ago, the local footpaths were rarely empty of walkers but today, very few people bother to come this

134

way. Thousands of birds and small animals have disappeared or died. There are already far fewer butterflies and bees. Bigger animals, such as deer, have disappeared completely. There is no food for them and the wickedly high and unsightly barbed wire fences which have been erected make life too dangerous for them. The Duke's personal public relations officer, still based in London, is busier than ever publishing bits and pieces of news about the Duke's ventures. Apparently the anti-personnel landmine industry is doing well these days and the Duke is doubtless celebrating an increase in the number of limbless children around the world. 'His Lordship,' says the PR representative, 'remains keen to be regarded as 'just one of the locals'.' He is, she says, very approachable and willing and available to open fetes, galas and gymkhanas as and when required. She adds that Her Ladyship will be available to judge babies and cakes at fetes and other public events. Antoinette and I are thinking of inviting the Duke to open our greenhouse door which warped during the winter and has been giving us some difficulty recently.

6

There is news today that His Great Righteousness, the Duke of Gloucestershire (aka the Duke of All He Surveys), is planning to go into sheep farming. The word is that he has placed an order for no less than 30 lambs and may buy another half a dozen later if all goes well. It is to be hoped that they find enough grass to eat on the post-apocalyptic landscape which is all that now remains of what used to be a pleasant looking smallholding. Antoinette and I have done some rough back of the envelope sums and we reckon that the farm's costs on equipment and labour mean that each sheep will have to fetch something in the region of £12,500 when it is sold. This is, unfortunately, a little more than usual market prices at the moment. Never mind, no businessman expects all his ventures to be profitable. The public relations officer has published photographs of the Duke and Duchess in their new garden. The Duke is wearing something with a collar made out of ermine and the Duchess, reclining on a plastic sun lounger, is wearing a bikini which appears to have been made out of a couple of pieces of thin parcel string and a yard and a half of pink cotton thread. Antoinette and I are disappointed that neither of them appears to be wearing appropriately regal headgear.

7

It has been reported that the average bra size increased from 34B to 36C during the last decade. If things continue at this rate then by the year 2054 the average bra size will be 48F and car windscreens will have to be moved further forward.

8

According to *Fortune* magazine the universal language of business comes from America. Ah, er, um, I don't know how to tell you this, boys and girls of *Fortune* magazine, but have you not noticed that the language is, er, called English? We English folk don't have much to be proud about these days. If you take all the credit for our language we will have nothing left. Even the most rabid Scottish nationalists speak English (though, it has to be admitted, some of them don't do it terribly well).

9

A 93-year-old woman who refused to be bathed by a male care worker has been told that she may need a psychiatric examination to see if she has a problem with men. She was told that it would be an infringement of the male carer's human rights if he was not allowed to bathe her. It isn't difficult to see why people are leaving Britain by the million.

10

Mickey Spillane was one of the best-selling authors of all time. He wrote the immensely successful Mike Hammer stories, which delighted millions of readers and annoyed lots of snotty critics. I've just found an old cutting about Spillane which reminds me of the time a literary figure approached him at a party and said: 'I think it's disgraceful that of the ten best-selling books of all time, seven were written by you.' Spillane responded instantly with: 'You're lucky I've only written seven books.'

It's not widely known that Spillane, who wrote very hard-boiled stories, was a Jehovah's Witness who was fond of animals and refused to allow hunting on his land.

11

I've been having awful trouble with the GMC. Although I don't practice medicine (in that I don't hang a stethoscope around my neck every morning) I still need to be registered and licensed. A few years ago I took my name off the register because I didn't want my address publishing in the medical directory. Inevitably, critics who didn't like my books started claiming that I wasn't a proper doctor. On television and radio and in newspapers and on the internet people accused me of being a fake, a quack and a fraud. Because they couldn't find my name on the register they assumed that I didn't have a medical degree. And so, to avoid this steady stream of libellous abuse, I arranged to put my name back onto the register.

And now things have got tricky because I don't fit neatly into the GMC's revalidation programme. I don't have masses of patients or colleagues to vouch for me because I work alone at home, sitting behind a keyboard. I did write to the GMC right at the beginning of their venture into this brave new world of licensing, explaining my situation. But they have, inevitably, ignored my requests, warnings and protests. And now they don't know what to do with me. But they have sent me a huge sheaf of paperwork to fill in.

They have, for example, asked for details of all my motoring offences. They have asked for details of a 1984 speeding offence. And they have demanded an explanation for a £5 fine I received in 1977 when an officious policeman spotted me hurrying to a suspected heart attack patient who had serious chest pains and a history of heart disease. I had switched on the car's hazard flashers to help me get through rush hour traffic and this, of course, is a traffic offence – the sort of thing likely to bring down western civilisation. The policeman (who was not related to the patient with the chest pains) insisted on taking me to court and the magistrates (who were also not related to the patient with the chest pains) fined me £5 but did not endorse my licence. The form collectors at the GMC clearly regard this 37-year-old motoring offence as having a bearing on my fitness to practice medicine though intelligent people might find this difficult to understand.

I have spent several hours today searching through old boxes of files to try to find the information they so desperately need. I am sure this will make the world a safer place for patients everywhere.

12

I complained of feeling tired this morning and Antoinette took me to the shelves where the books I've written are collected. 'That's why you're tired,' she said. And I suppose she's right. But if I'm feeling tired, John Creasey must have been exhausted when he died. He wrote 564 novels in 40 years. He once finished two books in six days and during his life he used 25 pseudonyms. I feel shattered just thinking about it all. Some self-styled literary folk (mainly those who've never actually written a book) might sneer at his output but the sheer physical and mental effort involved must have been incredible.

13

Children are to be banned from building sand castles on the beaches of Europe this summer. This daft new law comes straight from the office of an EU bureaucrat who has presumably been heavily lobbied by representatives of the Sand and Mud Castle Building Union (Dusseldorf branch). Or maybe it was lobbyists from the Association of Beach Buggy Drivers (Malaga branch), fed up with having to drive their buggies around sand castle ruins. It will have been the result of lobbying from someone. The EU never does anything without being pushed into it (or out of it) by a bunch of highly paid lobbyists. If the EU is banning something they will invariably claim that it's for 'health and safety' reasons. But it isn't really. It's because a group of rich bastards have hired some lobbyists. If anyone at the EU cared a damn about health and safety they'd ban dogs from all parks and beaches, or at least enforce laws requiring owners to pick up after their dogs have defecated. Every year countless children are bitten, disfigured and maimed by uncontrolled dogs and scores go blind because they've contracted toxicariasis from canine faeces. No one does anything about these very real and very serious health problems because there isn't a lobby group representing the interests of children at risk but there are lobbyists representing dogs and dog owners.

14

The quasi-tragic news is that the Duke of Gloucestershire appears to have gone bust. Too much equipment and not enough logs, perchance. A number of men arrived today and drove away a wide variety of vehicles. Two low loaders were involved and there was much cursing as the drivers struggled to squeeze their vehicles down the lane. Padlocks have now been put on gates, lambs have disappeared and there is talk that someone will be along to roll up the barbed wire and take it back to the barbed wire shop. Even the Duke's website has been closed and the public relations lady has been summarily silenced. I am told that even the social media outlets are no longer buzzing with news. Alas, the Duke has, like the birds, stopped twittering. How many decades will it take, I wonder, for the hedgerows to recover and for some more trees to grow? I'll give the squirrels extra nuts to hasten the process. They always 'plant' far more than they remember to dig up.

15

Google, the evil search engine company which has done infinitely more harm than good but managed nevertheless to make its irresponsible, witless employees rich beyond all sense and understanding, has been told that it must remove stories which are inaccurate, or which people find unreasonably distressing. Google (whose employees generally seem to think they are far brighter than they are) and its sycophantic defenders do not approve, of course. Many people who have doubtless never been exposed to public criticism claim that this is censorship. Google has waved two fingers at the new law by ensuring that extra publicity is given to news items which are pulled from the search engine. I'm totally in agreement with those who want news stories about them to be removed from the search engine. I no longer do any interviews and if I could wipe my name from the internet I would happily do so.

In my youth I was encouraged by my publishers and agents to insist that newspapers which printed wildly inaccurate pieces about me publish corrections. There have been a good many of those over the years – largely because many of the articles about me were written by, for or at the behest of drug company lobbyists anxious to discredit me. Over the years a surprising number of stories have been followed, a week or two later, with apologies and retractions. I never asked for libel damages but I did demand that false accusations were withdrawn.

But these days there is no point in bothering to insist that an apology is published. The problem is that while search engines will pick up an original news story or feature article they do not pick up any corrections which might have appeared subsequently. And there is absolutely nothing that the libelled individual can do about this. The difficulty and cost of suing a search engine would be ruinous.

So I never key my name into Google or any other search engine. And I never look up other people either. I know just how inaccurate and misleading these search engine results can be. (The general value of search engines was destroyed when it became possible for companies, lobbyists and pressure groups to influence their positions on the list of sites which appear when a particular enquiry is made.)

16

Many, many years ago, when I was still wearing short trousers and believed in Father Christmas, the tooth fairy and the integrity of our judiciary, I wrote an article pointing out that a number of foreign trained doctors working in the National Health Service did not quite match up the standards required of British trained doctors. I pointed out that a high proportion of the doctors getting into trouble for incompetence or naughtiness were, to put it bluntly, foreign. To say that this article did not go down terribly well with the medical establishment and the forces of political correctness would be an understatement of heroic proportions. So I was interested to see that a study by University College in London has found that the majority of the 88,000 foreign doctors working in the health service would fail exams if they were held to the same standard as British doctors. Over 1,000 doctors a year are licensed by the General Medical Council after passing an examination which assesses their clinical and language skills. (The language skills test produces some odd results. I once met a foreign doctor who thought that quinsy was a consequence of over-enthusiastic infertility treatment.) But the new study showed that around half of the doctors who were given licences would fail to reach the standards expected of British doctors. It is, therefore, perhaps not surprising that although foreign doctors make up only a third of NHS doctors they account for two thirds of the doctors struck off each year. The study was commissioned by the GMC itself after the charity/quango had been criticised by the British Association of Physicians of Indian Origin which claimed that the GMC failed too many doctors from overseas.

17

We have been in Paris for two days and we were woken this morning by the pigeons flapping at the window and doing a good deal of cooing. We haven't been here for a while and when I put out the bird food yesterday morning it was several hours before the pigeons and the sparrows turned up. The pigeons, however, are bright enough to realise that when they get fed once it means that we are in residence and they will be fed again – every morning and every afternoon. We buy them bird food from the pet supplies section of the local supermarket and they very much approve. So, if they haven't been fed by 9.00 a.m. they land on our sixth floor windowsill and wake us up. The sparrows dance around between the slow and steady pigeons, darting here and there with the speed of lightning. Feeding the birds may be illegal but it is a human right and a joy to the soul. The last time the police arrived we kept quiet and didn't open the door. The French plod had, I suspect, been called by one of the other residents who disapproves of the birds being fed. (As the French found in the 1940s there's always one miserable informer in any building.) The Paris police are hardly likely to break down the door to deal with a suspected case of bird feeding are they?

18

We did bugger all today. And absolutely nothing happened. We sat in the apartment, listening to music, reading books and playing games. It is, from time to time, quite wonderful to squander a day in such a luxurious way. Both of us felt surprisingly refreshed and invigorated by the rest. Everything happens at such a pace these days that it is occasionally necessary to turn off the telephones (even the mobile ones), ignore the internet and leave the mail uncollected. The important thing is not to be suckered into just checking the emails 'to see if there's anything urgent'. There almost certainly won't be anything urgent but there will almost certainly be something annoying that someone else regards as important. It can wait a day.

19

We wandered up to Les Invalides and walked around the cloisters. We then sat in the small park near to the church where Napoleon is buried. It is only a few yards off the beaten track but hardly anyone ever goes there. We sat for an hour watching the sparrows and the firebugs. I'm sure that both Antoinette and I had more important things to do, but I am equally sure that neither of us had better things to do.

20

We caught the train back to England. We sat in our usual seats, at a table for two, and across the aisle the table for four was occupied by a bunch of rock musicians. I didn't know who they were but Antoinette recognised them. They are, apparently, hugely successful and renowned for being exceptionally noisy and raucous on stage. This is, by coincidence, the second time this has happened and they were once again the quietest, politest travellers I've shared a carriage with for a long time. One worked on a laptop computer. The other three read books and magazines and drank water and fruit juice. I don't wish to embarrass them so I will not mention their names, or the name of their group. A quartet of salesmen or a family with a couple of squabbling children would have made far more noise and been far more of a nuisance. This incident confirmed our experience that if you want to travel quietly, in dignity and in style then you should choose rock musicians as your travelling companions. On our last train journey, a week ago, four old age pensioners sat opposite us. They were disgraceful and embarrassing and screeched and shouted endlessly and generally behaved like hooligans. By the time we reached our destination they were all as pissed as newts.

21

We visited an acquaintance in a nursing home. It was an awful place. The residents were sitting in rows of plastic chairs staring at one another. Apart from some coughing and wheezing and a little occasional moaning the place was silent. It was awful. It reminded me of residential homes I visited when I was a young GP. I remember once suggesting to the matron in one of them that it might be a good idea to dig up the huge expanse of lawn at the front of the property and to allow the residents to grow vegetables and flowers. It would, I suggested innocently, be good exercise and a great hobby – as well as providing the nursing home with supplies of fresh vegetables and flowers. The response was immediate. The matron could not have been more appalled if I had suggested organising weekly ecstasy raves. The residents might injure themselves. There would be serious health and safety issues. There would be massive insurance problems. It could not possibly be done. I was startled and disappointed. (This was in the 1970s when 'health' and 'safety' were just beginning to rear their ugly heads.) I did, however, go back to the idea in the second of my books about Mrs Caldicot. In *Mrs Caldicot's Knickerbocker Glory* the residents of her nursing home dig up the lawn so that they can grow whatever takes their fancy. Fiction is sometimes far more fun than real life.

22

I've just seen my favourite ever newspaper apology. This appeared in the *Financial Times* under the heading *Apology to His Excellency Sheikh Khalid bin Ahmed al Khalifa*. Here is the text of the apology:

'An article about detainees at Guantanamo Bay in FT Weekend…was mistakenly accompanied by a photograph of Sheikh Khalid bin Ahmed al Khalifa, foreign minister of the Kingdom of Bahrain, with a caption that incorrectly described him as 'Khaled Sheik Mohammed: among five detainees on trial'. We apologise unreservedly to His Excellency Sheikh Khalid for the error and any distress caused.'

I'm surprised Sheikh Khalid doesn't now own the *Financial Times*. Maybe he does.

23

If I bit someone in the street I would be arrested. Why don't footballers get arrested when they bite, kick, gouge one another on the pitch? It is hardly surprising that football fans behave like lunatics if they see their heroes behaving badly – and getting away with it. Bad behaviour on the pitch was virtually unheard of when professional footballers were paid £14 a week and had to have additional jobs in order to buy food for their ferrets.

24

Back in England we have weeds in our grass which are waist high. I thought I could stick it out longer than this but the weeds have called my bluff and I have reluctantly arranged for our lawn mower to be serviced.

A reviewer claims that my medical books are unfair and that Britain's National Health Service is a wonderful organisation whose staff provide the best medical care in the world. This sort of complacent nonsense enrages me. The NHS is a bureaucratic monster which does far more harm than good. Here, taken from my mail bag, are just a few of the reasons why I believe the NHS is well past its sell-by-date and should be put out of our misery.

1. A woman of 93 was dumped at the wrong address by an ambulance crew. She fell and broke both hips while trying to walk the five miles to her house. She had told the ambulance crew that they were dropping her at the wrong house but they ignored her.

2. A 51-year-old woman was forced to sleep in a wheelchair for 15 months because bureaucrats working for a hospital trust decided that it was too dangerous for nurses to lift her into bed. The woman the nurses couldn't or wouldn't lift weighed just eight stone.

3. Administrators told a consultant surgeon to operate on non-urgent patients (including one wanting breast augmentation) before dealing with patients with cancer. The order came so that the hospital would meet Government waiting list targets.

4. A schoolboy who lived two miles from a major hospital was taken on a 100 mile round trip to have his broken wrist set. He was turned away by three hospitals and spent nine hours in agony.

5. A woman of 92 lay on a pavement for more than an hour with a broken leg. The hospital to which she was eventually taken was just a few hundred yards away.

6. A 75-year-old woman who was found dead in her home had been waiting five hours for an ambulance.

7. A black woman had a foot amputated in an NHS hospital. She was told that if she wanted a black artificial foot she would have to pay extra because black artificial feet cost more than white ones.

8. Two surgeons removed a patient's one remaining healthy kidney. Neither of the surgeons had checked the patient's notes or records or consent form. The surgeons were suspended for just twelve months.

9. When five bureaucrats visited a woman at home to assess her care requirements she fell down on the floor while trying to show them round. Although she begged them to help her to her feet none of them offered her a hand. Bureaucrats aren't actually in the helping-people business.

10. Asylum seekers now routinely choose to go back home if they fall ill – because it is widely recognised that medical care is better almost anywhere outside the UK. The asylum seekers return after medical treatment because the benefits system in the UK is second to none.

26

I've received a rather snotty letter from someone at the GMC called Lindsey Westwood who is in charge of the Revalidation programme for all doctors and who tells me that if I wish to be registered and licensed as a doctor then I must follow the GMC's procedure, even though it is patently clear to anyone over the age of two that it is quite impossible for me to follow their procedure. She has the gall to question whether or not I need to be licensed since I no longer stick my fingers into strangers' orifices. (I have already explained exactly why I need to be licensed.) After wandering around on the internet for two minutes I was dumbfounded to find that just two years ago Ms Westwood (who is now pontificating about how doctors should be licensed and who is, it seems, in charge of the whole revalidation programme) was working for the Traffic Penalty Tribunal as an appeals manager. Before that she worked for AIG (an insurance company). I find it absolutely staggering that the person the GMC have put in charge of checking the fitness to practice of every doctor in Britain was previously checking parking tickets.

I've sent this reply:

'Thank you for your letter which, I'm afraid, I found rather pompous, patronising and just plain rude.

There are two basic and crucial problems with your revalidation scheme in general. First, you are wasting doctors' time on frivolous, pointless box ticking. The forms are endless and require the collecting of vast amounts of paperwork. This means that doctors have far less time for patients. Any honest GP or hospital doctor will confirm this in private. Less time for patients means a poorer service. I'm not surprised that the GMC distrusts the NHS and provides private health care cover for its employees. Second, older doctors are now forced to retire completely instead of working part time. This removes a vast number of experienced doctors from the available pool and is the reason foreign doctors are being flown in (at enormous expense) to provide locum cover. I know a lot of people like to be treated by bright young doctors who have been trained in the latest ways but I would always prefer an older doctor who has had the time to acquire intuition, instinct and wisdom. All that skill has now been lost; tossed aside as unwanted. (Older doctors are also far more likely to know, at first hand, a little about pain. Young doctors, who've maybe never been ill, are too likely to be blasé about pain.)

At a time when the EU's Working Time Directive limits the number of hours doctors can work (NHS hospitals employ highly paid bureaucrats to make sure that doctors don't work more hours than allowed) those older doctors, flexible and prepared to work part-time, are needed more than ever. It's difficult to avoid the feeling that the whole revalidation procedure was designed to give the GMC more power and more money rather than to protect patients. If you don't understand all this then I suspect you have very little idea of exactly how health care works in practice and I fear you don't recognise the harm the GMC's absurd revalidation policy is doing to the nation's health. (I realise that your previous job was dealing with parking tickets). It is well known (though I realise the GMC may deny this truth) that revalidation was set up in an attempt to prevent another Shipman. It's less well known that instead of preventing another Shipman (which it patently will not do) revalidation will be a far greater killer than Shipman himself. Shipman killed retail. The GMC is now killing wholesale. The whole revalidation scheme is arrogant, disorganised, unprincipled and out of touch and is designed to remove creative, thoughtful doctors rather than 'bad' doctors who might harm their patients. It will do nothing whatsoever to stop doctors with murder in their hearts. And it will do absolutely nothing to weed out corrupt, incompetent or ignorant doctors.

As far as my specific situation is concerned, I fear that you have misunderstood your role and assumed a sense of authority to which you are not entitled. The GMC's job is solely to protect the public from incompetent and dishonest doctors. I'm a qualified doctor and how I choose to practise medicine is up to me. Your job is simply to make sure that I do my job honestly and honourably. You can easily do that by assessing my published work. I simply want to be treated fairly and in the same way as other doctors. I found your comment that you 'will not be producing a bespoke solution which will allow you to keep a licence essentially on your own terms' extraordinarily rude and, moreover, it seems to me to illustrate just how completely you have failed to understand our respective roles. I have never asked to have a licence on my own terms. All I ask is that I am treated fairly; in the same way as any other doctor. It is not my fault if you have designed such a rigid revalidation procedure that I do not fit into your scheme. As you have confirmed I gave you plenty of warning of my situation. I cannot produce forms filled in by colleagues and patients but I do think it is reasonable to expect you to judge my competence according to my work. I've never heard of the Independent Doctors Federation or any commercial providers and I have no intention of joining a Federation so that I can satisfy the GMC. I just want to be treated as fairly as psychiatrists, GPs and dermatologists. A refusal to allow me a licence would, I believe, be contrary to Human Rights legislation and employment law and would suggest that the GMC is officious and highhanded and determined to exclude originality and creativity from the profession. It is not your place even to consider whether I should or should not be licensed for my work. It is your job to administer the rules which decide whether or not I am safe to be licensed for the type of medicine I practise – writing books. The GMC added licensing to registration and I need both. It is now your job to devise a form of appraisal that fits my work and not my job to change the way I practise medicine so that I can fit your form of appraisal.

My own revalidation will be a good opportunity for us all to assess the relevance, validity, suitability and effectiveness of the GMC and to debate the GMC's revalidation programme in Parliament and in the press. I look forward to this and I hope you do too. '

27

A new study has suggested that men may suffer more when they have the flu because higher levels of testosterone weaken the body's immune response. A study by Stanford University School of Medicine found that women tend to have a stronger antibody response to the bug which causes influenza than men do and that this response gives them better protection against the virus. It seems likely, therefore, that men are more susceptible to bacterial, viral, fungal and parasitic infections than women are. It's curious that nature gave men stronger muscles and bigger bones and yet equipped them with a weaker immune system.

28

All our utility suppliers want us to go entirely online. They want to stop sending us bits of paper showing how much we owe and how much we have paid. Instead, they will send us an email occasionally. Some companies insist on our accepting email invoices. There is no alternative. I have resisted the pressure to have all our utility bills online because I know that if the HMRC's countless myrmidons want to see my expenses receipts they will expect bits of paper. Today, Antoinette pointed out another problem with having our utility bills sent on the internet. She points out that if we want to open a new bank account (or prove our identity for any other purpose) we will need utility bills. And since many banks and other places won't accept photocopies it is unlikely that they will accept invoices we've printed ourselves.

29

Our mower has come back. A man in a van brought it back and it arrived together with an invoice. Checking with the website of a well-known purveyor of lawn cutting machinery, I see that it cost £37 more to service the mower than it would have cost to buy a new one. If the mower doesn't start next year the sensible thing will be to order a new one and dump the old one in the long grass at the top of the garden. I reckon we can 'lose' a couple of dozen mowers before they become too obvious. Or maybe I could fasten the dysfunctional mowers together with brown parcel tape and send them off to the Tate Gallery as a piece of Modern Art.

30

I'm delighted to see that my warnings about antibiotics seem to have filtered through to the medical establishment. Whenever I write about anything new I find that I am ignored, ridiculed and attacked and then, a few years later, people are falling over themselves to claim credit for the idea. I have for decades been warning that the growth in the number of antibiotic-resistant organisms will result in the return of infectious diseases that we had thought conquered. Sadly, as usual, my fears have been ignored, ridiculed and attacked.

But it seems that things are changing at last. Speaking at the World Health Assembly, the UK's Chief Medical Officer, Professor Sally Davies, said: 'If we don't take action, in 20 years' time we could be back in the 19th century where infections kill us as a result of routine operations. In the last five years we've seen a steep change in the level of resistance...and in some cases a doubling of the death rate.' The World Health Organisation itself agrees with my 30-year-old assertion and claims that the crisis with antibiotics is 'bigger and more urgent than the AIDS epidemic of the 1980s'. They point out that 'a child's scratched knee from falling off their bike, common bladder infections among the elderly in care homes and routine surgery to replace broken hips could all become fatal as antibiotics are becoming increasingly useless'. I can't imagine why it's taken the WHO and Professor Davies so long to realise this but I hope they will have more luck than I have in persuading people to take this threat seriously. There are two simple reasons for this problem. First, doctors overprescribe antibiotics and dish them out like sweets. And the average prescribing doctor has no idea whether to use antibiotics for five days, seven days, ten days or a fortnight. Second, vets dish out antibiotics by the truckload because farmers give them routinely to their animals. The drugs aren't used to treat infection but because animals which are given antibiotics tend to produce more meat and, therefore, fetch a higher price at market. Only yesterday I received a letter from a reader telling me that in the farmer's field behind his house the cows stand shin deep in their own faeces. The farmer keeps his cows 'healthy' by having them treated constantly with antibiotics – provided by a compliant and wicked veterinary surgeon. The problem, of course, is that the widespread use of antibiotics in this way means that more bacteria become resistant. In addition, the problem is exacerbated by the fact that antibiotics then get into the food and water supply. The abuse of antibiotics by people who should know better is one of a number of problems which are far more important than the politically popular but scientifically unsustainable climate change theory. We may laugh and sneer at the strange things doctors did a century or so ago, when leeches and arsenic powders for stomach problems were common remedies, but the truth is that many of our modern practices are just as daft. Today's doctors, who have sold their souls to the pharmaceutical industry and the government (in return for not too much work and oodles of cash) do a lot of crazy things. Surgeons now sew up the stomachs of greedy people (to stop them getting fat) and they remove perfectly healthy breasts from perfectly healthy women (so that they won't develop breast cancer which could be avoided by dietary change). And doctors everywhere prescribe far too many antibiotics.

31

Cricket is in a bigger mess than I thought it was. Startling new evidence confirms that the game is moribund and has about as much of a future as the Liberal Democrats. At great risk to myself I ventured into a large newsagent to investigate the state of our true national game. I was looking for a now endangered species: the cricket magazine. I decided that the best way to measure the popularity of the game would be to count the number of cricket magazine titles available. There weren't any. There were 23 different magazine titles dealing with cycling, 16 magazines dealing with boxing and wrestling and six specialising in carp fishing. But no magazines dealing with cricket. There were, to my astonishment, 10 different magazines dealing with tattooing which seems now to be more popular than television or gardening. But there was nothing about cricket.

I found an assistant and asked if the cricket magazines had, perhaps, all sold out. 'Cricket?' he said, looking bewildered. 'Magazines on cricket,' I repeated. He shook his head and called over a more senior colleague. She looked thoughtful for a moment and then rummaged around among the football publications and the yachting magazines. 'I think we used to stock one or two,' she said. 'But I haven't seen any for a long while.' She pulled a magazine on walking out of a well stuffed rack. 'We've got quite a few magazines on walking.'

'No thank you,' I said, wondering why someone would want to buy a magazine on walking. I've been doing it since I was one but I've never wanted to read about it.

'We've got magazines on bowls,' she said. 'And curling.' She pulled out a magazine on curling and showed it to me.

'But nothing on cricket?'

She shook her head. 'We've got darts, snooker and ice hockey magazines. And quite a few on triathlons.'

'Anything on synchronised swimming?'

She moved across to a group of magazines dealing with swimming. She picked one out and handed it to me. A bunch of grinning synchronised swimmers smiled at me from the cover. It occurred to me that if there isn't one already then there will soon probably be a magazine on drowning.

The game that once ruled the hearts of all Y chromosome owners has become a sporting anachronism; a minority sport, competing with tiddlywinks for a corner of the nation's weakly beating heart. Morris dancing is more popular and has taken over as the quintessential English activity. I left, quite depressed, and outside the store, handed the swimming magazine I felt I had to buy to a scowling East European selling the 'Big Issue'. She looked at it and then at me. 'Now you can offer customers a choice,' I told her 'And anything's better than the *Big Issue*'.'

It is clear from this scientific study that the people running cricket these days are as lost as if they were facing Deadly Underwood on a drying, sticky wicket. There are many possible reasons for this sad state of affairs but, as a working hypothesis, and I don't mean this to sound rude, I think it is probably fair to assume that the massed administrators of our sport have a collective IQ rather smaller than the late and lamented Harry Pilling's shoe size. They sold the television rights to our national game to a station controlled by a naturalised American and now seem surprised that schoolboys are more likely to study baseball statistics than cricket averages. Counties wanting to stage Ashes Test Matches need to bid so much for the rights that some now have the same sort of financial health as Grand Prix circuit owners. Cricket's administrators have, generally speaking, managed cricket with the sort of business acumen usually, and probably unfairly, associated with the whelk stall industry.

I fear that the majority of cricket clubs may go bust within the next five years. Already, many seem, like race courses, to be dependent on mid-season pop concerts to pay the bills. The members are leaving; tired of paying through the nose for a handful of matches and the chance to be abused by snotty gatemen. That rather woeful invention, 20/20 cricket, will soon die an unnatural death and the county secretaries will be sticking their fingers down the backs of the sofas in the executive boxes as they search for funds with which to pay their club's massive debts.

The big media managers haven't helped much either. Which idiot decided that the majority of cricket commentators and correspondents had to be retired cricketers? When the BBC hired Trueman and Bailey to whinge between overs on Test Match Special it was an inspired move. Fred puffed and huffed (sometimes at the same time) and Trevor pontificated. They operated singly but were the best double act since Lindwall and Miller or Hobbs and Sutcliffe. But Fred and Trevor were there as cherries on top of the ever present fruit cake. The real stars of the show were, of course, Arlott and Johnston; professional wordsmiths and erudite entertainers. Writing and commentating well require special skills and they both had them in abundance. The producers who cram old cricketers into commentary boxes seem unaware that with the solitary exception of Jack Fingleton, none of the great cricket writers or commentators ever played international cricket. I know that Henry Blofeld nearly did but there's a vast gulf between nearly and did. Neville Cardus played league cricket as a medium paced off break bowler but his speciality was apparently 'a quick one aimed straight at the batsman's penis'. La Swanton had his own side, of course, but I doubt if he ever lay awake waiting for the selectors to call. His average for his three county matches (13.4 against university sides) hardly gives him professional status.

It is true that most of the great cricketers of the past had newspaper columns, but everyone reading them knew damned well that the newspapers relied on proper journalists to glue the words together and turn them into sentences. And I suspect there were quite a few cricket playing authors who never quite got round to reading the books their ghosts had written for them. Today, however, it seems that the primary qualification for a cricket broadcaster is to have played a few games for England. And since the selectors have, in recent years, tried to scatter caps with random generosity there are a good many former players lying around waiting for the call. Heavens above, former captains are hardly thin on the ground either. Most of these retired cricketers would be better suited to coaching public school boys or running sports shops in the East Midlands. The result is that the quality of cricket writing has diminished at an alarming rate. And the quality of cricket broadcasting has deteriorated even more rapidly.

The basic problem is that retired sportsmen tend to be self-obsessed and to love nothing more than to talk about their greatest moments on the pitch. 'Ah, that shot reminds me of the time I hit Lillian Thomson through the covers in 1974. Let me tell you about that…'.Test Match Special has become a parody of a once great programme. The listeners who switch on do so more out of habit than anything else. The original TMS succeeded because the broadcasters managed to persuade us that we were invited guests, sharing their day out at the cricket. It worked because the men at the other end of the airwaves were professionals who could paint pictures with words. Today, there is a lot of a ho ho hoing about the sticky cakes and too many tedious interviews with bankers and celebrities passing through. I live in hope that a commercial radio station will buy the rights. Anyone will do it so much better than the BBC, the EU's official broadcasting unit.

I really don't understand why there is this enthusiasm for stacking studios and press boxes with former players. Drama critics aren't all retired actors. Political correspondents aren't all retired politicians. So, why should the cricket media be dominated by former cricketers? Maybe they're cheaper than proper writers and broadcasters. Hire one, get one free. The result is that the only time cricket gets newspaper coverage is when the universally acclaimed Kelvin Patterson has his nails manicured or reports an exceptionally successful bowel movement. (I wouldn't have picked him for England if he'd averaged 200 in Tests and been able to bowl all day at 100 mph. I may be wrong, of course, but he seemed to me to be the sort of fellow who ought to be playing football rather than cricket.) But the selectors fired him and now they're going to have to find another way to keep Lord Piers Morgan interested in cricket.

Other than Kelvin's antics, cricket today has a terrible image. It is, of course, dull, po-faced, pretentious and self-important but there are also too many bad aspects to it that cannot be avoided. Players and officials seem to have forgotten that amateur cricketers play to amuse themselves but that professionals play to entertain the paying spectators. Cricket is a branch of show business when played for money and the aim should be to send the punters home with songs in their hearts, smiles on their faces and memories tucked away in their souls.

Another mistake has been to give in to the armies of the politically correct and to try to give equal status to women's cricket. The patronising assumption that women should be allowed to do everything that men do is, of course, an utter nonsense and rests on the matching assumption that women get a raw deal in modern society. (Look at the facts: the Brussels Broadcasting Corporation's outrageously sexist radio programme Woman's Hour is all about women. And yet there is no matching programme for men. Can you imagine the BBC broadcasting a programme called Man's Hour? The magazine *Men Only* is all about women too. But if anyone ever produces a magazine called *Women Only* it will, I suspect, be full of recipes, knitting patterns and sound advice on feminine matters. I rest my case.)

Women's cricket undoubtedly has a place somewhere. But not on this planet, thank you. It's even more of a freak show than synchronised swimming. It certainly isn't cricket as we know it. I honestly doubt if a world XI of test playing women cricketers could give a decent school side a match worth playing. I know we aren't even supposed to think things like this but cricket is, by nature, a man's game in the same way that floor gymnastics and show jumping are sports best enjoyed by women. The breast stroke is a women's event because it was invented so that women could swim without getting their hair wet. Fast bowling is best done by men simply because they do it so much better.

The final problem is that the public now know that cricket is fixed and run by the bookies. No one knows how many matches are fixed but we all know that many are. If you know that some matches are fixed but you don't know which ones, then all matches become suspect. And that changes everything.

So, what is to be done? Well, we have to accept that cricket has changed. We have to move with the times. Let no one accuse me of having my feet in the mud or my mind stuck in the past. If cricket is to succeed we have to be bold and imaginative. The forthcoming demise of 20/20 cricket shows that the fickle public must be drawn in with newer and greater attractions. Falling gate figures show that dancing girls and caterwauling popsters no longer pull in the paying punters. But the answer isn't difficult to find. The awful 20/20 cricket was never really cricket or sport. It was circus time. And so we must offer a more entertaining circus. We must learn from the Romans and allow the spectators to play a bigger part in the game. At the end of each match let them vote (by text or email) for the worst player on each side. And then (and this is the touch of genius) those two players will be put on spits, roasted and served to the crowd. A giant pig roast without the expense of buying the pigs.

Cricket clubs can do a deal with the phone companies and get half the call revenue, and then make even more money by selling off bits of their worst player, wrapped in a bun and covered in ketchup. What a thrill for everyone. And what an incentive for the players to do their very best on the field of play.

Two players won't keep a big crowd fed, of course. And most county sides probably won't want to lose more than one player per match. So I have another suggestion, perfectly in keeping with the mood of the modern game. I got the idea from North Korea, where Jang Song Thaek was executed by his nephew for 'failing to applaud with sufficient enthusiasm'. Cricket clubs with financial aspirations set up some CCTV cameras and spectators who applaud without vigour are then selected for roasting.

The spectators, having paid to get in, then pay extra to eat one another!

If that's not commercially viable, I don't know what is. Maybe cricket has a future, after all.

June

1

EU supporters claim that patriotism is for scoundrels (and, because they don't understand the phrase, Little Englanders). Since whatever the EU's fascist supporters believe in, is bad then it is clear that if we are going to do the right thing we must all become more patriotic. I suspect, indeed, that patriotism is the only political leaning now worth having.

2

I wish grapefruit growers would give up producing fruit with tiny seeds (they usually promote them, erroneously, as 'seedless') and go back to producing the ones with proper, decent sized pips. The growers started producing grapefruit with smaller seeds because they believed that people hated having to fish the pips out of a grapefruit they were eating and would happily swallow the smaller seeds in the mistaken belief that they were harmless. The problem for me is that I'm a doctor and I know damned well that the smaller size seeds are perfectly proportioned to catch in my appendix. Because of this risk I have to fish them all out and put them on the side of my plate when eating a grapefruit. This takes forever and is a very messy business. Bring back grapefruit with pips big enough to use as pellets with rubber band catapults!

3

A friend of mine has been miserable for days. He used to run one of those small seaside hotels where the windows won't close properly in the winter and won't open at all in the summer. He retired some years ago, selling the hotel to a developer who converted it into small flats for social security beneficiaries. Today, at last, I persuaded my friend to tell me what was worrying him.

'I got onto the bus and a young woman stood up and offered me her seat,' he said softly. There was a long, long pause. 'I suddenly realised that I must look old,' he confessed.

He told me that until this incident on the bus he had assumed that when young women smiled at him it was because they fancied him. Now he realises that it's because they feel sorry for him.

My friend is 87-years-old and, like most octogenarians, comes equipped with a fair few wrinkles.

4

Broadcasters used to regard cricket as an art. These days they like to pretend it's a science. Computer graphics are supposed to tell the viewer what the ball would have done (or would not have done) and a whole range of modern visual aids (such as Hot Spot and Hawk-Eye) second guess the umpires and give any viewer the chance to be a critic. I know I am old-fashioned but I miss the old days of John Arlott and Jim Laker who, when commentating, would talk only when they had something useful to say. When sport is televised there often isn't much need for any commentary. The picture tells the story. Sadly, today's commentators think they're failing in their duty if they don't fill every second with some pointless tittle tattle. They read out their own tweets and talk incessantly about themselves and their achievements. They may well have degrees in gym and umpiring and coaching tiny tots but they have no love for the language or mastery of their newly chosen art. Oh, for the bad old days when the silence would occasionally be broken only by the quiet snoring of John Arlott sleeping off a second bottle of claret.

Am I the only person to be fed up of the incessant wittering of celebrities? These days no luncheon or tea interval is allowed to pass without an actor or politician sharing with us their pointless, humourless anecdotes. In the bad old days television producers would fill in the tea interval with a pre-recorded reading of some piece of literature or poetry. One week there would be a reading of a cricket match from Dickens. Another week someone would read a little A.A.Thompson. And occasionally John Arlott would read out one of his own cricket poems. You don't hear all that much literature on Test Match Special or Sky television these days. Actually, I don't hear much of anything. I neither listen nor watch.

5

I'm now the proud owner of a pair of pince nez which have been fitted with prescription lenses. I bought several pairs of pince nez at a couple of auctions and took the best frames along when I had to have my eyes tested. The optician seemed delighted to be faced with an unusual challenge and today I collected the results of his work. My new pince nez are spring loaded and extremely comfortable to wear. They are very light, come with a neat and very old case and fit easily into a waistcoat pocket. I can't imagine why more people don't choose to wear them. They will, I fancy, be quite a potent weapon. I look forward to peering over them at tax inspectors, customs officers and other assorted bureaucratic riff raff. Considering that the lenses had to be specially tailored to fit the tiny frames the cost wasn't prohibitive. (Why is it, I wonder, that opticians are allowed to charge so much for an ordinary pair of spectacle frames. The spectacles which can be bought for a pound or two at supermarkets are often better designed and better made than the spectacles which opticians sell for a hundred times as much money.)

Best of all, however, the optician told me that I do not have macular degeneration. I was surprised, delighted and puzzled at this news but the optician showed me the scans which proved beyond doubt that this is one disease I do not have to worry about. So, why was I told that I did have early macular degeneration just a few years ago? Was it just incompetence? Or did the optician who told me this, and who encouraged me to take special (expensive) tablets to slow down the condition, simply have a product to sell? If so then her behaviour was criminal and she should be disbarred and put behind bars. I've had several years of completely unnecessary worry. I do have a cataract developing but compared to macular degeneration that's a walk in the park.

6

Obama's tenure as President of the United States of America will be remembered for wars, lies, assassinations of innocent Americans and Olympic class hypocrisy. He produced widespread disappointment and disillusionment among the naïve and trusting folk who thought they'd found an honest politician, and who must by now have realised that politics is all about campaigning and has nothing to do with governing. He has now announced that Britain must remain a member of the European Union. The sentiment is not surprising. It was, of course, largely to please the Americans that Britain entered the damned Common Market in the first place. I wonder how Obama would like it if we had a leader who told him what policies America should follow.

7

I saw a picture of the audience at a Google developer conference. (I have no idea what one of these is, and no interest whatsoever in finding out.) Every one of the audience members was a nerd straight out of Central Casting. All were male, all under 40, all wearing black T-shirts and all the sort of sad folk that hale and hearty grown-ups try to avoid whenever humanly possible. Just looking at the picture I knew, just knew, that all of the Google developers play video games all night long, spend all their money on computer magazines, speak in incomprehensible jargon and are infinitely more stupid than they think they are. Around 75% of them will, in due course, be arrested for peeping, exposing themselves or serial killing. The picture reinforced everything I already knew about Google and its fans.

8

A national report (called, tellingly, *Poverty and Social Exclusion*) has concluded that people should be officially classified as poor if they 'don't have what they think they need and what people around them have'. If the report had been published on the 1st of April I would have assumed it was a not very good practical joke. But it's real. People already think that they are poor if they don't have at least one late model motor car for every adult in the family, a widescreen television set in the living room and subsidiary sets in the kitchen and all bedrooms, a subscription to Sky television (according to many self-appointed experts a subscription to satellite television is now one of life's essentials, along with daily bread and a roof), trainers with flashing laces, a tablet, a laptop and at least one fancy mobile phone per person. The tragedy is that social policy is devised according to these damned reports. When everyone feels poor there is bound to be dissatisfaction, unrest, envy and misery.

9

It has been known for years that men and women who are married are likely to enjoy better health, and live longer, than people who are single. Now, researchers at Harvard Medical School have shown that the blood pressure of people who are married falls slightly at night. A night-time drop in the systolic pressure is, apparently, associated with a lower incidence of heart disease. Single folk do not have this night-time fall and are, therefore, more likely to die early. Curiously, the researchers do not seem to have conducted any research into whether or not it matters if the marriage is a happy one.

10

An independent bookshop sent an email ordering copies of all my Bilbury books for a customer. We've received a number of such orders recently and I have no doubt that these are coming because of the success of the e-Book sales on Amazon. Some of the orders are probably coming from public libraries which have had requests for the books from their patrons. I sent an email back to the bookshop telling them that the books are now out of print. I could not help also pointing out that over the years I had done everything I could to persuade bookshops to stock my self-published books but that virtually all of them had refused to take any shelf stock at all – even though they could return any books which they didn't sell. As a self-publisher I sold a fairly huge number of books (with quite a few individual titles selling more than 50,000 copies each in hardback in the UK alone) but hardly any of these were sold through bookshops. The few that were sold through bookshops were sold only as a result of customers wandering in and ordering the books directly. The problem, of course, was that small bookshops were just as reluctant as the large chains to take books from a small publisher – even though they could easily order the books from any one of the major wholesalers. I told the assistant from the bookshop which had wanted to order the seven books in the Bilbury series that the books are now only available as kindle books on Amazon (where, I'm delighted to say, all seven have been in the Amazon bestseller lists.) I find it difficult to have any affection for bookshops these days and I confess I hardly ever go into one (though I am an enthusiastic customer of second-hand book shops – especially those which are privately run). Shops selling new books are closing faster than pubs and in my experience most of these shops deserve to close. They have been exclusively loyal to the big publishers selling cookery books and gardening books and television tie-in books and now those markets are shrinking rapidly. The big publishers are giving up and struggling to make a living selling e-Books. Bookshops will also die. The wholesalers will go too, for they have huge warehouses with nothing to store. (A man working at one major wholesaler told me, quite seriously, that they planned to start wholesaling e-Books.) The whole traditional publishing industry will die. Still, it occurs to me that there are some advantages for authors. In the good old days an author had to sell his book to an agent who had to sell it to a publisher who had to persuade a wholesaler to stock it and bookshops to take copies on a sale or return basis and the bookshop then had to sell the book to book buyers. As I have discovered over the last quarter of a century, self-publishing is quite different. The author sells straight to the reader – cutting out all the parasitic middlemen. And e-Book publishing is particularly well suited to self-publishers. Indeed, any author who allows a traditional publisher to handle his e-Books is barking mad.

11

The headlines this morning mostly read *Statins Could Reduce the Risk of Breast Cancer*. Oh dear. I really do despair. It appears that the drug companies which have managed to persuade the Government to give British doctors bonus payments in order to persuade them to prescribe these damned things for eight million healthy individuals (in order to prevent heart attacks) are planning to improve their profits still further by telling doctors to give the pills to all women with breasts. (Drug companies tried to do this with a drug called tamoxifen. The plan was that all women would take it to prevent breast cancer. I put a spanner in the works by revealing that the drug actually caused cancer and that it seemed perfectly possible, therefore, that it might well kill far more women than it saved.) It appears that scientists have noticed that there is a link between high cholesterol levels and breast cancer and so they want women to take the drug in order to reduce their cholesterol levels. It's a brilliant argument except for the fact that it has more holes in it than a fishing net. Apart from the fact that statins cause horrendous side effects, and that the jury is still out on whether or not reducing cholesterol is a good idea, the plain fact is that the incidence of breast cancer would plummet if women ate less fatty food and, in particular, gave up, or cut down on, eating meat. Today's farmers fatten up their animals because they've noticed that when you get paid by the pound an animal which weighs more fetches more cash at the abattoir. They haven't noticed, or don't care, that fatty meat means a dramatic increase in the incidence of cancer among their consumers. So, the bottom line is that statins are potentially dangerous and there is a much easier, far safer way to reduce the risk of breast cancer. Nevertheless, I have absolutely no doubt that before long the drug companies will have persuaded the Government to pay doctors extra to prescribe statins for all breast bearing citizens. The next step will be for the medical profession (and its drug company paymasters, the people pulling the strings) to increase the number of diseases for which statins are essential and the age at which people should be taking these drugs. The plan, already, is for statins to be given to 40% of the entire population – most of whom are healthy. This is utterly appalling. How can any doctor in his right mind recommend giving such dangerous drugs to so many people in the hope that they might, just might, prevent an illness? Whatever happened to the old principle of 'First do no harm'? Why do doctors do this when those with functioning brain tissue must know that patients could improve their health, and dramatically reduce the risk of illness, by changing their diet? The answer, I am afraid, is that most doctors have been bought by drug companies. And drug companies will make billions out of this dangerous nonsense. I've exposed this appalling practice for many decades and now realise that no one in the profession or the media seems to give a damn. I would write a book specifically outlining the hazards associated with statins but, sadly, I know damned well that no one would buy it. The final step will be for the profession (backed by its drug company paymasters) to persuade the Government that patients should be 'encouraged' to take the drugs, by being told that if they refuse them they will not be allowed to claim benefits, to leave the country, to renew their driving licences or to use the NHS. And then, the final, final step will be for the drugs to become compulsory, with the police arresting anyone who refuses a prescription or cannot prove that they have dutifully taken the pills they have been prescribed. We are well on the way to that scary endpoint. George Orwell must be standing up and shouting: 'I told you so!'

12

Those readers who were for some reason offended by my book *Oil Apocalypse* (which described the peak oil crisis in detail) and who still delight in writing to me every time a new bucket of oil is discovered, might like to know that last year all the oil exploration companies in the world discovered just 13 billion barrels of oil. That may sound a lot but it was the lowest rate of discovery for 62 years. And between us we all managed to use up 33.5 billion barrels of oil in the same period. You don't need to be terribly good at sums to work out that we are using up oil faster than we're finding it. Moreover, the real key in this whole issue is the EROEI – the Energy Return on Energy Invested – which measures the amount of usable energy acquired from a resource compared to the amount of energy required to extract that usable energy. A falling EROEI means that prices of energy, and everything which relies on energy for its production or transport, will rise. Whenever we buy anything these days we are effectively buying oil and prices are going to rise remorselessly. When Saudi Arabia first extracted oil their returns were 100:1 (they produced 100 times as much energy as they used up) but today the average is 14:1. The strange thing is that few of my books caused as much anger as *Oil Apocalypse*. Several people who hadn't even bothered to read the book wrote Web blogs condemning it. One or two didn't like my prediction that we are heading for a pre-industrial age because as the cheap fuel runs out so our world which has been built on the availability of cheap energy obtained from oil, must change dramatically. The standard objection is that when the oil runs out we will be able to drive around just as well in electric cars, hydrogen cars or hybrid cars. None of the proponents of these transport modes ever seems to be concerned about the fact that they all rely on the existence of an energy source. We would none of us be moving around much if we drove cars which relied upon the electricity provided by sunshine or the wind. Some critics were angry because they simply didn't want to have to face the truth but at least one outspoken critic got red-faced and apoplectic because he felt that my book on the peak oil crisis was selling more copies than his. His answer to this distressing situation was to write a piece on his website explaining why he wasn't going to read my book and telling his readers why they shouldn't buy it either.

It's sad but these days the internet has made it increasingly difficult to sell original books on disturbing or controversial subjects. This is partly because the internet makes it easy for the prejudiced and the bigoted to come out of the woodwork and do their best to suppress whatever they do not like, find inconvenient, consider threatening or simply disagree with. A nasty review can finish a book's prospects within hours. And, of course, it is far too easy for the envious, the bitter and the twisted to do their best to suppress other people's work.

13

The Financial Conduct Authority (entirely useless and expensive Quango no 2827637 in an endless number of similar taxpayer funded organisations) has investigated the poor returns savers receive on their money and has concluded that it is the fault of savers for not shopping around for better deals. The employees of the FCA clearly live on an entirely different planet to the one the rest of us inhabit. Has anyone working there ever tried to move money from one bank to another? Thanks to the absurd anti-money laundering and anti-terrorism rules it would be easier for a pub football club to qualify for the World Cup finals than it is for an ordinary punter to open a new bank account.

Indeed, I have no doubt that the banks, knowing that their customers no longer feel any loyalty to the bank which holds their money, use the anti-money laundering and anti-terrorism regulations to make it as difficult as possible for customers to close or open accounts.

And have the decerebrate buffoons at the FCA not noticed that if you find a bank offering a better rate of interest it will, within minutes of you producing your passport, gas bill and inside leg measurement, cut the rate of interest to the lowest of any lender on the planet?

14

We were getting into bed. Antoinette was clearly worried about something and eventually I managed to persuade her to tell me what was troubling her.

'How long can the brain go without oxygen?' she wanted to know.

'No more than three minutes.'

'I thought as much,' she sighed, unhappily. She plumped up two pillows, put them behind her and sat up in bed.

'So why is that worrying you?' I asked.

'I always lie on one side and I'm worried that I'm compressing the arteries taking blood to my brain,' she said. 'If I do that my brain won't be getting enough oxygen. And I'll develop dementia.'

I looked at her and tried to think of something reassuring to say.

'When you lie on your leg or your arm it goes white doesn't it? And that's because the blood isn't getting through.'

I nodded.

'So if it happens to a limb why shouldn't it happen to your head?'

I started to say something.

'When your leg isn't getting enough blood it feels funny and so you so move it, don't you?'

I nodded.

'But how would I know if I was asleep and my brain wasn't getting enough oxygen? I'd be asleep so I wouldn't know would I?'

'But...' I started to say.

'I'm going to stay awake all night,' she said. 'That way even if I am lying on my head I'll know if it doesn't get enough blood.'

15

Antoinette has bought a new digital watch which, if you press the right buttons in the correct order, also tells you how fast your heart is beating. Antoinette is very good at understanding electronic devices and I am not. I suspect this may be because I am considerably older than she is and, as I once explained, spent my formative years at infant school scratching my alphabet and sums on a piece of slate, which I wiped clean not with a touch of a button or an India rubber but with a damp rag. It is a long walk from such primitive tools to mastering a watch which can tell you what time it is or if you are dead. I am not, however, the only person who finds these devices something of a challenge. While we were both in another room an American visitor who has been staying with us for a few days, and who is something of a known hypochondriac, decided to try out Antoinette's new watch for himself. He strapped it onto his wrist and pressed the buttons he thought he'd seen Antoinette press. Moments later, I heard him call out in dismay. We hurried into the room to see what was wrong with him.

'You'd better ring for an ambulance', he said.

'What's the matter?' I asked. He looked well enough to me. He was just as pink as ever and he wasn't sweating.

'I think I'm having some sort of ventricular tachycardia attack,' he told us. He pointed to the watch. I looked at it and then looked at him. 'My pulse is never that fast,' he said. He was now hyperventilating and there was panic in his eyes. 'Do you have ambulances over here?' he asked. 'Yes, we have ambulances,' I told him. 'But you don't need one.'

He looked at me, puzzled and clearly alarmed. 'My pulse is 156!' he cried, pointing to the watch. 'It's never been that fast.' I unfastened the watch and removed it. 'That's the time,' I told him. 'It's four minutes to two.'

16

I rang the stockbrokers at Lloyds Bank. Before I could deal I had to give my account number, numbers from a 'secret' code number they had given me, a password, my date of birth, my bank account number, my bank sort code, my nationality, details of where I was born, details of where the money I wanted to invest had come from, the country where I pay tax, whether or not I pay tax in other countries and numerous other things which I have now forgotten. By the time I'd finished I couldn't remember why I had telephoned in the first place and all these nonsensical questions had taken so long that the price of the share I wanted to buy had probably changed quite dramatically. I intend to close this account. In the past I have often thought that there is no such thing as a dumb question – just dumb answers. I am now convinced that I was wrong. Lloyds Bank has mastered the art of asking dumb questions. If anyone on the Board of Directors of this disgraced bank is paid more than £2.50 a year then they are being egregiously overpaid.

17

In 1985, in Cork, a man called Bernard Murphy, who was an independent candidate standing for his council elections, advised electors to back him at the bookies and then vote for him. Mr Murphy won his seat and the local bookie had to pay out £20,000.

What an absolutely brilliant idea. Mr Murphy's manifesto seems to me to have been far more honest and profitable for the electors than the manifestoes published by any of the established political parties.

18

We are in Paris and the EU Commissioner for Burgling and Mugging has had his wicked way with the City of Light. At night the street lights now go out and so Paris, which acquired its soubriquet when it became the first city in the world to have gas lit streets, has become the City of Darkness. The Parisians are not impressed and since the French have a history of starting good, productive revolutions I do hope this will trigger an uprising against the fascist EU.

Still, the EU has not yet succeeded in stopping birds singing to one another. This evening we heard two nightingales exchanging tunes. What a joy.

19

Five shops in our small street have become offices since we were last in Paris. It is clearly cheaper to rent a shop, and use it as an office, than it is to take space in a purpose-built office building. Now, sadly, those buildings have plastic blinds hanging down behind the windows and all the passer-by can see is a clump of people crouched over computer screens. Happily, however, one small shop (wherein used to sit a man making mattresses by hand) has been taken over by a man who polishes shoes for a living. There are samples of his work in the window. I think he must glaze shoes with sugar because even a pair of gentleman's brown brogues is as shiny as a pair of patent leather dancing pumps.

We caught the bus down to St Germain. Antoinette, who has taught herself to play, took some music with her and played 'Bright Eyes' and 'Let it Be' on the piano upstairs in Shakespeare and Company (the bookshop in sight of Notre Dame Cathedral). She played beautifully and I have never been prouder of anyone or anything.

20

I read in one of the French newspapers that lace underwear has officially been banned in Russia and Kazhestan. Fancy lingerie is, it seems, regarded as a threat to the State. This, I think, tells us everything we need to know about those two countries. How does the state benefit if women and eonists are all forced to wear bras and knickers made out of itchy, brown canvas? And what sort of State is so flimsy that its very security can be threatened by the sort of underwear women choose to wear?

21

Rousseau (the French philosopher not the fat singer who used to sing while dressed in a tent made out of picnic rug material) said that men are good and that it is too much government and too many laws that make them bad. I think he was probably right. You can see it happening before your eyes. The EU has created so many absurd laws that everyone is now a lawbreaker. I very much doubt if I know anyone who isn't a criminal. The trouble is, of course, that when the law cannot sensibly be obeyed the citizens lose all respect for it. The same thing happened in America during Prohibition. People ignored the one law and lost respect for the other laws. We can rely on just one thing these days: if the morons in Brussels, Westminster and our local council offices can find a way to mess things up and make life more complicated and more unpleasant they will find it and then make it a law. Today, thanks to the idiots in charge, everything in the UK is more expensive and of poorer quality than elsewhere. Our utilities, our transport, our rabbit hutch housing (thrown up to satisfy government targets and satisfying absolutely no standards of any value), our clothing and our food are all of poorer quality than are the products sold in France, for example. Government in Britain today means privilege (for them), waste, hypocrisy, exploitation, suppression and manipulation. Our infrastructure is crumbling and only the skills and integrity of Victorian architects and builders are keeping it standing. The public have been forced through scepticism and into cynicism and through pessimism and defeatism to a fearful surrender to authority. We can't change anything anymore because no one in authority listens and so we have no voice. Anyone in Britain who seeks truth and justice is likely die young of a broken heart; disillusioned and destroyed by a daily torment of disappointment.

I confess that I have a slight problem with authority (and although I am at heart a complete softy I do my best not to let them know that)

168

and there's a lot of it about these days. The basic problem is that our politicians are not very bright but are very corrupt. Most are also rich and privileged and don't believe in democracy because the idea of politicians having to do what the people want them to do scares the hell out of them. The average modern politician leaves university at 21 knowing absolutely nothing about real life or the real world. Thanks to Daddy's chums at the bank he or she gets a job as a 'special adviser' to a Government politician (though heaven knows what use a 21-year-old university graduate is as a special adviser) and five years later he or she is adopted as a parliamentary candidate and becomes an MP.

I have seen a good many politicians over the years the present batch are, without a doubt, the worst. This morning I tried to describe Nick Clegg, former professional eurocrat, former MEP, enthusiastic Europhile and currently (as I write) leader of the Liberal Democrats.

(People vote Tory because they want things to stay the same. People vote Labour because they want the Government to keep giving them money. But who the hell votes Liberal Democrat? And why?)

I thought about it for a few minutes and then realised that Clegg is the sort of smug, hypocritical, sanctimonious, two-faced kid who was teacher's pet and a sneak. People can't stand Clegg not because they don't like his policies but because they don't like him as a person. He's whining, self-pitying, sanctimonious and as smug as a Salmond – and those are just his good points. Traitorous lies disguised as sanctimonious piety.

We've all known a Clegg in our lives but I feel I can sum him up quite accurately in three words: lying little shit. Most countries have detestable politicians but only Britain has a Clegg. (Plus, we also have a back-up in the form of Vince Cable – the man whose rank incompetence with regard to the Royal Mail privatisation has so far cost every man, woman and child in the country £20 each in real money.)

Our misfortune is that we are far too polite to enjoy the concept of schadenfreude and so when Clegg and Cable are finally ejected from office (as all politicians are) we will wave them goodbye with crocodile tears in our eyes. There is no word in the English language to explain the concept of schadenfreude (the cruel delight Germans feel when their foes are brought down with woes) and we are in any case too easily embarrassed to enjoy it. And then, of course, there would be the guilt.

22

Antoinette and I were sitting in a park near to the Eiffel Tower, watching the birds, and feeding them. We watched a crow dip bits of hard baguette into a small puddle, in order to soften them before eating them. A dunking crow! We watched another crow pick up an abandoned crisp packet, hold it by the closed end and empty out the remaining bits and pieces of food. I doubt if there are any members of the Liberal Democrats who could manage that. Crows are remarkable birds. They hang around in groups (or 'parliaments') but recognise and respect one another's ownership of scraps of food. If a crow has food in its beak, no other crow will try to take it away. This is firmly in contrast to the behaviour of pigeons who squabble and fight over food. If a pigeon can take a piece of bread from another pigeon's beak it will do so.

Suddenly, a sour looking man came over and shouted at us. I don't like being shouted at, or told what to do, and so I pretended not to understand him, smiled and held up the box of cage bird food I was holding as offering him some. The man scowled and did not seem impressed. He said a lot of things I did not understand but which did not sound complimentary. The world is full of busy bodies these days. I took out my wallet and offered him a five euro note to go away. He became very cross at this so I offered him ten euros in the hope that this would make him so cross that he would explode. Unfortunately, it made him crosser but he did not explode. He hurried away.

'Where's he gone?' I asked Antoinette.

'He said something about fetching a policeman,' she replied. 'There's one just over there.' She pointed to a gendarme a couple of hundred yards away.

'Shall we go?' I said, distributing the remainder of the bird food. 'The sun has gone behind a cloud and I'd like a cup of tea.' I put the empty box (the evidence) into a bin and we went home.

We are now wanted criminals again. I will wear a different hat next time we go out and I very much doubt if we will be recognised.

'What is the worst they could do, if they catch us?' I asked Antoinette. 'They could, I suppose, tear out my fingernails, shoot off my knee caps, nail my tongue to the table, stick hot needles in my eyes and cut out my liver, but that's about it.'

Antoinette looked at me and raised an eyebrow. 'They could go through last year's expenses receipts and ask you questions,' she pointed out.

I shuddered.

23

The total number of medical practices in England has fallen again. In the last ten years it has dropped from 8,830 to 7,960. The reason is simple: there are huge financial incentives for doctors to group together in large practices. And so doctors in single-handed practices are closing their doors and joining in with bigger practices so that they can share their costs and set up expensive telephone systems which require patients to press one (if you require a repeat prescription), press two (if you have an insurance claim), press three (if you wish to speak to the dispensary), press four (if you are bleeding to death) and so on. Many people living in the country now have to travel miles to their nearest doctor – and they are exceedingly unlikely to be able to persuade a doctor to visit them at home. The Government, the medical establishment, the bureaucrats and the drug companies all like bigger practices, which they regard as more efficient and easier to control. Drug companies like to have doctors all grouped together in one place because it makes it easier and cheaper for their reps to visit them. The GMC's revalidation scheme, which requires doctors to obtain gold stars of approval from medical colleagues as well as patients, makes life almost impossibly difficult for doctors working by themselves. And, of course, the EU, being an overtly fascist organisation, is constantly trying to get rid of everything small. The eurocrats don't approve of small hospitals, small schools, small businesses or small medical practices.

24

The French believe that life begins when work ends but the British have come to dread retirement because they know that Society (with a very definite capital S) will regard them as worthless; a burden to be ignored, pushed around and got rid of as soon as possible.

The French, however, look forward to retirement very much. A neighbour in our apartment building has joined a local drama group. She speaks her very own brand of English, looks a little like Dame Maggie Smith and must be 75-years-old if she's a day.

'Jessica Tandy was 80 when she got her Oscar,' she told us with a knowing smile and something of a wink. We both told her we hoped she didn't have to wait that long. She was very pleased by this. We wonder, however, if she may not be a little innocent for thespianism. She once admitted that until she was in her late sixties she thought that a bisexual was someone who got their sexual kicks from riding a two wheeled conveyance, that a condom was a small apartment and that a denture was a small amount of damage to the bodywork of a motorcar. Until we put her right she also thought that the phrase 'the pen is mightier than the sword' referred to the might of the male organ, as in 'the penis is mightier than the sword'.

25

Immigration is continuing to soar. One in ten people living in Britain doesn't speak English as their main language and there are now 800,000 permanent residents of England who don't speak a word of English. Most of them work for call centres. The countries queuing up to join the EU (and, therefore, have free access to our benefits system) include Turkey, Albania, Kosovo and Bosnia. They have a combined population of just under 100 million and income levels just under a third of ours. That should be fun. The Migration Advisory Committee has, incidentally, admitted that the concentration of low-skilled migrants has already put great pressure on health, education, transport and housing services. Well, I never. What a surprise that is. How and why, I wonder, does it take politicians and quangos years or decades to see what even quarter-witted citizens could see aeons ago? And while immigration soars, emigration is growing too. There are now five million Britons living abroad. That's the largest diaspora of any developed country. Many of those are young, hard-working professionals who have left Britain because it no longer feels like home – or a good place to bring up their children.

26

Increasing numbers of school children are allowed to wear their own clothes (instead of school uniform) when sitting examinations. The idea, so I'm told, is that children will relax more when wearing their own clothes. This is, however, a daft idea for two reasons. First, the last thing anyone should be when taking an examination is relaxed. Adrenalin is an essential ingredient for those trying to perform well. Second, we remember things far more easily when we are in precisely the environment where we learnt them. So, for example, we remember what we've been taught far more effectively if we take an examination in the classroom where we studied. And we remember more effectively if we are wearing the clothes we wore when we learned. So, school teachers who allow children to take examinations while wearing jeans and T-shirts are making a huge mistake.

Talking of children, I also learned today that the basic cost of bringing up a child in Britain is now estimated to be £227,000 a year. That's after tax and it is for one child. Two children will cost the best part of half a million pounds over a 20 year period. That is assuming that the child doesn't go to a private school, require expensive orthodontic treatment or have piano lessons. This now means that the only people who can afford to have more than one child are the very rich and those couples who live on benefits.

27

Farmers and politicians are still arguing that badgers cause tuberculosis in cows and must, therefore, be killed. When, I wonder, will these people look at the scientific evidence before opening their mouths? The fact is that tuberculosis has always been a slum disease, caused by overcrowding and poor diet. It is a slum disease when it affects humans and it is a slum disease when it affects cattle. Cows develop tuberculosis when they are kept in overcrowded conditions and not fed properly. But no farmer is going to admit this. It's much easier (and more profitable) to blame badgers and claim compensation from the Government.

28

Am I the only person on the planet who finds it odd the way tennis players' families seem to have nothing else to do but to turn up and watch match after match after match? Don't these people have lives of their own? Don't they have jobs to do and homes to run? Professional tennis players (and this applies to other sports but particularly to tennis) are working when they're on court. Do mothers and fathers and brothers and sisters and aunts and girlfriends go to the Old Bailey every day in order to watch Nigel their barrister hero strutting his funky stuff in front of judge and jury? How many parents spend their lives sitting in the bank watching Albert accepting paying-in slips and counting out money? Would Judy be sitting in a corner if Andy worked in an estate agency?

29

A man tried to sell us some insurance but he wore a clip-on bowtie. I would never do any sort of business with a man who wore a clip-on bow tie or, for that matter, one of those awful ready tied concoctions which go round the neck on a piece of elastic.

30

The Government has spent over £4 million trying to wipe out the ruddy duck, which is apparently its proper name and not merely a mild form of abuse. The official plan is to exterminate the creature and hunters are being paid £1,256 by taxpayers for every duck they kill. Amazingly, the Royal Society for the Protection of Birds is supporting this bizarre extermination. Apparently, the Government wants to kill all the ruddy ducks because they breed with an endangered Spanish white headed duck. It seemed slightly odd to me that we were getting rid of one type of duck to save another, and that British taxpayers were having to foot the bill to please the Spanish, and then I realised that the whole thing stinks of the European Union. I have no doubt that this is yet another bizarre example of the EU in action. We would all be much better off if the Government paid hunters £1,256 a head to exterminate eurocrats. If my money was being spent on exterminating bureaucrats in Brussels I would be a very contented taxpayer.

I don't understand what the RSPB is doing supporting this bizarre slaughter of the ruddy duck, but I am pleased to see that a recent edition of their magazine includes an article criticising the Maltese who kill gazillions of birds every year for no reason whatsoever except that they can. About twenty years ago I wrote a couple of columns criticising the Maltese habit of killing migrating birds which use their island as a picnic spot. I ended up receiving such serious death threats that policemen came to see me and Interpol became involved. The Maltese did everything they could to shut me up. I was formally accused of racism and the newspapers which printed the articles were, inevitably, reported to the Press Complaints Commission. If it is true that you can judge a man not by his friends but by his enemies then I am well positioned.

I do wish, however, that the RSPB would do more than acknowledge the problem of what is happening on Malta. One of the reasons migrating birds are endangered is the fact that when the birds stop off in Malta for a rest they are slaughtered quite pointlessly.

British charities (and the RSPCA is probably the worst example of this) have a bad habit of closing their eyes and sticking their collective fingers in their ears when it is politically or commercially convenient for them to do so. I find it shameful, for example, that the RSPCA will not even question the value of vivisection.

July

1

Our garden is full of bushes and flowers planted to attract butterflies and bees but we have seen very few of either so far this summer. We had masses of apple blossom earlier in the year but very little of it was pollinated and, as an inevitable result, we are going to have a very poor apple crop in the autumn. There are several explanations. Farmers haven't helped by cutting down hedgerows and using vast quantities of pesticide. Gardeners have done their fair share of damage by choosing to grow showy flowers with very little pollen and by spraying everything that moves with the horticultural equivalent of Agent Orange. But I wonder how much damage genetically engineered crops are doing – and how much more damage they will do in the future. Farmers, politicians and Monsanto lobbyists all keep telling us that there is no evidence to prove that genetically engineered crops will do us any harm. This is true, of course. No one has done any research to find out what damage these crops might do and so there is, inevitably, no evidence to show that they are dangerous. But what no one admits is that there is also no evidence to show that these damned seeds of the devil are safe. Our starving descendants will, I fear, be horrified at the way we played death poker with their future without having the foggiest idea how much damage we might be doing.

American fruit farmers have for decades had to rent bees to pollinate their crops. The bee owners cart their hives around from state to state because there aren't enough local bees any more. It's impossible to know just how fast things are going to deteriorate in the UK because no one knows how widespread genetically engineered crops are in Europe now that the EU has bowed to pressure from the USA. (In contrast, I was pleased to see that the Chinese recently rejected shipments of genetically modified corn.)

Meanwhile, it looks as if Antoinette and I might have to start bee keeping if we want to have apples in our small orchard.

2

A chartered accountant called Run Chai Pan is reported to have threatened HMRC staff members with violence and suggested that inspectors could be killed. He apparently told a female tax inspector that he intended 'hammering' one of her colleagues and would give her 'a good punching'. Another HMRC employee was warned that he would be killed if he entered Pan's premises. The accountant said that he would be within his rights to kill the tax official. Inspectors were told that they would be stabbed to death. As a result of all this the accountant was fined and warned that if he continued to behave in this way he would lose his membership of his professional body the ICAEW (the Institute of Chartered Accountants in England and Wales).

No one locked him up. No one stopped him being an accountant. They simply told him that if he didn't stop threatening to murder tax inspectors they would throw him out of his accountancy organisation.

3

The evidence that most of us are getting poorer, while scoundrels such as bankers get richer, is overwhelming. I spent the morning digging through some old statistics and produced some startling results. In 1950 the average wage was £364 a year, the average house price was £1,900 and a small, new car cost £80. Today the average wage is £25,000 a year but the average house price is £250,000 and a small, new car costs £10,000. In 1950 the cost of a house was just over five times the average wage and the cost of a new car was equivalent to less than three months work (before tax). Today, the cost of a house is ten times the average wage and a new car needs five months of work (before tax). We may all think that we are richer but that's just a trick of inflation. In reality, we are poorer than we were more than half a century ago. We may have more money but it won't buy as much as it did. Even over a shorter time interval things have got considerably worse. In 1993, a house cost around 22% of a good salary and a first time buyer could obtain a decent house for just three times his or her salary. Students had no debt (because university education was free) and the average savings rate was just under 5% before tax. Today, a house costs 35% of a good salary and a first time buyer will need to find over six times his or her salary to buy a property. Students have average debts of £17,000 to start them off in life and savers are lucky to get 0.5% on their savings. The same thing is happening in America. In 1968 the minimum wage was $11 an hour (allowing for inflation). Today it is $7.25 an hour

4

A rather odd friend of mine who collects porcelain thimbles and follows Australian rules football with an enthusiasm which borders on fervour, tells me that when he is feeling angry or upset and needs to lower his stress levels he telephones a Tourette sufferers helpline and swears at length at whoever answers the telephone. Once he feels better he simply puts the phone down and ends the connection. 'What can they do?' he asked, not unreasonably.

5

Sorting through some old boxes this morning I found an old black and white photograph of my Uncle Charlie. He was my favourite Uncle, not least because he was something of an eccentric. I never knew what he did for a living (it was, I suspect, something far too ordinary) but he told me that his ancestors were pirates and he made false teeth in his spare time and if that doesn't qualify him as an eccentric I don't know what does. I remember he drove an old black Citroen, the sort that Maigret favoured in the old black and white movies. He took me to my one and only football match (Walsall versus Port Vale) and I remember the outing for the fact that when he parked the car he didn't bother to lock it. 'Aren't you worried that someone might steal it?' I asked. 'Insurance!' he said, with a wink. I'd never met anyone else who thought that way. He smelt of cigars and frequented pubs and always seemed terribly raffish to a young grammar school boy. He and my Aunt never had children and often when we visited he would have small unusual presents for me.

I still have a Victorian compass which my Uncle Charlie gave me when I was a boy. It's a splendid little thing, the size of a pocket watch and fitted, indeed, with a brass watch chain loop. The compass itself is made of brass and it sits in a velvet lined leather case. There is a small button on the top which enables the user to fix the needle. It was scuffed and battered when my Uncle Charlie gave it to me and I doubt if he paid more than a shilling or two for it but it has, since childhood, been one of my most treasured possessions. It has always sat on my bookshelves where I can see it. Alongside it sits a small, red horseshoe shaped magnet in a blue and black paper mache box. Uncle Charlie gave me that, too. Real toys for small boys. Toys that fitted into a pocket. It was my Uncle Charlie who taught me that if you rubbed a balloon on your jumper (they were jumpers then, and not sweaters) it would stick to the ceiling and stay there for hours. No school teacher ever taught me anything as useful.

6

The NHS pension scheme has a deficit of £250 billion. That is twice the annual expenditure on the NHS. What's even more worrying is that this deficit is rising rapidly. Last year the pension scheme deficit went up by another £37 billion. None of this debt is officially part of the UK's national debt. Public sector pension debts are going to be a huge drag on the future and a burden for generations to come. As I pointed out some time ago, between a third and a half of all council tax payments go towards paying absurdly generous pensions for former council employees.

While public sector employees receive huge pensions, the state pension in the UK is one of the worst in the world. Just over 10% of our government spending goes on the state pension. Most countries spend two or three times as much but we cannot afford to spend any more because we give former civil servants so much loot when they retire. The real problem is that all the people who decide public sector pension policy enjoy generous public sector pensions. So nothing will change until the country goes bankrupt and no retired public sector workers receive any pension at all. My guess is that any public sector worker currently under the age of 50 should not expect to receive a pension – whatever he or she may have been led to expect.

As the bosses of the public sector unions realise what the future holds for their members there will, of course, be uproar, and a good many strikes. There are only about six million union members now in Britain but most of them are public sector workers. (Less than 15% of private sector workers are union members but nearly 60% of public sector workers are paid up union members.) Although most public sector employees earn more than private sector workers, have a much smaller workload, and work fewer hours they also believe that they are, for some reason, entitled to better pensions – paid for by taxpayers. And they will doubtless complain bitterly when they, and their leaders, eventually realise that their pensions are unaffordable.

7

I read today that there are 565,000 estate agents in Britain. That's what is wrong with the country: far too many bloody estate agents. The Government should organise a cull. Leave the badgers alone and get rid of the estate agents.

8

A friend of ours died recently at the age of 89. It was quite a shock because he was very lively and full of beans – both mentally and physically. 'He had a good innings,' said a man I know when I told him the sad news. Why do people always dismiss the deaths of old people? The fact is that most of us miss old people a great deal. The older they are, and the longer we have known them, the more we will miss them because they were a part of our lives for longer.

9

I read an article today in which a heavyweight writer (by which I do not mean a 'great' writer, but one who has consumed too many steak and kidney pies and who regards a three seater sofa as a suitable armchair) claimed that the Pankhurst clan liberated women. I disagree. Women were liberated by the English men who invented the washing machine. (Some American writers claim that an American invented the washing machine but they are wrong.) The first patent for a 'washing and wringing machine' was issued in England in 1691 and a drawing of an early washing machine appeared in an English magazine called *The Gentlemen's Magazine* in 1752. In 1782 a man called Henry Sidgier obtained a British patent for the first rotating drum washing machine and within a decade a man called Edward Beetham was selling 'patent washing machines' in England. The very first American patent for a washing machine wasn't taken out until 1797 by a man called Nathaniel Briggs though whether he re-invented Sidgier's machine all by himself or just copied out his idea in his best writing isn't clear since a fire at the American Patent Office destroyed all the records.

Feminists should remember that long before the Pankhursts and their chums started throwing themselves in front of horses and fastening themselves to railings, English inventors were making real strides forward in the emancipation of women, freeing them from the drudgery of the washtub.

Talking of feminists and horses, I am reminded that I discovered the other day that Carlisle race track has an annual women-riders-only meeting. How on earth can this be? Can anyone imagine the fuss if a race course organised a male-riders-only meeting?

10

It is said by people who claim to know these things that between us we now move more than eight zettabytes of data around the world every year. That is, apparently, equivalent to moving 80, three hundred page books per second for every person on earth. I feel slightly guilty about the fact that I don't think I'm doing my fair share in the 'moving information around' department. I've moved a few books in my time but I've never once managed to move 80 books in a second (unless moving books around in the back of the truck counts). This movement of information has been increasing for decades and the rate at which it is increasing is itself increasing. It's not surprising that we all feel dazed and slightly confused and bad about the fact that we can't keep up, or sort the wheat from the vast amounts of chaff which appears on sites such as Wikipedia, surely the only encyclopaedia in history to have been written almost exclusively by spotty 15-year-olds. (Wikipedia can't even define words accurately. Look up 'pandemic'.)

History has always been a product of a potent mixture of imagination, prejudice and wishful thinking. And it has always been what society considers acceptable. So, for example, if the Germans had won World War II, the holocaust would now be regarded as a great human achievement, up there with the pyramids and the hanging gardens of Babylon. It's all about attitude, interpretation and the position from which you start. But in the past whatever the interpretation might have been the facts usually bore some slight resemblance to what happened. However, things have changed dramatically and thanks to the internet in general the egregious Wikipedia in particular our descendants won't have any idea what really happened in years gone by.

It's not surprising that companies which cannot adapt fast enough go bust or that more people than ever are having nervous breakdowns. Personally, I think it has all got more than a bit silly. Most websites, most phone applications and most pieces of software are absurdly over-complicated and, as a result, are fiddly and clunky. The people who devise new software seem to be lost in their own tiny little worlds; they don't understand what real people want. Microsoft Word is the worst example of this and is an absurdly overcomplicated piece of software. I am lucky to get through an hour without my words turning red or completely disappearing because a stray finger has hit the wrong key. In the old days I would merely untangle my typewriter keys and carry on regardless. Now I pull out hair, beat my desk and cry for help. I have to fetch Antoinette so that she can get me back to where I was before the software screwed up. I strongly suspect that the problem is that the software designers just want to show how clever they are so that they can charge more and more for the junk they're selling. They are, I suspect, so arrogant that they see their products as an end rather than as a means to an end (which is what they should be). If a washing machine, cooker, car or television set were as badly designed and counter intuitive as Microsoft's product the world would come to a grinding halt. No one would eat, go anywhere or watch anything. Any why is the 'send' button right next to the 'delete' button? Isn't that really stupid? My old Word Perfect 5.1 programme was infinitely better than the overpriced rubbish Microsoft turns out. They don't even give you a measly CD these days. You have to go online to download their product. And if I see Bill Gates described as a philanthropist one more time I will scream. His company has carved itself a monopoly out of an overpriced, diabolical product which would not survive for five minutes in a fair and decent world. If Gates wants to be loved (which he clearly does) then he should stop fleecing his customers and start providing a better, more sensibly priced product. He would also do well to stop pushing deathly vaccines onto innocent people in Third World countries.

11

I recently wrote a medical novel which I called 'Sharp Practice'. I published it in hardback under the name Curtis Brown. This is the third novel I've published pseudonymously in the last year or so (the first was called '*Revolt*' and was written under the name Robina Hood and the second was called *My Secret Years with Elvis Presley* which I wrote as Tim Wood) and, like the other two, it hasn't been a rip roaring success. I published 500 copies of each book in hardback and the aim, knowing that books with my name on them tend to be tossed aside by snooty literary editors who think that self-published books are too awful even to touch, was simply to try to get some decent reviews. I was hoping that if the books got good enough notices I might be able to sell them to a paperbacker. Sadly, I proved yet again that first novels under pen names have very little chance of being reviewed widely enough to attract any attention. Most of the books I sent out ended up on Ebay or being sold on Amazon by literary editors and reviewers who supplement their meagre incomes by flogging off the books they are sent. I have, therefore, abandoned these hopeful but non-existent authors and republished all these novels as kindle books on Amazon. I've given them new titles and put my own name on them. (*Sharp Practice* has become *The Truth Kills* and *My Secret Years With Elvis Presley* has become *Is This What Really Happened?*). No sooner had I done this than, rather belatedly I saw an excellent review of *Sharp Practice* which had appeared in *Country Life*.

'This is a first novel by a pseudonymous GP and probably self-published – which might put you off,' writes Leslie Geddes Brown who, bless her little prejudices, probably realised it was self-published because it didn't come with a posh review slip or an invitation to take luncheon at the Ritz with a PR lady called Lucinda, Fiona or Phillipa. 'But in 228 pages, it rants hilariously at every organisation within sight. The author…takes a pop at the police 'and their ungodly spawn', the BBC, which 'never allows a balanced debate', *The Guardian* – 'if they gave out awards for sanctimoniousness, *The Guardian* would undoubtedly sweep the board' – and, of course, bureaucrats who are 'all soulless do-gooders, earnest box tickers… neat hypocrisy running through their veins'.

She generously goes on to say that 'it is very funny indeed' and 'If you want a GP's uncensored views about the NHS today, consultants, social workers and politicians this is your book'. All very nice of her but I'm puzzled by the bit about readers being put off by self-published books. Here, just off the top of my head, is a list of some authors who have published their own books: Beatrix Potter, Walter Scott, J. M. Barrie, Lewis Carroll, T. S. Eliot, Virginia Wolf, D. H. Lawrence, Honore de Balzac and Mark Twain. Recent bestselling authors who started out self-publishing include Vince Flynn and John Grisham. (Flynn's first book, which eventually became a huge bestseller, was rejected by 60 publishers before Flynn published it himself.) It would not take long to produce a list ten times that long.

Publishers and agents are a relatively recent innovation and are best regarded as parasites rather than as essential parts of the publishing process. Incidentally, self-publishing should not be confused with vanity publishing. *The Guardian* and *The Independent* newspapers, both of which make huge losses and require subsidies to stay alive, are excellent examples of modern, vanity publishing.

12

In the year 2010 Britain's national debt was £790 billion. By the year 2016 it will be at least £1.5 trillion. The annual deficit is huge and still rising. So much for austerity. I enjoy being in France (or, indeed, anywhere outside Britain) because Britain seems some way away and I can remember and rejoice in our cultural heritage without being sneered at as a Little Englander. England has no present and no future; the past is all we have.

13

I recently abandoned my VAT registration and no longer have to visit HMRC's incomprehensible website to fill in their wretched forms. I doubt if anyone, anywhere in the world, has ever designed a worse website than the one the tax people have created. It is as badly thought out and as impenetrable as their book of rules and regulations. Everything about the site is bad. Before I could even start I had to key in a 12 letter and number preliminary password and then a 12 letter and number second password. Some of it was in lower case and some of it was in upper case. And then, before I could finish, I had to put in more numbers. Who can possibly remember two passwords when each consists of a random jumble of a dozen mixed figures and letters? No one, I suspect. So, everyone has to write them down. And once you write down a password it stops being confidential and becomes entirely pointless. (It is, of course, something of a joke that HMRC should insist on taxpayers using such incomprehensible passwords for 'security' reasons since once they have got hold of confidential financial information they will probably lose it or sell it or pop it in the post or give it to a man on a bus in a scruffy raincoat.)

I really do loathe the tax people, not because I don't like paying taxes but because I don't like the way they collect it. They are now renowned for treating everyone as crooked; except, of course, for their good friends at Goldman Sachs (a prominent member of any decent citizen's list of 'worst companies in the world'). I'm not alone in regarding HMRC as contemptible. The whole organisation is run in just the same sort of way as one of those protection rackets that are so popular with Italian thugs and Hollywood screenwriters. 'If you give us your money we just might not break your windows/kick down your door.' And the people who work for the HMRC are taken from the same pool of dim thugs as provides the mindless idiots who work in security at airports and railway stations.

A friend of ours recently closed his business and made several people redundant because he simply couldn't cope with the incomparably bad HMRC website and couldn't afford an accountant. He asked HMRC if he could fill in their forms on paper but they said he couldn't. A recent survey of leading Chief Executive Officers concluded that the UK tax system is not fit for purpose and needs a complete overhaul. The UK has now overtaken India as the country passing the most tax legislation in the world every year. No one, not even the experts or the tax inspectors themselves, can keep up with what is allowed and what isn't allowed and the HMRC makes so many mistakes that if it were a taxpayer it would be serving 30 years in a maximum security prison for tax fraud. The HMRC's automatic VAT penalty system is so bad that nearly half of all the 17,200 fines it issued in 2013 were found to be wrong. Complaints about the HMRC go to an adjudicator's office which reported that for 2013 a total of 2,311 complaints were made – and 90% of them were upheld. The CEOs say that the Government would actually receive more money if they simplified the system but also concluded, however, that any attempt to reform it would be entirely futile because accountants, the Treasury and HMRC themselves like to keep things complicated so that only they know what is going on. If the tax system were replaced by something sensible the nation would save billions of man hours but thousands of accountants, civil servants and tax inspectors would have to find something useful to do with their lives.

Incidentally, I was interested to see that it has been confirmed that HMRC now pays performance bonuses to members of staff who turn up for work instead of staying at home or tottering along to watch the football. In addition, I see that HMRC, which had previously denied my report that they pay bonuses, now admits that members of staff who exceed their Soviet style target will receive a pay increase and a higher grade in their branch of the civil service (doubtless entitling them to a large hat rack and better quality carpet).

To all this must now be added the alarming fact that the arrogant HMRC has demanded the right to take money from taxpayers' bank accounts without the nuisance of having to go to court to obtain legal justification for taking the money. Giving these bozos the right to act as prosecution, judge, jury and debt collector is frightening; not least because the HMRC would do better if it were staffed entirely with dyslexic baboons.

Just the other day I read that the HMRC had added up the tax it had collected from Britons in a year and had made a small mistake with its sums. None of HMRC's hugely well-paid civil servants noticed the error until the Government organised an audit. How big was the error? Just £1.9 billion. If you or I make a mistake of one penny on our accounts we are likely to be threatened with everything just short of a nuclear attack. But when the hooligans at HMRC add up their accounts and make a mistake of £1.9 billion no one gets fired, fined or even told off.

And finally, the last bit of damning evidence suggesting that HMRC has lost the plot came in guidance notes they published recently. The notes state that 'taxpayers are not free to reduce their tax bills by lawful means'.

That should convince the few hold outs who were convinced that they were still living in a quasi-democratic country. Not so, I fear. The country is now being run by the stagnant pool dwelling creatures who work at HMRC and who have clearly decided that, until the revolution, they stand above the law. It certainly seems clear that HMRC staff regard both the law and taxpayers as beneath them in the food chain.

14

I took a pile of books and CDs to the counter at Oxfam in Cheltenham. I still have qualms about shopping at any of Oxfam's bookshops because I suspect they are putting a lot of old-fashioned private bookshops out of business. But today I succumbed to temptation and found a number of items I could not live without.

'Were you at the recording of *Gardeners Question Time* in Gloucester?' asked the volunteer at the till. I shook my head and admitted that it had not been my pleasure to be present at this important event. The volunteer, a tiny lady in her later years, was not deterred. 'A former neighbour of mine asked a question,' she told me with great pride. 'She was on the radio.' It is sometimes astonishing to see how pervasive the cult of the celebrity has become. This woman was genuinely preening herself because a former neighbour of hers had asked a question on a BBC quiz programme. I expressed my delight, showed that I was duly impressed, and left.

A few yards away, outside an empty store, a man was playing the saxophone. He was perfectly good enough to play in a band. I suppose he probably does. Many professional musicians add to their income with a little quiet busking. I always give money to any busker who is good and who has added a little something to the day, and although the town's central shopping area does tend to be littered with an unusually generous supply of beggars Cheltenham does have particularly good buskers. (Some towns seem to specialise in attracting awful buskers. Barnstaple in North Devon has some of the worst musicians in the country. I don't know if he still appears but there used to be an organist operating in the town centre who would wheel his organ around and sit and play very loudly. He was so bad that shoppers walked around with their hands over their ears and shop assistants within a quarter of a mile of where he played would stand mute and weeping, utterly exhausted and quite ready to slit their wrists if someone would only be kind enough to supply them with a razor.)

15

For the second time this year, we took our BMW into one of the many car washes run by Eastern Europeans. It was as always an impressive exercise. Two men squirted detergent onto the car and several more than used high pressure hoses to wash the car. Once the men doing the squirting and the hose operators doing the hosing had finished their work another pair cleaned inside the bonnet and around the doors. Finally, a bunch of blokes used sponges and cloths to polish the car. I couldn't help thinking that they looked like the sort of baddies who die wholesale in Steven Segal movies. It was a remarkably efficient operation, involving over a dozen men and probably at least matching the efficiency of the Germans who built the car.

16

The prostate gland was, I sometimes fear, designed to remind old men of their age, and to take away their dignity. Today, I received a letter inviting me to have a prostate screening test. I'm not surprised. I'm in the right age group to be targeted and prostate screening is big business today – promoted both by those who make money out of it and by well-meaning but woefully misguided campaigners. When the prostate screening test was first introduced in 1994 I was immediately sceptical. I was never convinced by the dramatic claims made for its efficacy. Much of the rest of the medical profession was, however, extremely enthusiastic and since then millions of men have had a PSA blood test to screen them for prostate cancer. (The explanation of my scepticism appears in a book I wrote with my wife called *How To Conquer Health Problems Between Ages 50 and 120*.)

The validity of this whole screening endeavour was officially and publicly demolished back in 2010 when the scientist who discovered the test wrote an article in the *New York Times* pointing out that he had for many years been trying to make it clear that the PSA test could not detect prostate cancer and could not distinguish between the two types of prostate cancer – the type that is likely to kill and the type that is relatively harmless. The PSA test merely measures how much PSA (prostate specific antigen) is in the blood. Those who sell prostate screening say that detecting high levels of PSA is significant and that a man who has a high PSA needs treating for prostate cancer. But that's not true. A man with a high PSA may well be perfectly healthy and, conversely, a man with a low PSA may well have lethal prostate cancer. And since many of the treatments for prostate cancer cause serious and permanent damage (including death) this is an important error. The scientist responsible for the PSA test, Richard J. Albin says that he never dreamt that his discovery would 'lead to such a profit driven public health disaster'. It is tragic that there are now studies which show that PSA testing can actually increase the risks of mortality.

I tossed the letter inviting me to have a PSA test into the rubbish. It is a great pity that the enthusiastic volunteers who put so much effort into promoting prostate testing don't spend their time and money trying to persuade surgeons to use new, better forms of treatment instead of sticking with the old, dangerous ones. For example, it is now well-established that removing a cancerous prostate gland by surgery has awful side effects. Most patients who have had the surgery can no longer have an erection and a good chunk of them lose control of their bowels. In contrast, high intensity focused ultrasound treatment seems to work incredibly well. But most cancerous prostate glands are still removed the dangerous, old-fashioned way. It would also be a good idea for campaigners to spend a little effort explaining to people that men who eat a lot of fat, especially animal fat, are more likely to develop prostate cancer. And that's not theory: it's proven fact.

17

There are two main disadvantages to being married to an author.

The first is that novelists are, on the whole, misfits. That's not surprising since they are adults with imaginary friends. I live in a world peopled by fictional characters who have personalities, homes and all the fears, ambitions and expectations of real folk. Mrs Caldicot, Henry Mulligan and Thumper Robinson are just as real to me as any of our neighbours. To be honest, I'd happily swap all our toxic and rancid neighbours for any bunch of characters from one of my books. I have nothing other than a heart, a spleen, a liver, two kidneys and another couple of pounds of assorted offal in common with any of the real people who share our neighbourhood.

I still haven't forgotten that one of our neighbours, a miserable looking old boot who used to clean our home when it belonged to our predecessors, was so miffed when we told her (most gently) that we would not need her skills with a mop and duster that she turned off the four stop cocks which allow water to reach our house. She then refused to tell us where the stop cocks were hidden; no doubt watching from her broomstick and cackling with glee as she watched us wander around the grounds looking for the missing taps. If they ever make strangulation legal she will be the first to go. She rolls her eyes into her head a good deal when discussing other people and I've always thought this to be the first resort of the verbally inept.

Most of the folk who live in our part of Gloucestershire are about as friendly as hijackers. The one thing they do have in common is that most of them shout rather than talk. I suspect they do this to compensate for the fact that so very little of what they say is worth listening to. They shout even if you're standing two feet away from them and always seem to own at least two dogs which never stop barking. I strongly suspect that there are more supercilious, condescending, smug, pretentious bores to the acre in the Cotswolds than there are anywhere else in the world.

The second disadvantage to being married to an author (to get back to my original point) is the ubiquity of ink. I never go anywhere without a number of notepads and several pens and so, inevitably, I always have ink on my clothes. I can pretty well guarantee that a new pair of light, summer trousers will have at least one noticeable ink stain within an hour of first being worn. The problem, however, lies in the fact that I don't just get ink on my clothes, I also manage to get it on Antoinette's clothes. Since I almost always have a pen in my hand (and, probably, a spare in my shirt pocket and a second spare in a trouser pocket) even a gentle embrace can usually result in the transfer of a noticeable quantity of ink. Today, I managed to get ink onto Antoinette's new white jumper within seven minutes of her putting it on for the first time. After offering the appropriate apologies, and offering to buy a replacement, I did point out that buying anything coloured white could be construed as rather reckless. Antoinette pointed out that she didn't really want to start dressing entirely in black until I'd taken my pens and notebooks with me to the great stationery shop in the sky.

18

The sweep came and looked exhausted. He told me that he was sweeping 60 chimneys a day and working until 9.0 o'clock at night.

'I thought this was supposed to be your quiet time of the year!' I said.

'It is,' he told me. 'I hate to think what it's going to be like in the autumn when most people decide they want their chimneys swept.'

He told me that he had got home one evening recently and found that he had over 100 calls on his telephone answering machine. All had come in that day.

'What on earth did you do?' I asked him.

He shrugged. 'I just deleted them all,' he answered. 'I couldn't possibly listen to over 100 calls and then ring them all back.' He told me that whereas a year or two ago he was busy in the autumn and quiet in the spring he is, these days, busy all year round but busier than ever in the autumn and winter. Last year a woman rang him at 10.00 p.m. on Christmas Eve demanding that he call and sweep her chimney because she had unexpected guests coming the following day. She also told him that £40 was too much to sweep a chimney. I don't think he went.

I suspect that more people than ever want their chimneys sweeping because many have decided that an open fire, particularly a log fire using wood culled from your own garden or sawn up from old scrap wood, is a cheap way to supplement expensive gas, oil or electricity central heating. (The health and safety bastards who've stopped pubs having open log fires have not yet managed to stop the rest of us having log fires at home.)

All good news for the sweep, I guess. Even I can multiply £40 by sixty. And then by five. And then by forty eight. (Allowing for a five day week and four weeks annual holiday.)

19

The fetes, pageants, carnivals and revels are coming thick and fast and the local marquee company (known as the 'Marquee de Sade') is doing a roaring trade.

One of the nearby villages held its annual fete today. It was opened by a local radio disc jockey who looked as though he thought he was famous. He never stopped bouncing around and Antoinette wondered if he had taken something invigorating. I told him I didn't think so and suggested that he was simply drunk on his own personality. Sadly, he seemed to be the only person present who knew who he was and so Antoinette and I felt sorry for him, pretended to be star struck and asked him for autographs. I am told that local radio disc jockeys will open anything (including cupboards and envelopes) in return for a cup of free tea and a biscuit if a small crowd can be promised. There were two local bands. One was called *The Crows' Feet*. Every five minutes or so they announced that they had a record out called *You're Looking Old Now, Babe*. ('It's on *Clenched Buttocks Records*', said the lead singer, as though this was of significance.) The other band, called *The Bouncing Boobs*, was an entirely female group. Not to be outdone they told us that their record was called *Two Black Eyes*. I may have got that the wrong way round. The band may have been called *Two Black Eyes* and the record called *The Bouncing Boobs*. I don't think it matters much either way because it didn't sound very good and I doubt if anyone will ever buy a copy.

There was a bottle stall (twelve bottles of vinegar, sixteen bottles of tomato ketchup, eleven bottles of the vicar's homemade wine and a single bottle of Tesco champagne); a guess-the-weight-of-the-cake stall (those in the know were only too aware that Mrs Dunwoody, who always makes the cake for this competition, makes exceedingly damp cakes which are invariably far more solid, and far heavier, than might be suspected); a stall where you could win a goldfish by throwing a rubber ring around a peg on a board (the goldfish on offer race round and round their bowls but they are clockwork because there is now, it seems, an EU law forbidding the use of goldfish as prizes at fetes and fairs) and a stall where, for a £1, angry or stressed visitors could rent three wooden balls to throw at a pile of old crockery (but they had to wear a hard hat and a pair of industrial safety goggles in case a piece of broken tea cup defied the laws of physics and flew backwards towards their heads).

And there was a 'stroke the cat' stall. A large, very fluffy Persian cat lay on a red velvet cushion and anyone prepared to pay 50 pence could stroke the cat for a minute. (Antoinette and I both had several pounds worth of delight at this stall.)

Far more fun than even the fluffy cat, however, were the sports events which had been organised. There were, in the very best tradition of such affairs, a sack race, an egg and spoon race and a three legged race. I was press-ganged into taking part in the sack race and smelt of fertiliser for the rest of the afternoon. For the record I came seventh out of a field of nine. The only contestants I beat were a fat lady, who collapsed after ten yards and howled with unseemly laughter, and a red-faced man in a heavy three piece tweed suit who was soaked with sweat after three yards and who finished nearly five minutes after the winner. The egg and spoon race ended in controversy when one competitor complained that another had used glue to enhance his chances and that he himself had been given a smaller spoon than anyone else.

And, unusual only in that neither Antoinette nor I had ever seen it before, there was a 'horse and jockey 60 yard steeplechase for married couples'. The rules were simple. Four rows of straw bales had been laid out on the course and the one half of each married couple (the horse) had to carry their other half (the jockey) over the bales as quickly as they could. Seven couples had signed up for this event which looked rather more suitable for children than adults. It was definitely one of those events which I would define as offering more fun to spectators than contestants.

Antoinette and I took up our positions half way down the course where we had a good view of both the start and the finish. Where else in the world could one watch such bizarre sporting events? The English founded just about every known sport there is, including football, rugby, cricket, tennis and tobogganing, and I couldn't help wondering if we might eventually see a version of the Married Couples Steeplechase in the Olympics.

It seemed clear from the start that one couple had a huge advantage over the others. He was over six feet tall and probably weighed in at 15 stone. He looked a little like a young Arnold Schwarzenegger might have looked after he had discovered the joys of pumping iron. She was a smidgeon over five feet tall and looked as if she weighed about as much as a half used bag of sugar. I suspected that if she removed the rather fashionable looking straw hat she was wearing her overall weight would halve. Both seemed to be in their early twenties and both looked as if they spent their evenings at the gym rather than the pub. He looked as if he could throw her over his shoulder and run a marathon in two hours. The other couples were all older. Four pairs were in their later twenties or thirties and one pair was in their forties. It was this older pair which looked least likely to reach the finish line, let alone to offer any serious competition for the winners. He was small, certainly no more than five feet four inches and probably no more than nine stones with his pockets full of change. He wore spectacles and looked a bit like the comedian Ronnie Corbett. His wife, who reminded me of a larger version of Hattie Jacques, the actress of Carry on Matron fame, was nearer to six feet tall and so solidly made that she gave the impression that she had been designed and built by a firm of shipbuilders. I didn't fancy his chances of carrying his wife as far as the first obstacle, let alone over it. I couldn't help thinking that there must be a better than evens chance that once his wife attempted to mount him he would simply sink into the ground and, like a tent peg under a couple of hefty blows from a mallet, disappear from view.

'They'd be 100 to 1 outsiders if there was a bookie around,' whispered Antoinette.

I thought for a moment. 'I think they'd probably be 200 to 1,' I whispered back. 'And that would be rather mean!'

As we spoke, the Arnold Schwarzenegger lookalike bent down so that his wife could climb up onto his shoulders. She was wearing a long, summer skirt which didn't make it easy for her to manage this gracefully but eventually she managed to clamber aboard. She looked very secure and smiled and waved to a group of friends who were shouting encouragement, as well as comments on her choice of underwear. The other contestants, all except our 200 to 1 runners, followed suit. They all managed it eventually though one or two riders did look rather unstable. One enthusiastic young rider had equipped herself with a proper riding whip and, with a few preliminary whacks, she made it clear she intended to use it to offer encouragement and not just as a prop.

I was watching to see if a very wobbly woman in a white trouser suit could manage to stay aboard her husband's rather scrawny shoulders when Antoinette nudged me. I turned my head and saw that the final couple were about to take their positions. To our astonishment, however, it was her not him who bent down and it was he not her who clambered up onto his partner's shoulders. This changed things enormously and I couldn't help wishing that there had been a bookie present, that he'd offered the sort of odds Antoinette and I had talked about and that I'd put on a fiver each way.

A moment later the vicar's wife blew a loud blast on an old-fashioned referees' whistle (the sort with a pea inside) and the race started.

The first ten yards went according to expectations. Young Arnold and his jockey set off at a tremendous pace and had cleared the first straw bale while the others were still making themselves comfortable. But, within a couple of yards, everything changed. The leading jockey suddenly realised that she was losing her straw hat and made the mistake of putting up not one but both her hands in an attempt to save it. As she did this she fell backwards slightly and, since her husband was still moving forwards as fast as his chunky legs would carry him, she completely lost her balance. A few seconds later she was lying flat on her back on the grass, her legs up in the air and her troublesome hat several yards away. The favourites were out of the race.

From that point on it was really a rerun of the tortoise versus the hare classic. Hattie Jacques, with an enthusiastic Ronnie Corbett urging her on, started last but gradually caught up and overtook the other contestants. And the unlikely couple duly finished as the winners. From our safe vantage point on the side lines, Antoinette and I both gave them a round of applause.

20

We have an injured jackdaw living with us. It has a badly injured leg and hops rather than walks. And although it can fly it can't fly very far. (Those who still argue that birds cannot feel pain might like to ask themselves why birds limp, or favour their good leg, when they are injured.) I did try to catch it so that I could take it to the vet but it quickly became apparent that my attempts were merely distressing the bird. So, now we simply try to make sure that it has plenty of food to eat. If it hangs around underneath the bird feeders, waiting for seeds that are knocked to the ground, it is quickly pushed out of the way by our family of five magpies, so we throw seeds down in the quiet corner of the garden where the jackdaw seems to have settled.

Sadly, I suspect that it will soon end up as supper for one of the foxes who visit every evening. I know this is all parts of nature's pattern but although the logical part of my brain finds it easy to understand the emotional part of my brain finds it enormously difficult to accept.

21

I have long wondered why laboratories take so long to produce test results. Patients can end up waiting weeks to find out whether or not they have cancer. Apart from the massive stress this causes the delay in obtaining the answers must inevitably mean a delay in starting treatment. Much of the time the delay is caused by simple incompetence. The results are available but they are sitting on someone's desk or waiting to be posted. There is absolutely no excuse for this sort of delay and the people responsible for it (doctors as well as clerks and receptionists) should be put in stocks on the village green and have rotten vegetables thrown at them.

Most people with pets will know that it is customary for vets to have blood test and X-ray results within minutes rather than days and hours rather than weeks and it seems to me quite absurd that human patients should be treated so much worse than animal patients. I have, in the past, sometimes managed to find a way past the system by the simple expedient of ringing the laboratory, introducing myself as a doctor and asking for the results for which a friend or relative has been waiting. I'm sure this is against some law or other and I have no doubt that the pen pushers at the General Medical Council would disapprove but I really don't give a fig.

Today's good news is that the whole business of testing blood samples is, at last, being given a good shake up by an American firm which can do valuable tests on just a few drops of blood, and produce the results within hours. If this new testing system isn't available in all NHS hospitals within a year then the responsible people at the head of the NHS should be taken out and shot.

22

The absence of bees in the spring means that we have the poorest apple crop we've seen for years. But it is now clear that we also have the biggest crop of nuts in human history. Our numerous beech and hazel trees are already laden with fruit. If our small army of squirrels tries to bury this lot they will be utterly exhausted by the beginning of October. And our big horse chestnut tree is going to produce a massive crop of conkers.

23

I've been a fan of the Macmillan Cancer Support organisation for many years and, generally speaking, I believe it is the only cancer charity that does any good. Actually, I strongly believe that the other cancer charities, which are very much part of the hideously cruel cancer industry, do far more harm than good. For reasons which I have described at length in my medical books the big cancer charity in Britain, called simply Cancer Research UK, should be closed down immediately. If it were closed, and its money used to buy simple television advertisements warning people that 'meat causes cancer' there would be fewer people dying from cancer than there are at present.

So, I was sad to see an advertisement on television for the Macmillan organisation's proposed World's Biggest Coffee Morning. In the advertisement a number of women (some of whom appear to be on the plump side of normal (I'm trying to be polite)) are seen enjoying a variety of scrummy looking cakes. Sadly, I fear that the people who organised the coffee morning, and who authorised the television advertisement, don't seem to know much about cancer. There is, I fear, plenty of evidence to show that people who eat tons of fatty and sugary foods (such as cakes) are far more likely to develop cancer. As, indeed, are individuals who are overweight.

The end result will, I suspect, be that the World's Biggest Coffee Morning campaign will make some money for the charity but will result in a noticeable increase in the incidence of breast cancer and bowel cancer among the women taking part. Probably not quite what was intended by a basically well-intentioned but perhaps misguided organisation.

24

My literary agent in Japan wrote today to ask me to send a photograph for the Japanese publisher who is printing my book *How to Stop Your Doctor Killing You*. This is the second time the book has been published in Japan. The previous Japanese publisher of this book let it go out of print some years ago and so now a new publisher is going to reissue it. My agent tells me that the publisher would like a picture of me in a white coat. Sadly, I don't think I have ever had my picture taken wearing a white coat. I certainly never wore one when I was a GP. I always thought that a white coat would act as a barrier between me and my patients and since suits always reminded me of bank managers and accountants I usually wore a sports jacket and flannels which I thought seemed fairly unthreatening. So, lacking a picture in a white coat I sent a couple of snaps which I have used before on book jackets. (To be honest I was tempted to ask them to just use a picture of anyone. A Danish publisher once used a picture of a very smart looking man as my author picture. He wore a tuxedo and black tie and had white hair and spectacles. Another publisher, obviously confused about my sex, used a photograph of a woman in a blue dress as my author picture. I really didn't mind in the slightest.).

Almost immediately the agent emailed back to thank me for the pictures and to tell me that he had scanned them and would return them to me straight away. This confused me enormously. Why would you bother returning an emailed photograph? Neither Antoinette nor I could work this out. It's good, nevertheless, to know that *How to Stop Your Doctor Killing You* is still alive and doing well around the world.

When I self-published the first edition around 20 years ago I went to Lisbon and my Portuguese agent took me to see a publisher whom he thought might like to publish my books. I put a collection of book jacket proofs down on his desk.

'I want that one now!' he said, immediately pointing a finger to the cover of *How to Stop Your Doctor Killing You.*

I started to tell him what the book contained.

'I don't care what it contains or what it's about!' he said, laughing. 'I just want to publish it.'

And so began a beautiful professional relationship. Before the company expired that same editorial director published nearly 20 of my books in Portuguese. Alas, like so many other publishing houses, they are no more; probably yet another casualty of the internet age.

25

Taunton in Somerset used to be one of our favourite market towns. But, like so much of England, it is going downhill at a frightening rate. Now that the main council car park has been sold to developers, there are very few places to park a car. I am constantly surprised by the way councils fail to understand that without decent car parking, town centres will die. When it is hard for people to park their cars they go elsewhere – either to special out of town shopping malls or to the internet which they can access while sitting on the sofa and watching the television.

In Paris, drivers tend to stop their car precisely where they want to be when they have arrived at where they want to go. They then leave their car wherever it is and go and do whatever it is they want to do. Cars are left parked on the pavement, on zebra crossings and, probably, on top of one another. But do this in Britain, where the pavements must be kept free for truck sized prams and mobility scooters, and your car will be towed away and turned into tin cans before you can say 'Hang on a minute, I'm just posting a letter!'.

In Taunton, visitors can park at the railway station (if they can find a space), at the cricket ground in the town centre (if there isn't a match on) or at the riverside supermarket (if they buy something and recognise that if they stay more than a couple of hours there is the danger of a chunky fine).

In the streets around the town centre the neat rows of red brick terraced houses, once a tribute to good architecture and solid building, are now ruined by ranks of wheelie bins and racks of plastic recycling boxes permanently stored in tiny front gardens. And the lower part of the main shopping street is now filled with little but charity shops. We hadn't been to Taunton for a while and whereas it was once colourful and lively it now seems drab and depressing.

Like most towns these days the council seem to have knocked down all the public loos – undoubtedly on the basis that they have to be cleaned occasionally and are, therefore, a drain on the coffers. This is yet another sign that life is deteriorating rapidly these days. Most towns have had public lavatories since the Middle Ages. In Gloucester, for example, it was way back in around 1300 that the local authority first erected latrines at the city gates. They put them there for travellers who were too tired to dig a hole or too refined to pee in the gutter.

In an attempt to save money, control money laundering and eliminate terrorism most towns have closed their public lavatories and these days travellers with bursting bladders must go into a café and buy a cup of tea before they can use a loo. And, in the long run, that merely perpetuates the problem.

26

'Is your husband all right?' a neighbour asked Antoinette. 'I saw him behaving very strangely in the garden the other day.'

These neighbours, who are enormously self-important, only talk to us when they want to complain about something, or think they might have some bad news with which to spoil our day. I've never really been able to work out precisely what he does for a living but I believe that his official job description is 'management consultant'. In olden times it used to be said, rather cruelly I sometimes thought, that those who can do and those who can't, teach. These days it could with great accuracy be said that those who can't run a business become management consultants and tell other people, who are running businesses, how they should do what they themselves cannot do. He is also a neatness fetishist. He spends 30 minutes a day cleaning his shoes, 30 minutes a day snipping the hair out of his ears and on Sundays he spends the whole day washing and polishing their vehicles. They both drive Audi motor cars with what look as if they are supposed to be personalised number plates (they have, however, bought cheap personalised plates and, I confess, we have been unable to work out what the letters stand for) and are awful gossips who delight in spreading nasty rumours. Whenever I am in their presence I always feel that I really should have a sharpened stake handy. They have three small yappy, growly dogs and a son who goes to an expensive boarding school. When he comes home for the holidays the son causes mayhem by riding around on a very noisy 50cc trials motorbike. The only time I ever spoke to him (to ask him not to ride his motorbike across an area of land I had planted with shrubs) he told me to 'fuck off' but since he goes to a posh school it came out as 'ferk orf'. This is the second time I have heard these words from a local child so I can only assume it is some sort of local dialect, or maybe a traditional Cotswold greeting. His mother has boasted to us that she enjoys writing nasty reviews about hotels, pubs, tourist attractions, films and books. She laughed when she told us this and admitted that she never says anything complimentary. She seems to regard writing bad reviews as some sort of sport, like shooting grouse or hunting foxes. The only thing of note about them is that they have very neat hedges. When they die they will be remembered for having had neat hedges.

In addition to his work as a management consultant he does a little wheeler dealing in land and once told me that he buys fields and trees from farmers and sells meadows and woodlands to dreamers. I have no idea what she does with her time but I'm thinking of starting a rumour that she works as a stripper in a pub in Gloucester. She's shaped like a barn and I would imagine that if she took her clothes off the customers would pay her extra to put them back on again, but I'll say she performs a novelty act as a speciality ecdysiast and does something spectacular with ping pong balls, indoor fireworks and a St Bernard dog. Actually, to add verisimilitude I think I will also start a rumour that her husband has served time for pandering. No one local will know what pandering is and they will all have to rush home and look it up in a dictionary. Or, more probably, search for it on the internet. Maybe I will also set up a website for her, offering her personal services 'at home or away'. Better still I will tell everyone that she has morning sickness and that this is something of a miracle since her husband had a vasectomy many years ago. I will then point out how curious it is that she is the only person in the area to have fresh bread delivered every day. 'The man who brings it must slice and butter it for her,' I will say. 'He always stays at least an hour.'

'In what way was he behaving 'strangely'?' asked Antoinette, unconcernedly. She knows that I have a vast 'behaving strangely' repertoire.

'He was waving his arms around and running from place to place as though he were having some sort of fit,' said our scary neighbour. She really is quite a frightening woman. Hammer films would have had her on long-term contract if they'd known about her. She could have played Frankenstein's monster without any make-up. When she walks into a room the temperature drops by ten degrees. If she dies she will need to be hung, drawn and quartered; just to make sure.

'Oh, I expect he was trying to get rid of a horse fly,' said Antoinette.

The neighbour, clearly disappointed by this mundane explanation, muttered something disparaging about the scruffy nature of our hedges and departed to annoy someone else.

When Antoinette told me about this I was reminded of the wonderful scene in Jacques Tati's first film *Jour de Fête*. Monsieur Tati, playing the village postman, is cycling along a country lane when a bee takes a fancy to him. The resultant un-choreographed dance, seen from afar, is an example of Tati, the maestro, at his very best.

But it also reminded me of something else.

201

A friend of mine called Dickson, who lived in a rather smart suburban area, was fed up with his neighbours, who would have all won gold medals for combined fascism and snootiness. Dickson reckoned most of them spend their evenings working out how many people you could cram into a railway wagon. He persuaded a pal of his called Norman to go round to all the neighbours with a clipboard. Norman is a psychiatrist and so has a rather strange of way of looking at, and talking to, everyone he meets. He could even make a traffic warden feel uncomfortable.

'I'm from the health and safety unit of your local council,' Norman told the people on whom he called. 'I just want to have a word with you about your neighbour Mr Dickson.'

The neighbours were, of course, all eager to hear more. Here was a great chance to get some gossip free of charge – and, from the sound of it, damned good gossip too.

'Mr Dickson suffers from a mental condition and has been a resident in several institutions over the years,' said Norman. 'We've been asked to keep an eye on him by the local police in view of his sometimes erratic and dangerous behaviour in the past. The psychiatrists are all happy that he is probably not dangerous now and it is a long time since he hurt anyone or did any serious damage. But we like to err on the side of caution.'

The neighbours, now alarmed rather than just curious, were all desperate to hear more.

'There really isn't any need for you to be alarmed,' continued Norman. 'But if I could give you just a word or two of advice?'

They all wanted the advice.

'Always be polite to him and don't do anything to anger him. If he behaves strangely then just ignore him. If he asks you for something then, if at all possible, I would suggest that you agree and do what he asks. And don't, please don't, mention my visit to him – or to anyone else for that matter.'

Dickson told me that after this he never had any trouble with any of his neighbours. They all smiled at him, waved when they saw him, wished him good morning or good afternoon as appropriate, and kept well out of his way.

There are many ways to get respect, but fear is certainly one of the quickest and most permanently effective. It is, after all, fear that stops people saying that they disapprove of gay marriage, that they don't like being frisked by foreigners when passing through British customs posts, that they hate having to speak in baby English when speaking to a bank clerk and never being able to get through to speak to a real person when ringing HMRC or a utility company. We are cowed and downtrodden by rules, laws and fascist officials. It is, I suspect, this general fear of being found politically correct which helps push people into attacking authors, hotels, restaurants and shops with such venom when they can do so anonymously, online.

I told Antoinette about Dickson and Norman.

'Do you know Norman?'

'I was at medical school with him.'

'Do you think you could get in touch with him?'

I said I thought I could.

Antoinette grinned broadly.

27

A bloke I know who is a specialist in prehistoric monsters (and calls himself a dinacologist) buys his reading glasses from a chain store and never pays more than £2 for a pair. He claims, not unreasonably, that since he only needs reading spectacles, and doesn't have anything much wrong with his eyesight, he really doesn't need to spend a fortune buying expensive frames and tailor made lenses. The last time we visited his home Antoinette and I had a little fun with him. We bought three pairs of spectacles from the shop where he buys his spectacles, making sure we picked the same frames that he buys but buying spectacles of three different strengths – none of them the same as the ones he currently uses. During the course of the afternoon we then substituted our reading spectacles for the ones he usually buys.

'These damned spectacles aren't strong enough,' he complained at first, trying but failing to read his paper.

'Oh, the lenses in those cheap spectacles warp if you leave them in the sun,' I told him. When he next left the room we changed the spectacles for a much stronger pair.'

He then naturally complained that the spectacles were too strong.

'Maybe your eyes are changing,' I told him. 'At your age eyes can sometimes change almost overnight.'

We confessed in the end, of course, and he was so relieved that he opened a bottle of bubbly to celebrate.

This reminded me of the time when Antoinette and I played a similar trick on a neighbour (at a previous house of ours) who was very proud of a new apple tree he had planted in his front garden. He was a pleasant fellow who did something for the council and looked like Bob Hoskins. His wife, I remember, was rather imposing and looked like Hillary Clinton. She managed a charity shop. It was a very small tree but the Mr Hoskins lookalike had high hopes for it.

Late one night Antoinette and I carefully dug up the tree and replaced it with a similar apple tree that was twice as high. When we saw the neighbour the next day he was so excited that I thought he would burst. He told us with great glee that his new tree was growing at a rate of three feet a day and he had worked out that within a month it would be as high as his house. We did not tell him the truth until a week or so later when we gave him back the small, original tree which we had been looking after in our own garden. Although he now had two trees he was very disappointed and we felt really bad about our practical joke for ages.

28

We went to Cirencester for the day. I was standing in front of the ticket machine in the car park, looking through the coins in my pocket in the hope that they added up to £3, when a man rushed up to me.

'Are you buying a car park ticket?' he asked, rather unnecessarily. I told him I was.

'How long are you staying?' he asked.

I didn't answer this straight away. I am allergic to strangers asking me questions because they bring me out in a rash of suspicions.

'Are you staying more than an hour?' he asked. 'Because I've got a ticket here with 45 minutes left on it.' He held out a car park ticket.

Just then a uniformed attendant wandered past. 'That's exceedingly kind of you,' I replied loudly. 'It would delight me enormously to be able to cheat the council out of a couple of quid. But unfortunately I need a ticket for three hours.' The man laughed out loud, probably because he didn't know that a council employee was standing behind him looking very peeved. He then tottered back to his car, at least sixty yards away. Kind gestures like this always make me feel warm inside.

It would have been a particular delight to take his ticket because the Cirencester car park is one of the worst in the entire world. One problem is that the spaces seem narrower than the spaces elsewhere, as are the aisles. Parking anything more than a pedal car is a nightmare. The other problem is that the ticket machines seem designed to cheat patrons out of their money. If you don't feed in the coins very slowly the machine accepts them but doesn't recognise them. The customer thinks he's paid for three hours but the machine prints out a ticket for one hour. I've been caught out by this twice already.

For no very good reason at all, this happy incident reminded me of the days when I used to drive a Volvo estate car. I used to stick the car park tickets on the rear passenger windows and then the rear windows right at the back of the car, but instead of removing them when they had served their purpose I just left them where they were. After a year or so there were around 150 car park tickets stuck to the windows. They weren't dangerous or impeding my view when I was driving but they gave parking attendants quite a job. I sat on a wall and watched one once: he spent fifteen or twenty minutes examining all the tickets, looking for the most recent and valid one. The ticket was there and the man from the Gestapo went away terribly disappointed that he could not give me a penalty ticket. I don't know why I suddenly remembered this. I find that as I get older, all sorts of odd old memories suddenly leap into the forefront of my mind and do a little jig to attract my attention.

After I left the car park I spent a pleasant hour or two in Cirencester queuing behind people who were buying incredibly small items with their credit cards.

In W.H.Smith's a man bought a newspaper with a credit card and from the way he examined it I got the distinct impression that he'd never seen a credit card before – let alone used it for anything more exacting than cutting a neat white pile of film star snorting powder. (I queue because I don't much care for the automated tills even when there are some, which there aren't in Cirencester unless they're hiding somewhere behind the mixed birthday cards. My original objection was that they were taking jobs but I also confess that I just can't stand the damned things. The last time I used one I found myself shouting at the automated voice which was telling me off in the sort of voice mental health nurses use when dealing with demented patients. A woman in the queue behind me looked very unamused and for a few moments I thought she was going to call the police. I would not be surprised to discover that it is illegal to shout abuse at computerised voices in shops.) In Mr Marks and Mr Spencers excellent emporium I queued behind a woman who paid for two bananas with a credit card. And when I gave up shopping and went to Caffè Nero for an Americano the woman in front of me there paid for a small expresso with a credit card.

My hope for a pleasant sit in the café was rather spoilt by the presence of an elderly gentleman in a panama hat and a striped blazer who was reading a book but, instead of reading it quietly to himself, was reading it out loud in the way that one might do to an invalid or a classroom full of primary school children. He was reading it not quite loud enough for me to hear what he was reading but just loud enough to be annoying and stop me concentrating on my own book. I suppose he must have practised to get the volume just right. I've seen him there quite often but I have no idea who he is or why he needs to read out loud. It did occur to me that he might be placed there as part of one of those televised pranks. It also occurred to me that it might be fun to be there if, one day, he reads this book out loud and finds himself describing himself.

After ten minutes of this auditory torture I left and walked round the corner to the upmarket store known as Poundland where I searched for and found a really cheap aerosol can of deodorant. Having tested a small squirt and convinced myself that the spray really was pretty pungent and foul smelling I bought two cans – though this was, I confess, only because Poundland was offering two for a pound and I was too embarrassed to try to buy one can for fifty pence. The store is, after all, called Poundland and not Fiftypenceland.

'We don't have any more free bags,' says the assistant at the till. 'Would you like a useful bag for 10 pence?' I told her I would like a useful bag for 10 pence and spent the next five minutes wondering what a not-useful bag looks like. Actually, my 10 pence bag turned out to be fairly sturdy and much better than those flimsy bags the supermarkets use, which would collapse under the strain if you tried to use them to carry a single empty match box.

As I left I was approached by a chugger. Cirencester has more chuggers than London has rats. 'I like your tie,' said this one, doubtless attempting to flatter me into signing up to pay vast sums of money to a charity which spends half its income on salaries and the other half on expenses. 'Thank you,' I said, walking on without even the slightest break in my step. One of the advantages of being old is that one can be superficially rude and get away with it.

29

It has been reported that the BBC has decided not to give equal air time to those who do not believe in climate change. In future it will give the majority of its air time to the lunatics and lobbyists who are convinced (for no very good scientific reason at all) that the earth is getting hotter because of man's activities. It may seem extraordinary that the BBC, which is paid for by taxpayers, should take a position on a subject about which neither it nor anyone else knows the truth but the organisation's vastly overpaid staff do this sort of thing all the time. The organisation seems to have arbitrarily decided that the EU is a 'good thing' (not surprising, since it accepts EU money with eagerness) and that genetic engineering, vivisection, vaccination and the eating of meat are all 'good things'. It would be no surprise to see the BBC broadcast a programme entitled *The Earth is Flat, Vaccination is Safe and Other Scientific Facts*.

A decent broadcaster would be far more interested in encouraging debate than in simply propagating well subsidised myths, but the BBC is not a decent or unbiased broadcaster and no one there seems to have the intelligence to work out that those who oppose public debate on these issues disapprove of free speech and open debate not because their arguments are strong but because their standpoints are indefensible.

The BBC staff seem not the slightest bit interested in the fact that those scientists who argue in favour of the official climate change position have falsified evidence, suppressed inconvenient truths, censored conclusions which do not fit their conclusions, withheld data which didn't fit the climate change theory and even threatened sceptical opponents with violence. Facts are rarely displayed objectively in the media these days but they are invariably distorted beyond recognition on the BBC which is, surely, the most hypocritical, sanctimonious media operation in the world. The BBC has established positions on just about anything you or I can think of and those positions are invariably taken not because of facts or logic, or even because of public opinion, but because of the views of a few prejudiced and bigoted journalists who, in turn, adopt their views after listening to the nonsensical outpourings of lobbyists and political thugs most of whom represent the establishment position and, therefore, the State.

(BBC news staff describe themselves as journalists because they cannot spell propagandists. Most of them are ethnically acceptable media graduates who have, I suspect, failed to find work on a newspaper but who have expressed the right mixture of sanctimoniousness and political correctness at their interviews.)

It is as though the people who work at the BBC believe that only the State is entitled to have its opinions heard.

The bottom line is that it is absolutely no use at all tuning in to any BBC programme hoping to hear the truth about the European Union (the BBC is aggressively for it), vaccination (the BBC is very much a supporter), vivisection (the BBC thinks it's wonderful), genetic engineering (the BBC thinks we should have much more of it), cutting the size of the State (the BBC, as a part of the State, is vehemently opposed to this) or, indeed, any other contentious subject.

The BBC has been bought lock, stock and valve and its opinions and editorial views will always reflect those of the most successful lobbyists and richest pressure groups. I suspect that the BBC promotes more myths, more misconceptions and more downright lies than any other news organisation in history. It is a tragedy that so many people around the world do not understand just how biased the BBC has become. Most understand that when they watch a news programme on a station owned by Rupert Murdoch they are getting a Murdoch view of the world. Very few, I suspect, realise that in comparison to the BBC the Murdoch empire is the very bastion of truth.

I very much doubt if I am the only person to have been effectively banned from BBC programmes for telling inconvenient truths.

I will be so delighted when non-payment of the BBC's licence fee is finally made a civil rather than a criminal offence. Once that has happened, as it surely must, I sincerely hope that no one will be stupid enough to pay the BBC any more money.

Not for nothing is the BBC now known by many as Betray Britain Comprehensively; it is a truly fascist organisation.

30

This is the day of the week when our rubbish is collected today and so today I used one of my new, foul smelling deodorant sprays. (I've decided that the contents are made from, or designed to smell of, canned French farts. Anyone wanting to establish a French Metro Theme Park should buy this stuff by the tanker load. I cannot, however, imagine why anyone would want to squirt it on or around their person.) I sprayed the stuff inside the black bags and on the outside of them too. As I was doing this, two women wandered past with an ugly pair of dogs. They did not look to be the sort of women who, when not walking their dogs, would spend their days worrying about hair, shoes and handbags. They were, I guessed, more the sort of women who would be into weight lifting and welding. They had probably spent nearly a minute getting ready to take the dogs for a walk. Actually, like most of the people we see, the dogs are taking them for a walk. I love animals but dogs are pack animals and the majority of dogs I see are uncontrolled; they, not the owners, are leader of the pack. Whenever you see a dog pulling at the lead, or running on ahead, you know you're seeing a dog which thinks it is the leader. And dogs can and do bite, maim and kill.

'What are you doing?' snapped one of them, in a surprisingly hoity toity manner.

I explained that I was merely spraying our rubbish so that the black bags would not be torn open, and the contents distributed far and wide, by badgers, foxes or magpies.

'You should put your black bags into proper bins,' she told me. She spoke as though she were telling a servant how to fold a napkin properly.

I explained that we had not been issued with bins because there was nowhere to put them. Our lane is so narrow that if we put out a bin the vehicle sent to collect the rubbish would not be able to pass by. Nor, indeed, would anything else.

'If that stuff you're spraying makes my dogs ill I will sue you!' screeched the woman, who had clearly not listened to anything I'd said. I doubt if she had listened to anything anyone said for at least a decade.

I started to explain again that I was simply spraying deodorant onto the bags and that as far as I know deodorant, however foul it smells, isn't toxic to dogs, but the woman wouldn't listen. Her dogs were running wild and, very politely, I asked her if she would put them on leads. This did not go down well. I doubt if I would have caused a bigger explosion if I'd asked her if she was a communist. She screamed at me that if I lived in the country I should expect to see dogs running round and barking and biting and generally doing stuff that dogs do when they aren't properly controlled. She then threatened to sue me for veterinary bills, distress and, quite probably, a sore throat. She then waddled away; her out of control dogs bounding ahead and doubtless looking for walkers to eat.

'It's good stuff!' I called, holding up the can. 'I bought it at Poundland.'

31

There is now a new disorder called 'Paris Syndrome' which strikes Japanese tourists visiting the French capital for the first time. The Japanese arrive with high hopes and great expectations and find it difficult to cope with the fact that the Parisians are often rude, over-bearing and insulting. Several tourists have had to be repatriated as emergency cases – broken by their experiences in cafes and souvenir shops.

I'm surprised only that the Japanese aren't prepared for the rudeness of the Parisians. It is not, after all, a new phenomenon.

During the Second World War, French President Charles de Gaulle met US President Roosevelt to try to persuade the Americans to join the conflict. But when Roosevelt, who spoke French fluently, tried to talk to the General, the tall and snooty Frenchman pretended not to understand him because Roosevelt spoke French with an American accent.

August

1

Someone I don't know well enough to call a friend but know too well to describe as a stranger and whom I would describe as an acquaintance if that didn't sound as though I were trying to distance myself from him (which, if I am honest I suppose I am but that doesn't mean that I am necessarily prepared to admit it) has bought himself a pair of these ridiculous Google glasses which enable him to take photographs and film everything he does wherever he is when he is doing it. They apparently even allow him to check his emails simply by glancing upwards. I really don't understand why anyone would want to buy or wear one of these absurd devices.

I always used to think of Google as simply one of the world's most evil companies (up there on the podium with Monsanto and Goldman Sachs) but I am now beginning to think of it as just plain stupid.

I have two main concerns.

First, when on earth is he going to find time to look back at the stuff he's been filming if he spends all his time filming everything he does? And when he does, will he film himself watching the films he's made of himself filming what the world looks like when he's cleaning his teeth? Where will this end? Where will all this digital dross be stored and how will anyone ever find time to organise a proper filing system for it?

Second, why on earth does he want to be able to look at his emails every two seconds. Does it really matter if the Vodafone statement has to sit there and wait for ten minutes? It's not going to go away. Millions of people now seem to spend vast portions of their lives texting and emailing one another but what do they have to say that is worth reading and what do they spend their time reading that is worth reading?

Third, how does Mr Google know that his damned silly glasses won't cause eye cancer? I bet they will and I'm a doctor and Mr Google isn't.

I really do despise the whole idea of Google glasses. If I see someone wearing a pair I have decided that I will accidentally bump into them, accidentally knock their glasses onto the floor and then accidentally stand on them. I didn't fight at the Battle of Curmudgeon to be filmed by some internet yahoo while I'm walking down the street and minding my own business.

2

A friend who is trying to sell a house rang me today. He was confused because his estate agent, who had been trying for some time to persuade him to accept an offer exactly £60,000 below his home's asking price of £299,950 (a discount of approximately 20%), had telephoned him to report that another buyer had offered £80,000 below the house's asking price. 'The house has only been on the market for ten days,' said my friend, who is the sort of person who believes the caller who tells him that they're doing a survey about energy prices and may be able to help him find a cheaper supplier. 'And I simply cannot believe that the offer the agent wants me to accept is the best offer I'm going to get.'

I told him that I suspected that his estate agent was trying the old 'low offer' trick to persuade him to accept the first offer that had been made. He sounded puzzled. 'It's quite a simple ploy,' I explained. 'The estate agent rings you with an absurdly low price in order to make you panic and agree to take the other bidder's offer. The very low bid isn't made by a real person. They know you won't even consider it so they don't have to worry about that. The bid is entirely fictional.'

'But why would they do that?' he asked. 'They're getting a percentage of the price I receive so the higher the price the more the commission.'

'The kind explanation is that they just want to persuade you to sell now so that they receive their commission sooner rather than later,' I told him. 'If you get a really low offer you will worry that your house is worth less than you thought it was and so you'll accept the better offer you've already been given.'

'That's the kind explanation?'

'Yes.'

'And the unkind explanation?'

'They're selling your house to a mate or a relative and they want them to be able to buy it cheap. If you think that you're only going to get £220,000 for your house then you'll be inclined to jump at the chance to get £240,000.'

My friend was shocked. 'But isn't that illegal?'

'Yes. But they are hardly ever caught. And estate agents aren't the most loathed people in the country for no reason.'

It is cheering to think that estate agents will soon go the way of lift operators and lamp lighters. It seems clear that the internet will before long do unto estate agencies exactly what it has done to bookshops and record shops and what it now seems to be doing to black cabs and hotels.

I have met many estate agents over the years and although most were superficially charming, in an Arthur Daley sort of way, and greasy enough to slide through a keyhole, I have never met one whom I felt I could trust to tell me the truth about whether or not it was raining. The business model for estate agents is truly absurd. They have no training and no qualifications and anyone with enough money to rent an empty shop can put up a sign and proclaim themselves to be an estate agent. If you want to set up shop as a hairdresser you probably need to spend years at a college and acquire a diploma. If you want to paint nails for a living you need to be trained and acquire a diploma. I have no doubt that if you want to empty dustbins for a living you will need to be trained. But if you want to become an estate agent you just need a cheap suit and a car. Estate agents have little or no specialist knowledge and often very little local knowledge either. You don't have to do O level estate agency before you're allowed to describe yourself as an estate agent. And yet estate agents charge 2% plus VAT for taking a few photos and, if you're lucky, agreeing to show viewers around the property you're trying to unload.

Estate agents have for years attempted to create a mystique about what they do (in the same way that solicitors like us to think that conveyancing is something complicated) but the bottom line is that although the amounts of money are greater, flogging a house is no more complicated than selling carrots, glasses of lemonade or second-hand books.

3

While sitting on a park bench today I read that it is now possible to build a pair of do it yourself Google glasses using a specially designed cardboard framework into which an ordinary mobile phone is fitted. I've seen a picture of the cardboard frame and it looks like something that Blue Peter would recommend making, using two toilet roll centres and an old cornflake packet, and getting Mummy or Daddy to help with the work requiring scissors. I do hope I see someone wearing one of these. What a hoot. I will photograph them and put the picture online. (I am kidding. I have absolutely no idea how one can put a photograph online. Photographs belong in albums, where they can be examined at leisure and in private.)

4

A kind reader has sent me a cutting from her local newspaper. A centurion, being interviewed and asked the secret of his longevity, replied: 'The secret is moderation in all things. I've never smoked more than 20 cigarettes a day or drunk more than half a bottle of whisky a day.' He does not mention good genes and good fortune. I celebrated this glorious piece of politically correct honesty with a glass of Laphroaig. I always let Antoinette put the water into my whisky because she invariably puts in too much. I then have to add a little more whisky. And then she adds a little too much water. And I have to put in a little more whisky. And before long I have a drink anyone could be proud to sip. As I sniffed and sipped, it occurred to me that life would be easier if someone would produce a weekly newsletter summarising the latest views on political correctness. It would be nice to know which views, words and jokes are likely to result in my being arrested or greeted with a hail of tutting and frowning.

5

Waitrose, the supermarket chain, has delivered our groceries each week for a few years now but every time Antoinette goes onto their website to place an order, the website keeps promoting offers that include meat products. I am astonished that any large company should have such terrible software. Surely, any decent programmer would have written software which could work out that those customers who never buy meat are probably vegetarian.

6

I bought a newspaper and a loaf of bread at one of the nation's few remaining corner stores.

'Would you like a woman for 22 pence?' asked the man behind the counter in an accent which suggested that when Pakistan play England at cricket he will probably not be cheering on the English side.

'No thank you!' I replied rather sharply. 'I'm a happily married man,' I added, rather pompously. I couldn't help wondering what sort of woman you can possibly buy for 22 pence. Even in Cirencester, where farmers' daughters abound, this seemed extraordinarily cheap. And I'm no prude, but it seemed alarming to know that pimping had become so open. And why 22 pence? It seemed a curious sort of price. Was it what is, I believe, called a 'loss leader' designed to hook me as a future customer? I am constantly confused by the world in which we live but this seemed to take both the cake and the biscuit.

'The magazine!' explained the shop assistant, looking cross rather than embarrassed. '*Woman* magazine. We have a special offer.' He picked up a copy of the magazine and held it up to show me. Now I was definitely embarrassed. I used to write for the damned thing when it contained long, serious articles rather than just lots of pictures but to be honest I'd forgotten it existed. 'Or you can have a *Hello* if you prefer,' he said. I told him a goodbye would do me nicely and left.

As I walked away from the shop I was very nearly run over by a huge mobility scooter being driven by a pavement hogging maniac. Why do they make these things the size of tractors? They don't need to be three feet wide and to weigh half a ton. It wouldn't surprise me to discover that they have four wheel drive and can tow a caravan. The small ones, which are far easier to manoeuvre on pavements and in shops, make far more sense. The driver of this one did not look to me to be in the slightest bit disabled though he was carrying about ten stone in excess personal baggage. I strongly suspect that 90% of the people who use mobility scooters really do not need them; most simply need to lose some weight. Similarly, I suspect that a similar number of people in nursing homes don't need to be there. Most, I would guess, end up in care homes because they have given up trying to cope with the administration of managing their utility bills.

They may also give up independent living in order to escape from their council tax bills and pressure from relatives who want to release the money tied up in their property. (An eccentric American millionairess called Huguette Clark spent the last 25 years of her life living in a private hospital in Manhattan. She was in good health but insisted on having doctors and nurses constantly on call. In addition to the fortune this cost she tipped heavily, giving her favourite nurse more than $30 million.)

7

I am tired of hearing famous individuals in sport and show business ascribe their success to hard work and determination. It happens time and time again and must be intensely irritating for the thousands who work hard and who are determined but who still fail to scale the peaks of their chosen profession. The truth is that the people who make it to the top often owe their success to luck more than anything else. Of course, they have worked hard and of course they have been determined but those are not the only factors which have led them to success. Singers, comedians and actors often hit the big time through serendipity more than talent or skill. They happen to be in the right time at the right place to be spotted. Racing drivers may get into Formula 1 because they are lucky enough to find a sponsor prepared to buy them a seat in a car. Athletes who get into the Olympics may do so because they are lucky enough to find a coach who will help them move in the most profitable direction. Hard work and determination are essential for success but they are by no means the only, or even the most important, factors. It's strange that people are always quick to blame bad luck when things go wrong but never eager to credit good luck when things go well.

8

'Is this the Roman city of Corinium?' asked a tall gentleman in a flowery shirt and beige slacks. We were standing in the car park in the centre of Cirencester. He was clearly foreign and even though he wasn't wearing lederhosen, I would, if I had to guess, have said that he came from Germany. Although it was quite a cool day he was sweating like a fat jogger in a heatwave.

'It is,' I confirmed. Cirencester used to be a Roman settlement and back in those days it was known as Corinium.

'Where is the city?' he asked, looking around at the public toilets, the selection of recycling skips and the police station. None of them looked terribly Roman or, it has to be said, terribly interesting, unless you needed a toilet in which case one of them would probably look very terribly interesting. 'How do we get to it?'

I pointed to a gap in the low wall at the far side of the car park. 'Go through the gap and then past the shop selling Roman mobility aids, past the Roman hairdressers and turn left when you come to the Roman estate agency. Wander up in that direction and within a couple of hundred yards you'll be in the middle of the Roman city of Corinium.'

'Thank you,' said the foreigner. He seemed pleased. 'And where do I pay for the car park?'

I pointed to the Roman Pay Here sign.

At that moment a flock of seagulls on holiday from Ilfracombe or Weston super Mare or somewhere wet and salty flew overhead. One of them deposited a large portion of guano on the man's head and he, muttering what I suspect was a mixture of foreign oaths and apologies, ran back to his car to fetch tissues.

I wonder if seagulls have competitions to see how many people they can hit on the head. When you stop and think about it, the number of times that guano lands directly on head or shoulders is way out of proportion to what one would expect. The birds must be taking aim and doing it deliberately. I once watched as a seagull's deposit landed slap bang in the middle of a creamy Cornish ice cream. The woman who was eating it was chatting to a friend at the time and absent-mindedly turned back to lick her icecream without looking at what she was doing. It was only my timely warning which prevented her acquiring a lifelong dislike of eating out of doors.

9

The son of a couple who live nearby was arrested (with a group of friends) for stealing a car. The youths were all drunk at the time and succeeded in crashing the stolen car and destroying both it and two other vehicles. The son was taken to court, fined and given community service. 'It wasn't fair,' the young man whinged, when I saw him today. 'The police and the people in the court made me feel like a criminal.' I'm absolutely delighted that he feels like a criminal. The country has been going to the dogs since they outlawed horse-whipping for dastardly young men who do bad things and then whinge when they are threatened with punishment. This isn't the first time I've heard a youth moaning about his well-deserved punishment.

10

What idiot at the Ministry of Transport decided that gradients on British roads should be measured in percentages? Today, I saw a sign on a hill telling me that the gradient was 20%. This meaningless nonsense, brought to us courtesy of the European Union, is now apparently replacing the traditional method of defining road gradients as, for example, 1 in 5 or 1 in 12. Everyone knew where they were with the old gradient signs. The new-fangled EU versions are a tribute to the memory of Adolf Hitler and Herr Funk and simply yet another sign that Britain will do anything to please the unelected, fascist eurocrats of Brussels. We didn't have to abandon our imperial measurements but we have and I suspect that it won't be long before mile posts become kilometre posts. The rood, the perch and the chain will soon be lost even to history.

11

I now spend so much of my life dealing with crap that if anyone asks what I do for a living I tell them that I am deeply involved in sewage. I sat in the garden, musing on this sad fact, and slowly my mood was lifted. Our bower seat is surrounded by trees and bushes which are still in blossom and the few bees who have belatedly turned up were working incredibly hard. I never feel worried by them, even though they may be working no more than a foot from my face. They do what they do, and I do what I do.

12

According to the Government's own website, it is, I am delighted to say, now against the law to let any dog (even tiny yappy ones) be dangerously out of control anywhere. The 'anywhere' includes public places and private gardens (including the dog owner's own home). According to the law a dog is considered to be dangerously out of control if it injures someone or makes someone worry that it might injure them. I believe that in general we have far too many laws (some of them downright silly and many virtually unenforceable) but this is one law that really deserves to be on the statute books. In recent years I have noticed that some dog owners seem to regard it as their right to march through towns, along country lanes and on footpaths with their dog off the lead and barking and growling at everyone in sight. They sneer at anyone who suggests that their dog should be on a lead and laugh at those who confess that they are afraid of dogs. These dog owners have made life difficult for millions and I am not ashamed to admit that I am one of the millions. I gave up cycling after I was attacked by two loose Alsations. The owner stood by and laughed as his dogs went for me. 'They don't like cyclists,' he sneered. 'You shouldn't be here.' Since we were all on a dedicated cycle track at the time it didn't seem to me that this was entirely fair. At least the baggy trousered bastard didn't tell me that his dogs didn't bite. ('My dog doesn't bite' has taken over from 'the cheque is in the post' and 'I'll pull it out before I come' as the biggest and most popular lie in Britain.) Still, those of who like to wander around without being sniffed and having your legs bitten can take comfort in the fact that the law is now very firmly on our side. Dog owners who break the law can be fined up to £5,000 and sent to prison for up to six months and may be banned from owning a dog in the future. If a dog actually injures someone the owner can be sent to prison for up to five years. And if a dog kills someone the prison sentence goes up to 14 years and the fine becomes unlimited. It is now against the law to allow a dog to run free on a public road. It is against the law to allow a dog to make a good deal of noise. It is against the law to allow a dog to foul a public space (or a neighbour's garden). Dog owners who let their dogs roam free in their own gardens will have to make sure that they have proper fences. I will not be slow to take advantage of this new law. If I see a dog which I consider to be out of control, and I am worried that it might injure me, I will report the owner. It will be a delight to see some of our arrogant and malignant neighbours locked up for six months.

13

The police in Northern Ireland have so little to do these days that they have apparently taken to patrolling the beaches in search of things to do. A reader has just sent me a newspaper photograph of two armed and uniformed policeman standing on a deserted beach waiting for a naked man to come out of the water. A police spokesman warns skinny dippers that they could end up with a criminal record and be placed on the sex offender register. The policemen not looking for naked bathers are busy arresting bottles of beer. The police in Holywood, Northern Ireland announced recently that they had seized 'approximately 1,000 bottles or cans of alcohol' in a single day. They didn't say what they'd done with it all but I'm prepared to make a guess.

14

Our friendliest neighbour, who is a lingerie designer (famous, apparently within the industry for the Asset Booster Cup), has a diploma in fashion history and probably knows as much about 19th century German lingerie as anyone in the entire South Gloucestershire area, saw me spraying our black rubbish bags with my toxic deodorant from Poundland. (Having looked at the can I am not entirely sure whether it is supposed to be a deodorant or an aftershave spray. Indeed, having used it I'm not entirely sure that it wasn't intended to be used as a fly spray. Or, perhaps, an oven cleaner. The odour still reminds me of the sort of smell that emanates from French public lavatories: all second-hand garlic and Gauloise.) He stopped and asked me what I was doing. I was tempted to tell him that the bags were going to a dance and that I was trying to improve their chances of picking up a couple of nice recycling trays but the folk who live in our village are not, generally speaking, well-endowed with humour so instead, in a moment of imaginative genius, I told him the truth.

'That's a brilliant idea,' he said, thoughtfully. 'I wish I could use that idea somehow.'

'Well, you can,' I told him. 'It's not copyright. Just buy some noxious aftershave and spray it on your bags.'

'It's a really good idea,' said the neighbour rubbing his chin. He looked terribly disappointed. 'Unfortunately we have room for bins at our house so we put our black bags inside the bins and we don't have any trouble with badgers or foxes.'

'Oh that's a pity,' I said, sympathetically.

'But it's a really good idea,' said the neighbour. 'I wish I could think of a way to use it.' He wandered off thoughtfully. He looked terribly disappointed.

15

An American laboratory has invented a wearable patch which can administer a drug and monitor variables in the patient's blood to see if the dosage is having the required effect. If the drug isn't working properly, or side effects are developing, the dosage can be adjusted automatically. There is talk, too, of fitting a cell-phone chip to the patch so that results can be sent automatically to the patient's doctor. Now this, surely, is what technology is for!

16

We assume, these days, that people are mentally ill when their thoughts or behaviour do not fit the patterns exhibited by those we know, or when they deviate from the thoughts and behavioural patterns widely regarded as acceptable. Anyone regarded as 'different' must receive treatment. This is a dangerous concept because it means that the exceptional individuals in our society are now being diagnosed as 'ill' and given medication which may seriously damage them and destroy their ability to create. The fact is that all great people are (almost by definition) sensitive and neurotic and (sometimes) paranoid too (in that sensitivity and fears lead to paranoia); they are like orchids in that they need warmth and lots of attention.

But doctors have a nasty habit of labelling such patients as 'officially' neurotic.

And no medical label sticks more firmly than 'neurotic'. Few labels do more damage. Get yourself labelled 'neurotic' and no one will ever take you seriously again. Nor will they treat you with respect. The best you can hope for is a brand of patronising sympathy, designed to make you feel about six inches tall. Most neurotics respond to this by adding extra shame and guilt to the burdens they are already carrying. The neurotic is the 21st century leper, constantly encouraged to feel 'unclean' or even incomplete.

The neurotic suffers twice. First there are the pains inherent in the neurosis and then, on top of those, there are the pains produced by the very real sense of self-doubt and self-criticism the neuroticism has inspired. The neurotic staggers from one crisis to another, perpetually hiding in the shadows of despair.

None of this is fair or reasonable.

Far from being a label to inspire contempt the word 'neurotic' should inspire love, affection, respect and admiration. For although our society does not trust neurotics, they are the very people who make up the heart and soul of the human community. It is true that neurotics are ridden with guilt and anxiety but they also tend to be exceptionally kind, gentle, thoughtful and courteous. Shyness is, in our society regarded as a fault and an illness (there is, you will not be surprised to hear, a special pill for it). But the unusually shy are often particularly aware of the needs of others. They try harder and often turn out to be exceptionally caring individuals. Neurotics are often obsessional too. Again, this is now an illness and there are drugs for it. But unless it reaches exceptional heights, obsessional behaviour doesn't usually do that much harm. And, on the contrary, the obsessional neurotic will pay great attention to detail and will be observant and watchful. Those are virtues not faults. What else? Well, neurotics are often described as being too imaginative. Imaginations may cause anxieties and tears but imagination means creativity and the production of music and literature and great art and architecture. The people we describe as neurotic are often the individuals whose creative genius we admire. Every great thinker, artist, writer was almost certainly also a neurotic. Without them the world would be a far less pleasant place.

It is, perhaps, about time we treated neurotics with affection and gratitude and understanding. Then, maybe, they would suffer just once and not twice for being neurotic.

It is not difficult to argue that neurotics are more evolved than anyone else. We gain enormously from the agony, the pain and the intense vulnerability endured by neurotics and yet, egged on by the professionals, we repay them with disdain, contempt and suspicion; we regard them as misfits.

How long do you think Mozart (the archetypal misfit if ever there was one) would survive in our society? He would be destroyed by the media and drugged into submission by the doctors.

It is worth remembering that at the other end of the spectrum to neuroticism lies psychopathy. And the odd thing is that we don't tend to regard psychopaths as needing treatment in our society. On the contrary, the psychopaths (the selfish, the uncaring, the insensitive) become the leaders in our world. In politics, industry and the professions it is the psychopaths who rise to the top. It is hardly surprising that the professions have all failed us.

Teachers control education, doctors control medicine and lawyers control the law and you would have to have your head stuck well into the sand not to agree that the leaders representing all these three professions have betrayed the public. Politicians simply dare not oppose them and, from their point of view, it's easy to see why not. There are nearly a million teachers and teaching assistants in the UK. Add in their families and that's a lot of votes. So education policies are determined by the teaching unions.

As an aside this means, of course, that it is the teachers' leaders who should take the blame for the high levels of illiteracy and innumeracy in the country. The latter is now so bad that I fear that anaesthetists are going to have huge problems with the present and future generations when they need putting to sleep. At the moment anaesthetists usually tell patients to count up to ten but most teenagers would hit a brick wall when they got to six or seven. 'Er... what comes after six?' Innumeracy is already a huge problem in shops. I am always being given the wrong change. Just the other day, in Cirencester, I was given £10 too much change. The two items I'd bought added up to £51 but the assistant had added them up in his head and come up with £41. I handed him back the £10. He looked at me as if I were bonkers (I may well be but for the purpose of this anecdote that is neither here nor there). 'You've given me £10 too much,' I insisted. With a great sigh he pulled out a calculator and added up the cost of the two items. He then turned the calculator round so that I could see my mistake. Sadly for him it showed that I was right and he was wrong. He took the £10, went very red and murmured a modest 'thank you'. If I had £10 for every time this has happened I would, well, have a lot of £10s.

Of course, we have to remember that neurotics and original thinkers have always been despised and oppressed in fascist countries.

The Nazis didn't think much of neurotics. And today the EU, the new proponent of raw, unfeeling fascism, doesn't have much time for the neurotic or the original thinker either.

17

It has been reported that British women do not exercise because they are worried that their breasts will bounce up and down if they do. And so they stay at home and watch television. The curious thing is that no other women, anywhere in the world, use the 'bouncing bosoms' excuse as a reason for not exercising. Maybe British women are better endowed. Or maybe they are more self-conscious. I'm sure that as I write a team of scientists will be negotiating a grant to conduct a thorough investigation and find the answer.

18

'When I was in my 20s,' said our friend D.J., 'I drank five or six pints of beer every evening, I smoked 40 cheap fags a day and I ate nothing except curries, chips and pies.' He looked thoughtful for a moment; remembering these halcyon days. 'I never had any health problems at all: no indigestion, no chest troubles, nothing. I was as fit as a fiddle.' He pointed an accusing finger at me, as though holding me responsible for what had happened to him. 'And now look at me!' he said. 'I live on salads and health foods. I eat yoghurt and cottage cheese and thin slices of wholemeal bread. And I suffer from indigestion and wind and I get out of breath if I cross the road.' He glowered at me. 'I haven't had a chip for a year,' he complained. 'I think you doctors are all talking rubbish. I should go back to the beer, the fags and the curry. I was healthy on that diet.'

19

In Cirencester I met a fellow who used to be a Punch and Judy man. He was playing the violin and had a hat on the ground beside him. He wasn't a very good violinist but he played with great gusto. I've stopped giving money to beggars, particularly young, healthy looking ones, but I happily give money to buskers. Unless they are really, really bad they make life better for us all. I put some money into his hat and, since I was going for a coffee, I asked him if he wanted a drink and something to eat. We walked to a nearby café and as he ate he told me and his wife had for thirty seven years toured English seaside towns with Punch, Judy, the policeman, the dog and a string of sausages. He had been the 'professor' and his wife had worked as the 'bottler', calling in the audience, introducing the act and collecting the money afterwards. They lived in a camper van and towed the Punch and Judy tent and paraphernalia in an elderly trailer with a canvas cover. 'We didn't get rich,' said the man. 'But it wasn't a bad life. We made a lot of kids happy and had some adventures.'

He told me that they now lived in a small, rented flat within walking distance of the town centre. I'd expected him to tell me that they had to retire because of opposition from the politically correct gestapo, the self-appointed forces of law and order who disapprove of old-fashioned entertainments such as Punch and Judy because they don't like people having fun. (I have heard them say that they disapprove of Punch and Judy because it glorifies wife beating violence. This only goes to show how little they know. In most Punch and Judy scenarios the wife gives just as much as she gets. Judy can look after herself. It is largely the policeman who gets the worst end of the stick.) But, to my surprise, it wasn't this that finished them, but the fact that they simply couldn't make ends meet. 'Councils started to demand huge fees to let us operate on the beach,' the professor told me. 'And the audience would pay us in pennies. My wife would go round with the box and when we emptied it after a show we'd have earned a pound in copper, with a few five pence coins from the more generous patrons.'

I said I was sad to hear this and he added that he earned more busking than he'd earned from the Punch and Judy show. I asked him what had happened to the puppets and the tent they'd worked in. He told me that they'd sold the whole lot for £500 to a young couple who intended to hire themselves out for children's birthday parties. He said he'd heard that they were doing very well. He told me that they set up on someone's lawn, or even in the living room if it was raining, and got paid £100 for an hour's work. 'They do two or three shows most Saturdays and a few during the week and make a decent living at it.'

I bought him a large piece of fruit pie and another coffee and bought myself a second cup of coffee. 'It's the councils who are killing off all the things people associate with the seaside,' he told me sadly. 'They charge so much for the donkey concession and the deckchair concession that no one can make any money. The council staff who do the negotiating seem to assume that the council is entitled to all the takings – leaving no wages for the people doing the actual work.'

I gave him £10 so that he could buy his wife a bunch of flowers from one of the market stalls. He told me that he'd wait until the end of the day because the flower seller always sold off flowers at half price when he was packing up ready to go home.

20

Another local village held its fete a couple of days ago and one of the contests was a scything competition. A local farmer, with a field next to the church in the grounds of which the fete was being held, had roughly marked out areas of a field where grass needed to be cut. Each contestant paid £1 for the right to rent a scythe for half an hour. The winner, the contestant who cut the most grass, received a bottle of Tesco's own brand champagne. This very much reminded me of Mark Twain, whose hero Tom Sawyer allowed his chums to pay (in such currency as unfinished apple cores) to paint the fence he was supposed to be painting. Sawyer sat in the sunshine and watched and supervised after cleverly 'allowing' the other boys to pay for the privilege of painting a stretch of fence.

If we had a better crop of apples this year I would be tempted to organise something similar for our orchard this coming autumn. Sadly, however, the un-pollinated blossom failed to turn into apples and we will be lucky to have enough fruit to make a pie and to keep the birds, badgers and squirrels happy. The one bright spot is that a particularly productive bramble has grown up into one of our trees and now we have apples and blackberries growing on the same branch. 'We just need a custard bush nearby,' said Antoinette, dreaming of apple and blackberry pie.

Sam, the clever and unusually well-read farmer with the well scythed field is exceptional in almost every way. He is friendly and sensible and although his family seems to own a large portion of the county he is remarkably down to earth.

Sam, who is a widower, is 72-years-old and technically he is properly known as young Sam. He lives with his father who is 95 and known as old Sam. His own son, who is 50, is known as the younger Sam. (There is another son, not as old as the younger Sam, who lives and works in London and who is known as Gerald because his name isn't Sam.)

Young Sam's father, old Sam, buys young Sam a train set every Christmas (and has done so for 66 years). Old Sam's own father, also called Sam, died at the age of 102 and when that happened it made life easier for everyone. Before that there were four generations of Sams and the youngest of them was known as the boy Sam. When one of the Sams dies the others all move up the pecking order. So, when old Sam finally moves on to better things, young Sam will become old Sam and younger Sam will become young Sam. It took me months to sort all this out in my mind and I feel quite proud of myself for having done so.

The only other person I've ever known who was called Sam was a teacher of mine when I was 13 or 14. His name was Sam Treadwell and he was paid to teach us Latin but we found the subject tedious and none of us ever paid much attention to him. He had a foul temper and used to keep one of those wooden blackboard rubbers in his hand at all times. If anyone annoyed him he would hurl the rubber at them. He did this as if he were throwing a baseball and had, over the years, become quite accurate. At the end of one of his lessons, we smeared tomato ketchup on the wall at the back of the classroom and hid one of the boys in the stationery cupboard. When the next master came into the classroom to teach us English he noticed the red smear on the wall and demanded to know what had happened. 'Mr Treadwell threw the blackboard rubber at Soames and killed him,' said a boy called Stourbridge, who in due course became a captain of industry. 'He made us bury him in the playing fields.' The English master went very red and ran from the room in a panic. He returned five minutes later with the headmaster in tow. By then, of course, all signs of the red smear had been removed and we all denied any knowledge of the story Stourbridge had told.

21

'I've had five wives,' said an old man I met in a pub. He looked to be at least eighty-years-old. 'And they've all been infertile. Not one could give me a child.' He grinned at me, strangely proud of this apparent perversity of nature. 'What do you think the chances are of that happening, doctor?'

I smiled, nodded and said nothing.

22

Every day I fill up at least half a dozen bird feeders and two squirrel feeders. (To help them through the summer months, we give the squirrels hazelnuts, which we put into two specially made wooden boxes. The squirrels have to lift the lids to retrieve the nuts – some of which are shelled and some of which are still in their shells.) I always wear plastic gloves when handling the feeders and I have just discovered a new supplier. A company in China will post me 100 plastic gloves for £1. More and more of the stuff sold on Amazon now comes direct from China. I don't know what Chinese postage rates are like but my guess is that they are considerably lower than Royal Mail charges. The irony is that the Chinese company just dumps all its packets on a plane which carries them to England. Royal Mail, which receives nothing for its efforts, then has to do all the hard work. I am afraid I have absolutely no sympathy for Royal Mail which I believe to be an incompetent company run by buffoons.

The gloves which arrived today are huge. Most of the people who had reviewed the product on Amazon complained bitterly about this fact but since they were women and presumably had small hands I regarded their criticisms as encouraging rather than discouraging. (Generally speaking, I take absolutely no notice of reviews on the internet. We know of an excellent hotel whose owners have been destroyed by cruel and wildly inaccurate internet reviews which, they suspect, were written by local competitors.)

The gloves are so huge that each one would probably make a sleeping bag for a family of five Orientals. The ordinary Chinese worker must be puzzled when they contemplate the clothing they make for sale to Westerners. Shoes are constructed the size of canoes, panties are built to fit unbelievably rotund bottoms and bras are made for breasts so big that to the Chinese they must seem as though they deserve their own post codes.

23

A chap with whom I studied, and who is now a hospital consultant, told me today that he, and a number of his colleagues, are genuinely worried about their job security. Apparently, quite a few NHS hospitals are sacking older consultants and replacing them with younger, cheaper models. My friend tells me that he knows several consultants who are so concerned and angry about this that they are reluctant to train junior doctors and are concentrating on building up their private practices. I find this genuinely alarming. Young doctors have always acquired much of their learning, and most of their practical skills, from the older doctors with whom they work.

There are, of course, many precedents for older doctors keeping their skills secret. The Chamberlen family, who were the first doctors to use forceps to deliver babies, kept their secret for two centuries. It was Peter Chamberlen who invented the obstetric forceps, a device which revolutionised the way a doctor could help a pregnant woman with a difficult delivery, and he and his descendants refused to share details of how the forceps were made and how they worked. I find it sad and rather alarming that today's doctors are now apparently keeping their skills and knowledge to themselves in order to protect their wealth and status.

24

A fellow I know who is a vet told me two odd stories today. They both concern dogs and both revolve around simple misunderstandings. The vet swears that they are both true stories. The first concerned a man who took his Labrador to the surgery. The vet picked the dog up to carry him into the examination room but almost immediately said: 'I will have to put him down'.

'Why?' demanded the panicking owner. 'What's wrong with him? Why do you have to put him down? Can't you save him?'

The vet quickly explained that as far as he knew there was nothing seriously wrong with the dog. 'I had to put him down because he's heavy,' he explained.

The second story is just as silly but much sadder.

A man took his dog in to see the vet and complained that the animal had been barking all night. 'Can you put him to sleep, please?' asked the man. 'I'm exhausted.' He then went home to try to get some sleep.

The vet wasn't happy about the man's request but being old-fashioned, and believing that the customer is always right, he put the dog to sleep. He was, therefore, shocked when the man returned a few hours later and asked to have his dog back.

25

I see that the police have been told by the Government that in future they must be polite to members of the public. Indeed, policemen (and policewomen) who are not polite will risk being fired.

What a sad state of affairs it is when public employees have to be told that they must be polite to their employers.

26

The honours system in the United Kingdom is truly incomprehensible and indefensible. Knighthoods and peerages are handed out to some of the most undeserving rogues in the country. Most of the people who are given these gongs have done nothing more than they would have done anyway – they certainly didn't do anything special or dedicate their lives in the service of others. People don't become millionaires or film stars so that they can be remembered in the honours list – they become millionaires or film stars because that's what they want for themselves.

Many of the corporate bastards who are 'honoured' in this way have done nothing more honourable than give a chunk of their shareholders' money to a political party or a politician's slush fund.

In practice, nothing has changed since the days when a country nonentity, a poor local squire with a modest home and pride for sale, would receive a peerage and 20,000 acres for allowing his wife or daughter to be shtupped by the King. If the wife or daughter were particularly luscious, and the shtupping especially enjoyable and memorable, the squire might be made a Duke. Nell Gwyn famously threatened to drop her baby out of an upstairs window unless the father, Charles II, made the baby a duke. The baby was duly made Duke of St Albans.

The tragedy is that the people who really deserve to be honoured, the people who have worked for their community without reward, or given their lives for people or animals, are invariably ignored.

But recently I did hear a lovely story today about one such individual. Cyril had spent his life in the village where he was born and he had worked tirelessly to protect the village and the area around it. He had single-handedly emptied the village pond of sludge, supermarket trolleys and bedsteads. He had restored the war memorial. And he had given a portion of his garden to be used as a children's playground. He had even paid for the installation of swings and a roundabout. I doubt if anyone in the country has ever done more for their community than Cyril has done. People had tried repeatedly to have his name put on the honours list. But all attempts had failed.

Three month ago Cyril, who was already blind with macular degenerative disease, was diagnosed with a pancreatic cancer. He was told that he had only a few months to live. It looked as though he would die without the honour and recognition everyone thought he deserved. And then a local celebrity, a rock group member who had been given an M.B.E. some years earlier, for some undefined services and for reasons which even he didn't quite understand, heard about Cyril and decided that he would do something about it. He paid for a fake letter and envelope to be printed (ostensibly from the Palace) and he arranged for the local postman to deliver it to Cyril's home.

And since Cyril was too ill to go to London to collect his 'fake' M.B.E. he helped arrange for a presentation party, which included the Parish Council chairman and the vicar, to present him with the medal. Cyril was plainly delighted. He was overcome with pride and cried real tears of joy. Two days later he died a happy man.

After his death, but before the funeral, one of Cyril's neighbours took the medal round to the rock star's home. She said she thought he would want it back since Cyril no longer had any need of it. But the rock star thanked her and said to her that the medal was now Cyril's and would remain Cyril's for ever. He told her that the medal was to be pinned onto the lapel of Cyril's suit and buried with him. And so it was done. And justice was duly served.

27

I read today of a bra designer who resigned from her position at the company where she works. 'I wanted more than just a supporting role,' she is quoted as having said.

28

A reader of mine wrote to tell me a strange but true story. Purely to get out of the rain one day a few months ago, while on a walk near his home, he joined a party of people he didn't know and wandered into a chapel of rest. He stayed for the funeral, sang a couple of hymns and listened to a few kind words spoken about the deceased. When leaving he signed his name and address in the book of condolences simply because it would have looked rather odd if he hadn't done so. He then forgot all about the incident until he received a letter from a firm of solicitors handling the deceased's estate. The person who had died had apparently left a will instructing his solicitor to share out his estate among all those who had attended his funeral. And so my reader found himself £17,857 better off.

'It was,' he wrote, 'the most profitable hour I ever spent in my life.'

He is now planning to share the money among half a dozen charities.

29

We went to Gloucester, though I can't remember why. It's a strange city. We always get lost there, even with our wonderful new satellite navigation device, and we got lost when we're out of the car too. We even have difficulty finding where we've parked the damned thing.

Gloucester does, however, have a good supply of unusual shops. Apparently, it has always been the same. Back in 1936, the poshest store in town was called Bon Marche and you could buy everything there – you could even walk out with an aeroplane. The shop sold odd little planes called 'Flying Fleas' which were designed by a Frenchman who claimed that his machine had a range of 200 miles and could land in a field or a garden anywhere. It sounded wonderful but unfortunately there was a snag and the darned thing had a tendency to crash. This didn't stop people buying it, of course, for there were no online reviewers in those days. Eventually early health and safety busy bodies had it banned.

It had rained all morning and the streets of Gloucester were awash. This reminded Antoinette of the old rhyme: 'Doctor Foster went to Gloucester in a shower of rain. He stepped in a puddle, right up to his middle and never went there again.' I read somewhere that the Dr Foster in the tale was actually King Edward I who, in 1278, was visiting the city to set up some sort of new taxation system. It was so wet and muddy in the city centre that the king's horse got stuck. The locals had a great time laughing at the hapless monarch but Edward was peeved and sensibly vowed never to visit Gloucester again.

Mind you, if he didn't have a satellite navigation system it probably took him weeks to get out of the darned place.

On our way back from Gloucester we stopped to watch a village cricket match. I'm not sure whereabouts it was, but it was definitely somewhere in Gloucestershire. It was dusk and the light was poor but village cricketers will always play on in the darkness. I once watched a match which was illuminated by the headlights of two dozen cars parked around the boundary's edge. As the match continued the lights dimmed as batteries died and I couldn't help wondering who was going to take the owners home. I also once sat and watched a village cricket match in a thunderstorm. I stayed in the car with the windscreen wipers going full blast. The players, drenched to the skin, refused to leave the field though I suspect they could hardly see where they were or what they were doing. The ball must have been almost impossible to hold.

Today, we sat on the grass, a few yards away from the pavilion, and enjoyed some wonderfully entertaining sport. These were clearly men who played the game for fun rather than in the hope that they might attract the attention of the England selectors. The wicket keeper of the fielding side was the oldest man I've ever seen take to the field in any sort of cricket. He was very small and had two short legs. His legs were so short that he had to walk very quickly in order to get where he wanted to be and I suspect that if he wanted to cross a room he would have to set off five or six minutes before he wanted to be where he wanted to be. He seemed slightly blind and very deaf. The captain of his side had such little faith in his abilities behind the stumps that he stationed a permanent long stop behind him, close to the boundary. The wicket keeper, I was told, suffered from arthritis, angina, diabetes and such a terrible case of athlete's foot that he was not allowed to use the dressing room showers.

When the captain of the batting side declared, one of the batsmen who had been called in was furious.

'You might have let me go on,' he shouted. 'I could have got my first hundred!'

'You'd only scored 24!' the captain pointed out.

'But I was batting so well,' complained the unhappy player, with feeling.

He meant it too.

30

We were in the household department of a store in Cirencester. 'I'd like a couple of those big jugs!' said a woman to a friend, pointing to a selection of oversized milk containers which were displayed on a shelf. Just then another woman, previously unseen, came out from behind the display racks. She was blushing bright red and trying to cover her enormous bosom with her handbag. It was clear that she had a cleavage so deep that anyone who had the temerity to yodel into it would have to wait four or five seconds before the echo came out.

31

An American friend (a genial fellow who is a master of the single entendre and who mixes metaphors like barman mix cocktails) told us that he, like most of his fellow countrymen, receives only ten days of paid leave a year. He was reporting, rather than complaining, and his comment was inspired by surprise at the amount of holidays normally taken in Britain. Moreover, he told us that nearly half of all Americans don't take all the holiday to which they are entitled. I checked on this and he's absolutely right. Astonishingly, nearly half of all Americans take only two of the ten days holiday to which they are entitled. Friends of other nationalities have told us similar things. No other country in the world gives employees as much holiday as the UK does. It is no wonder that productivity is so low that we are in a never ending decline.

Even when they are at work a frighteningly high proportion of the workforce spend their days twittering, reading their emails, posing for selfies and messing around with their Facebook pages. Amazingly, the average Briton now sends around 12,000 private texts and emails every year. This is the TTF generation (Twitter, tattoo and Facebook). Today's generation can't take a photograph of a monument, a wild animal or a sunset without putting themselves into the picture.

September

1

Antoinette and I both love the nearby village of Bourton-on-the-Water.

Cotswold villages do have the most wonderful names and many (Stow-on-the-Wold, Upper and Lower Slaughter and the three Sodburys – Chipping Sodbury, Old Sodbury and Little Sodbury – to name but a sample) sound as if they were invented by P. G. Wodehouse in a particularly fanciful moment. There really ought to be a village called Loose Chippings.

Bourton-on-the-Water, however, was named by someone with no time for flights of fancy. The village has the river Windrush running through the centre of it and that's the end of it. Apart from the river, which features on most picture postcards and all tourist photographs and is the site of what is, I believe, the world's only annual football match played in water, Bourton has two wonderful tourist attractions: the model village and Birdland. The former is a magnificent creation which is a great place to take friends and visitors coming to the Cotswolds for the first time. The model village, which is quite rightly Grade II listed, is a one ninth scale replica of the centre of Bourton-on-the-Water and all the tiny houses, shops and churches are built in local Cotswold stone. The river is there, complete with miniature bridges, and there are flowers and trees in the gardens. Stand close to the churches and you can hear the choirs singing. And there is even a model of the model village itself.

It is, however, Birdland which drags us back to Bourton time and time again. There are herons nesting on the river and there is sometimes a stork standing guard by the gate. Inside there are many wonderful birds to see – including my personal favourite, the wonderfully named White-Bellied-Go-Away-Bird. There are crowned cranes, elegant waders, owls and, of course, a plentiful supply of penguins. And behind the main part of Birdland there is the magnificently wild Marshmouth Nature Reserve.

Every time we visit Bourton-on-the-Water we think seriously about buying a cottage there but after a walk through the village, and a quiet cup of tea in one of the many splendid cafés, we always abandon the idea. Even out of season the village is full of tourists and, inevitably and quite naturally, the local tradesfolk cater almost exclusively for them. As a result the majority of shops now sell souvenirs and little else and if your shopping ambitions stop at toy models of London buses, solar operated models of a waving Queen and holographic posters of friendly polar bears you will be well pleased. Similarly, if you are looking for a card, pen or mug to give to a much loved teacher or hugely adored teaching assistant you will have no difficulty in finding an ample selection from which to choose. But locals wanting a decent selection of shoes, socks or a good book to read probably have to travel some distance to find what they need.

A generation or two ago Cotswold villages used to be pretty well self-sufficient. And no Cotswold village would dare show its face unless it had at least one decent second-hand bookshop. These days too many local shops cater mainly for the Japanese tourists who arrive by the coachload to take photographs and, of course, to buy those model London buses and delightful, solar operated models of the Queen forever waving, which were probably manufactured no more than a few miles away from their homes. Sadly, the second-hand bookshops have pretty well all gone; sacrificed on the altar which is the internet. I don't blame the shopkeepers at all. They have to make a living. But I suspect they're sad too.

The residents of Bourton-on-the-Water are renowned throughout the Cotswolds for believing that putting a live pigeon underneath the bed of someone who is dying will keep them alive. I suspect that this belief may now be a thing of the past but who can tell.

2

My distrust of the NHS grows ever stronger. The thousands of bureaucrats who control the nation's health care provider seem to me to specialise in two things: lies and waste. I have long believed that the NHS is run by and for the drug industry. Doctors' postgraduate education is designed, managed and administered by drug companies and drug company serfs. Orders which come down from the Department of Health, the British Medical Association and the General Medical Council are effectively designed to expand the profits of the drug companies. Vast amounts of money are spent on providing drugs which do more harm than good (but which are enormously profitable) and when costs need to be cut the patients who are targeted are the ones who have little power – such as the elderly and the mentally ill.

Vast amounts of taxpayers' money is spent on providing cosmetic surgery, fertility treatment and other optional extras but there is never enough cash to pay for care for cancer patients or to provide vital services for pensioners or those with serious mental disorders. Vast amounts of money are spent on ineffective (and potentially hazardous) screening programmes and on treating non-existent diseases. Today, I read that even more money is now going to be spent on ADHD which seems to affect at least 100% of all the nation's children. The truth, unpopular though it might be, is that ADHD is an imaginary disease, devised by drug companies to find a commercial use for large quantities of otherwise toxic defoliant. It is not a medical disorder; it is a disorder of disappointment resulting from the thwarted ambitions of parents who feel more comfortable if their child's failure to read or write, or to behave like a small, civilised human being, can be blamed on a disease rather than poor parenting or poor teaching. Like so many other disorders it was invented by psychiatrists working for drug companies searching for 'diseases' to cure with otherwise useless drugs. (If you think I'm exaggerating, just check out how new diseases are 'invented'. The American Psychiatric Association simply publishes new diseases in its *Diagnostic and Statistical Manual of Mental Disorders*. Every year the list of diseases gets longer and in the words of a former chairman of the task force which puts the Manual together: 'pretty soon all of us may be labelled mad'.)

Gordon Brown (the star of my book *Gordon is a Moron*) has argued that Britain's greatest historical achievement is the NHS. I believe he says this partly because he has never worked in it and partly because when he uses it he does so with the protected status that helps him avoid nine hour queues in casualty, six month waits for an appointment with a hospital consultant and waits of a month or more for blood test results.

3

There is, it seems, much talk in the USA about the lack of free speech in the West. The unstinting efforts of the Homeland Security bullies to stamp on anyone daring to open his mouth and question

America's absurdly misdirected security operations mean that very few journalists, politicians or ordinary citizens are prepared to stand up and make themselves heard when the latest piece of nonsense is unveiled. The truth, of course, is that free speech in America has always been in rather short supply. We should, perhaps, all remember that the Sedition Act of 1918 made it a crime to say anything critical about the war effort of President Wilson's administration.

The only difference today is that 'security' is now regarded as a catchall excuse for any totalitarian, oppressive action the State, or any State employee, may choose to take. It's the same in the UK, of course. If the rubbish isn't collected on time it's for security reasons. If a train doesn't run or a road is closed it is for 'security' reasons. If all the rubbish bins disappear from London's streets (with the result that the pavements and gutters are strewn with discarded wrappers, newspapers and drinks containers) it is for 'security' reasons. If travellers must be strip searched, fondled and humiliated it is for 'security' reasons.

4

Curiously, it seems that we all have many rights we didn't know we had. I'm accustomed to being told that we all have the right to free education, free water, free legal representation, free books and so on but I was surprised to see a political advertisement today telling me that we all have the right to play.

Oddly enough, no one ever talks about our having a right to free food.

5

Our groceries were delivered by a new driver today. He moaned at some length about the fact that we live at the bottom of a steep and narrow lane. Worried that he might return to the store, complain to the manager and have us expelled from the Waitrose delivery list, I told him that the store's other drivers, including several young women, had no difficulty whatsoever in driving up and down the lane. The moaning driver was taken aback at this and seemed extremely upset that he should find it difficult to do something that young women had found easy and had managed without a murmur of protest.

'Well, if they can do it, I can do it without any problems!' he stated rather indignantly.

I don't think he will be complaining to the manager and so I suspect our deliveries will be safe for a while yet.

6

I was riding my bicycle along our lane when a woman who lives nearby imperiously called me in to help her gardener pull out a tree stump. It took us half an hour and by the time we'd finished I was exhausted and unpleasantly hot and sticky.

'Do you do much in the garden yourself?' I asked her.

'I do the pointing,' she said.

I was impressed and looked around, expecting to see some neat mortar work. 'Which walls have you done?' I asked.

'Oh not that sort of pointing,' she replied, haughtily. 'I point like Beverley Nichols.' She extended an arm and a finger and pointed imperiously. 'Plant that here and put that there.'

The miserable old bat may well be good at pointing but she didn't thank me for my efforts. And nor did she offer me a drink.

7

We're still working our way through the sale of a property we no longer need. It still amazes me, after all these years, that it takes so long to complete a property purchase or sale. The procedure really doesn't have to take as long as it does. When I bought Publishing House (the office building where I ran my publishing business for two and a half decades) I completed the purchase in a single day. I saw the building in the morning and by close of play I owned it.

These days most solicitors and estate agents would have a fit if you asked them to move that quickly. But, in reality, there is really no reason that buying property should take so long. The truth, of course, is that solicitors, estate agents, surveyors, the local council and the mortgage brokers all want to drag out the whole sorry exercise so that they can justify their absurdly inflated fees. How can an estate agent justify his 2% fee if a property sale is completed in a week? How can the local council justify the vast fee they charge for a 'search' if it doesn't take them 16 weeks to press a button and send an email? How can a surveyor justify his massive fee if he doesn't spend hours reporting on the weather, the outlook and the quality of the decorations?

And so it takes weeks of painful stress to complete a sale or a purchase.

(Why, incidentally, are the websites run by estate agents so ineptly put together? Why are there so rarely any decent key word search engines? If an estate agent allowed folk to put in seven key words, and provided the requisite software, potential buyers would be able to find the house of their dreams very speedily and efficiently. If we must have the internet in our lives let's at least make it do what it can do best.)

8

I discovered today that up until recently it was illegal for French employers to prevent their staff from drinking wine while at work. Anyone with a job was entitled to have a bottle of red close at hand, just in case he or she felt their blood alcohol level drifting down towards sober. Spoil sports have now got rid of this law and, I have no doubt, replaced it with a dozen far more boring ones.

9

An American government study has found that a significant number of people who have undergone treatment for cancer during the last few decades may not have actually had the disease at all. The report, commissioned by the U.S. National Cancer Institute, and published in the Journal of the American Medical Association, says that many patients were just plain old-fashioned misdiagnosed. It is estimated that millions have been falsely treated for cancer and have been killed with chemotherapy, surgery and radiation. Many women have been treated for breast cancer when they didn't have anything seriously wrong with them. And many men have been treated for prostate cancer when, in fact, they had a condition that would not have killed them. The bottom line is that millions of people have been killed not by cancer but by treatment they never needed.

I have written about this problem in a number of my medical books (most recently in *Do Doctors and Nurses Kill More People than Cancer?*) but, sadly, an embarrassed and infuriated medical profession has suppressed my arguments. I very much doubt if the profession will take any more notice of the U.S. National Cancer

Institute than they have of me. And so doctors will continue to be one of the three big killers – up there alongside circulatory disease (heart attacks and strokes) and cancer.

The cancer industry, led by hugely rich charities, is a deadly disgrace. The bottom line is that half of all Britons will be treated for cancer during their lifetimes but half of those treated for cancer won't actually have it at all.

Over the last century or so it has become increasingly clear that the key to defeating cancer lies in understanding the human body's immune system, but when, just 20 years ago or so, I founded a website devoted to explaining the intricacies of the immune system, the site was immediately attacked by the cancer industry.

10

'Revenons à nos moutons!' said the Frenchman.

We had been discussing the planned painting of the hallway in our apartment building and had strayed a little and ended up talking about the city's decision to turn off street lamps during the night.

Puzzled, I stared at him. Let us get back to our sheep? What the hell was he talking about. Together we worked it out in the end.

'Revenons à nos moutons' is the way the French say: 'Let us get back to the point'.

It's funny how different languages have different ways to create idioms.

We talked of one or two others. 'Il ne faut pas réveiller le chat qui dort' (literally 'Don't wake the cat who sleeps') is the equivalent of our 'Let sleeping dogs lie'. 'Il croque la vie a pleines dents' (literally he munches life with full teeth) is the equivalent of 'He lives life to the fullest'. The phrase 'avoir du monde au balcon' literally means 'to have people at the balcony' but the practical translation is 'to have big breasts'.

Foreigners are all odd, of course, but surely the French are the oddest of all.

'Revenons à a nos moutons!' said the Frenchman again. I looked at him and smiled. We resumed our discussion about the painting of the hallway.

11

Madame Rolande, a woman living in our apartment building in Paris, is in her fifties and works at the Mayor's Office as an important administrator. She has six Christian names. Her full name is: Domenica Irma Nathalie Philippine Clarisse Aurelie Rolande. All these names appear in full on her mail box. She explained to us that her father had five sisters and one brother (called Philippe, of course) and that he had hoped that if she was named after them all, a few might remember her in their wills.

'And did they?' asked Antoinette.

Madame Rolande smiled and shook her head. 'They are all still alive and in good health,' she replied. 'They show no signs of leaving the world.' She shrugged. 'I do not like any of them but I have spent a fortune buying them presents at Christmas and for their birthdays.'

'But there is one thing you have must have already inherited,' said Antoinette.

Madame Rolande looked puzzled.

'Good genes!' explained Antoinette. 'If they have all lived long lives then you too will probably live a long time.'

Madame Rolande nodded and smiled at us. 'That is possibly true!' she agreed. 'But if they all live until they are in their 90s then I will be in my late 60s when, and if, I inherit anything. It will be a little late to have fun.'

'But a useful pension fund?' I suggested.

She pulled a face and, rather reluctantly, nodded. 'I suppose that is so.' She didn't seem terribly thrilled.

Madame Rolande then also told us about something that had happened in the building since we had last been in Paris.

It appears that a couple who had rented an apartment on the fourth floor had fallen out with just about everyone. They had, in particular, fallen out with their landlord and with the people who lived in the apartment below them. They had exacted their revenge by disconnecting the waste pipe underneath the bath just before they left the building for the last time. The inevitable result was that when the new tenants took their first bath all the water poured into the flat below, drenching the unfortunate residents and their belongings.

'This was too much,' said Madame Rolande. She told us that it is accepted practice for residents to go on holiday and leave their radio or television switched on, with the volume turned up high, if they are upset with their neighbours. 'But this thing with the water was not acceptable,' she said, shaking her head with clear disapproval.

Not for the first time we are pleased that our apartment is on the top floor. If anyone is going to be drenched by dirty bath water it is not going to be us.

12

We sat in a café today doing a little idle people watching. It occurred to me that whereas the English put food onto the backs of their forks, where it is bound to fall off (especially if the food involved happens to be peas) foreigners use their forks like slightly leaky spoons. And Americans, of course, whose left hands are of no use at all when dining, use their forks as a combination knife and spoon. Why do they bother with a knife at all? I'm not criticising. But I am bewildered. Why not simply have a spoon and be done with it? A spoon with a cutting edge would be perfect. I seem to remember that camping shops sell suitable multipurpose cutlery for those hardy folk who like to spend their holidays shivering or sweltering under canvas.

The bottom line is that there are doubtless many other countries which produce better food and better meals than we do. But there is no doubt at all that the English have by far the very best table manners.

13

The Germans are so worried that England might leave the EU (and leave Germany with even bigger bills to pay) that they are now claiming that Winston Churchill would have wanted us to remain members of the new United States of Europe. Apart from being damned cheeky this is, to use a technical term, 'a complete load of bollocks'. It was well known that Churchill loathed the idea of the European Union. In 1962 Field Marshall Montgomery found Sir Winston Churchill sitting up in bed smoking a cigar, shouting for more brandy and protesting against our proposed entry into the Common Market. It would be nice if the EU's supporters would occasionally get their facts straight. But when lying has been so effective I suppose it's difficult to see why you should stop.

14

One of the many things I enjoy about Paris is the fact that I can understand what most people are saying to me in shops and cafes. My French isn't good but theirs is usually excellent and at least we are both speaking the same language. In London, and indeed many towns and cities in England, I frequently find myself talking to people whose command of English lies somewhere between poor and non-existent. And since my command of Polish, Romanian and other East European languages is completely non-existent we simply have no language in common.

As a result of the high levels of immigration it is possible these days to obtain most of the joys of travelling in a foreign country without leaving home. I like foreign countries, and many of the people who live in them, but when I go abroad I never try to impose my culture on them and I always try hard to speak their language. It would be nice if a few more of our imported residents made a small effort to learn a few words of our language.

Critics will, doubtless, accuse me of being a Little Englander but that will probably be because they don't have the foggiest idea what a Little Englander really was. And I cannot see why I should be ashamed of my patriotism.

Talking of which I couldn't help noticing that the Embassy opposite our apartment building has another brand new EU flag flying. There are two flags outside the Embassy. One is the national flag of the country concerned (and it is a rather sad, sorry looking thing in traditional flag material). The other flag, which seems to be replaced at very regular intervals, is the EU flag. It is silk and shiny and always looks very smart.

15

Wandering around the Champs de Mars we spotted a crowd. This was not the sort of ghoulish crowd which gathers at an accident but the sort of curious crowd which gathers around a street entertainer. We wandered closer. The police in Paris are forever moving on most of the traditional street artists (the statues, the jugglers, the clowns, the musicians and the tumblers) so it was good to find one who'd managed to evade the heavy hand of the French P.C. Plods.

But it wasn't a street entertainer (at least, not in the true and proper sense). It was a scam artist practising the oldest street scam in the book: the shell game (in which the mechanic moves a pea around between three shells), also known as the find the lady card trick (in which a Queen card and two other cards are moved around, usually on an upturned cardboard box). I've been fascinated by this scam since I watched men working it in Oxford Street over half a century ago. I was, I think, 14 when I first worked out that the bloke in the crowd who seems to keep winning is a stooge, working as part of the scam.

This, however, was no ordinary scam. Within five minutes I had spotted six stooges – the individuals in the crowd who appear to be ordinary members of the public, merrily winning and losing their money, but who are there merely pour encourager les autres. Most, like the mechanic looked Romanian, but although a couple of them were pretty easy to spot, several were well disguised. One female stooge had dressed herself up in a huge straw hat and a Bolero jacket and she carried an expensive looking handbag. A white male wore a typical outfit for a lager drinking English tourist and carried a small rucksack with him. Every time he won money he high fived everyone he'd been standing near to in the crowd. The stooges weren't difficult to spot: they were too quick to lose money they'd won, they didn't worry enough when they did badly and they didn't look particularly pleased when they won. And the stakes were high. The minimum stake per play was 100 euros, often boosted by rapid doubling of the bet to 200, 400 or 800 euros. The mechanic was using three metal cups and a strange, fluffy looking ball which would be easy to hold inside a cup or to move about.

Every time a stranger won, the six stooges would crowd in; ostensibly to check out the result of the game but in reality to intimidate, to confuse and to give the mechanic time to disguise the position of the ball if it should be necessary. Most of the losers were young tourists, clearly gambling with money they could ill afford to lose but pulled along by the prospect of making easy money. The majority were female.

By my reckoning the mechanic had won around 1500 euros in the 10 minutes we'd been watching when he suddenly stopped, stood up and walked swiftly away. Another individual, a ferret faced little chap, leapt forward and picked up the three cups, the ball and the mat on which the mechanic had been playing. While the mechanic shot off one way, the ferret faced chap fled in another direction and five of the six stooges disappeared in other directions. The sixth stooge, the woman in the posh looking hat, stayed for a while to comfort one of the teenage girls who'd lost 100 euros from her travel money. There was, it seemed, a risk that the girl might go to the police. The older woman, the stooge, talked her out of it and then she too left.

Antoinette and I followed her, guessing that the entire group would meet up somewhere not too far away. Sure enough, after a walk of about a quarter of a mile, the woman in the hat joined up with the mechanic, the ferret and the rest of the stooges.

Our curious small adventure didn't end there, however.

Within a few minutes we spotted another crowd. A second mechanic was working the same scam and he too was accompanied by half a dozen stooges. We watched as one of the stooges, a white-haired fellow, a heavy winner, suddenly walked away and moved across to a fat Romanian who was standing nearby, talking on a mobile phone (presumably to a spotter posted to give advance warning of the approach of any police). The white-haired winner handed a thick wodge of notes over to the fat Romanian who slid the money into his pocket. The stooge then rejoined the game.

Two or three minutes later one of the stooges from the first game turned up and reported to the fat man who took the money he was given and directed the stooge to the second game. Clearly, the fat man was operating quite a sizeable business, and moving his players around to keep the customers confused.

What a pity that the police spend all the time harassing genuine street entertainers (who provide an excellent service for tourists and locals) and too little of it watching out for crooks and conmen. I reckon that this small gang were probably taking 30,000 to 50,000 euros a day out of the Parisian economy. The money they conned out of tourists was money that would have otherwise been spent in restaurants, cafés and shops.

16

I learned three things today.

First, someone who knows nothing at all about chess can win one match, or at the very least get two draws, if he plays against two grand masters at the same time. How? It's surprisingly easy. The novice arranges that one of the masters starts the first match (using the white pieces) and he himself starts the second match (again using the white pieces and making the same first move as the first grand master). From then on the novice merely mimics all the moves the two masters make. This effectively means that the second master will be playing the first master and vice versa. The result is bound to be that the novice either gets two draws or one win.

Second, if you have two locks on your front door you should always leave one of them unlocked. If someone tries to break in he will assume that both locks are locked and when he tries to unlock them both he will be forever unlocking one and locking the other.

Third, a person with a good, solid, regular heartbeat may sometimes be able to help an individual with an irregular heartbeat – simply by taking their pulse. Undeniable but inexplicable, serendipitous cardiac synchronicity.

17

When shop assistants demand my name and address, I usually give them their own address. The shop assistant never notices. And now, when websites demand my telephone number I give them a number belonging to Google or Yahoo or one of the other large American computer companies. I hate giving out my telephone number to people. They might ring me. Worse still, they might get one of their machines to ring my number.

Talking of telephones, I hate it when people promise to ring me back straight away but fail to do so. When they do this I sit by the telephone for hours waiting for the call. Ten days later they ring when I am in the bath. The telephone always goes when I'm in the bath. I think it's connected to the water supply in some weird and wonderful way.

18

I had an email from Debretts reminding me to fill in a form confirming my details for their annual book *Debrett's People of Today*. I suppose they want to be sure that I have not yet snuffed it. I tried to fill in the form online but failed miserably to pass the first hurdle. I sent them this email: 'I'm afraid I have forgotten my user name and password. I've also forgotten whether I filled in and posted the form you sent me. But I know it's Sunday and the Prime Minister is called Churchill so things aren't too bad. Can you help?'

They were kind enough to send me the details I required and to assure me that since I clearly seemed pretty well on top of things they would be happy to keep my name in the directory.

19

A reader who works at the reception desk in a large provincial hospital wrote to tell me of a curious experience she had recently. A couple approached the desk. He looked very stern and rather cross and she looked worried. He was holding a baby which looked no more than a few days old.

'There is no one at the baby changing room,' complained the man. He spoke quite good English but was obviously East European.

'I'm afraid there isn't usually anyone there,' my reader told him.

'But we want to change the baby,' he said.

'If you need help I could find a nurse,' suggested my reader.

'We want to change the baby,' insisted the man. 'This one is not good.'

I went cold,' said my reader, 'when I realised that they didn't want the baby changing, they actually wanted to exchange it!' She asked why they wanted to change the baby.

'It does not sleep well. It does not eat well. It is not a strong baby. We want to change it.'

'That is your baby?'

'It is the one we were given. But we want to change it.'

'I'm afraid we don't change babies,' said my reader.

The man looked very unhappy and muttered something. The woman looked relieved. They left.

Life is far more curious than fiction. I would never dare make up anything which sounded so unbelievable.

20

I was walking along the main shopping street in Cheltenham when my telephone rang. It was Antoinette. We had separated in order to do our shopping separately.

'Can you come and get me, please?' she asked.

'What's the matter?' I asked, anxiously.

'I don't feel well. I nearly fainted.'

'Where are you?'

'In that shop called The Works.'

I knew where she meant. It's a shop that always has a big sign outside saying 'Everything Must Go'. I always think this is a silly sign because of course everything must go. It's a shop. They don't want to keep all their stock, do they?

I was less than two hundred yards and ran there as fast as I could go. I don't do much running these days but I can still hurry when I need to and nothing stands higher on my list of 'need to' than a cry for help from Antoinette.

My wife did not look well. She was leaning against a table piled high with cheap paperbacks and looked very pale. I reached for her wrist and took her pulse. It was fast but regular.

'Have you got any pains?'

She shook her head.

I asked her a few more questions. There were no signs or symptoms of anything serious. 'Have you eaten anything since breakfast?'

'No,' she replied. 'And I didn't have any breakfast. I didn't feel hungry.'

'It's probably a hypoglyaemic attack,' I explained. 'Low blood sugar. You need something to eat.'

'Can you help me out of here?' she asked.

'Of course,' I said. I put my arm around her and helped her walk slowly to the door.

'Thank heavens we're out of there,' she murmured, when we got outside.

I looked at her.

'I was terrified I'd need an ambulance. I really wouldn't want to be known as the woman who fell ill in The Works.' She paused, and shuddered. 'Suppose I'd died in there?' She smiled at me. 'Marks and Spencer would be OK I suppose,' she joked. 'House of Fraser would be better. But not The Works.'

I spotted an empty bench a few yards away and led her gently towards it. When she'd sat down I took a bar of chocolate out of my pocket, unwrapped it and gave it to her. 'Eat this,' I told her.

Within ten minutes she was looking and feeling better.

'I'll be fine now,' she said. 'Would you say that was a funny turn?'

'Sort of,' I replied. 'You could call it a swoon, if you like. One of those things Victorian ladies were always having.'

'Oh that sounds rather good,' she said. 'But I wish I'd had it somewhere a bit more up-market than The Works.' She stood up. 'Maybe I should carry smelling salts with me?'

'A bar of chocolate might be more sensible if you're going to miss breakfast.'

'You won't write about this, will you? I don't want any of this in one of your books.'

'Of course not,' I assured her, with as straight and stern a face as I could muster.

We drove back home via the part of Cheltenham known as Montpellier. There is a large and very grand lamp there which was erected in 1885 to commemorate the death of General Gordon in Khartoum. I don't know why folk are always so keen to commemorate the deaths of famous people but they are and so they do.

An organising committee of Montpellier residents appealed to the public for funds but the men and women of Cheltenham weren't as keen on remembering the departed General as had been hoped and the public donated only £20 which was a tenth of the cost of the lamp. The organising committee had to find the other £180 which must have been a bit of a shock. Once the lamp had been erected there was a row about who would pay to light it. The gas company said it would cost £22 a year and the council said they wouldn't go higher than £15 a year so they compromised and lit just two of the three bulbs which must have resulted in a lot of people complaining to the council that one of the lamps wasn't working.

Everything went wrong with that damned lamp.

The granite base didn't arrive until later and the ironwork wasn't strong enough to hold the three lamps and had to be reinforced. Then someone invented electricity and the damned thing had to be converted from gas. With all these problems it is hardly surprising, perhaps, that no one remembered to add a plaque commemorating General Gordon and it wasn't until 1933 that the council got round to having one made and fixed.

There isn't much else to say about Montpellier.

Actually, there isn't much else worth saying about General Gordon, either.

21

People complain about taxes in Britain but I don't think we've seen anything yet. As I explained in my book *Stuffed!* Britain's national debt is so vast (and is continuing to rise) that at some point services are going to have to be cut heavily and taxes are going to have to rise even higher.

The problem is: who is going to pay the higher taxes?

It has been shown many times that when governments raise taxes beyond a certain point the amount of money the Treasury receives actually diminishes. People either find ways to reduce their tax bills or they simply stop working.

I suspect that the extra money is going to be raised by a mass of stealth taxes. The Government will hope that we won't notice 2% here and 3% there in the same way that we might notice a plain and simple 10% rise in income tax.

There will be fees for getting up late in the morning, licences for wearing shoes and all sorts of weird and wonderful new taxes. There will be masses of new regulations and directives and we will have to pay to obey them and pay a fine if we don't.

No one will notice or care that none of these fees or licences or expensive regulations will make life better or safer.

(Nursing homes are a perfect example of the disparity between regulations and quality. Nursing homes are licensed, judged, and given ratings, according to a whole range of mechanical regulations. There must be so many fire alarms, the doors must be so wide, the staff must have knowledge of the latest regulations concerning chair height and tap water temperature and so on, but no one ever attempts to measure the amount of respect or kindness shown to the residents because these are intangibles and are therefore impossible to assess with forms and computers.)

The big problem, of course, is that in our new world of benefits and entitlements all these new taxes and fees will fall on a relatively small number of people.

I was staggered when I discovered that nearly two thirds of all households in Britain now receive more in the way of public services and benefits than they pay in tax. That is, of course, unsustainable. And so the result is that for workers and savers the financial future is a bleak one.

These days, too many people think only of what they can get out of life without working, and so those who do work will have to pay taxes and fees and licences to cover the rising cost of their benefits – as well as to try to settle the nation's enormous debts.

T. S. Raffles, the founder of Singapore, once wrote: 'I have chalked out for myself a very varied and diversified course; but what is life without variety? And what is existence without occupation?'

Raffles was right: work is an essential part of a healthy life. But he would be shocked to know that today far too many people seem content to exist without occupation or, indeed, much in the way of variety.

22

I saw two nurses walking in the street today. I knew that they were nurses because they were both wearing their uniforms. They were, however, some distance from the nearest hospital or medical centre.

I am constantly surprised and dismayed by just how ignorant medical professionals are about infection.

It is by no means uncommon to see nurses wandering through the streets like this. I suspect some of them expect to be treated deferentially because they are shopping in their uniform. But wandering around in work clothes is a very dangerous habit for nurses and those who do this should be put in prison for attempted manslaughter.

Nurses are not expected to wear uniform because they look pretty in them, or because the uniform saves them getting blood and gore on their own clothes. They are expected to wear clean, freshly laundered uniforms to minimise the risk of their taking infection into the hospital or clinic where they work. And, equally, they are expected to take off their uniforms before they leave the hospital so that they don't take hospital infections out into the world.

Killer bugs are now commonplace in NHS hospitals (which are, without a doubt, the dirtiest hospitals in the world, and are the only ones where antibiotic-resistant bugs are commonplace) and it is because nurses don't understand the first principles of hygiene that these killer infections are becoming increasingly commonplace outside hospitals.

My knee has been playing up badly again. If it were a toaster I'd send it back and demand a refund, though to be fair I doubt if much kitchen equipment would be around at the age my knee has reached. I really should take it along to a hospital but I'll stay away for as long as I possibly can. It got bad when we were last in Paris. We had a taxi ordered to take us from our apartment to the Gare du Nord but the driver couldn't get through because much of Paris was blocked and closed so that women runners could jiggle and joggle around the streets. Why they couldn't do their jiggling and joggling in the Bois de Boulogne I cannot imagine. I can only assume that they wanted an audience. Like many folk these days they probably didn't think that they would actually be doing something if there is no one to watch them. Anyway, the result of the blockage was that we had to walk a mile to the nearest Metro and then struggle up and down a vast number of steps. Worse still, the metro itself was crowded with thousands of exhibitionistic, hairy-legged lesbians who'd finished their running and wanted to go home for a dry biscuit and a yoghurt. It was a nightmare and my knee, which suffered badly, has still not recovered from the enforced yomping up and down all those Metro steps.

23

The EU has decreed that fat people must now be officially treated as disabled. The obese, the plump and the rotund must, in law, be treated in exactly the same way as paraplegics or amputees. They must be entitled to disability benefits and they must be given consideration in exactly the same way that society looks after the genuinely disabled. This is patently wrong. Why should people who have indulged themselves and allowed themselves to become overweight be put in the same category as people who have lost limbs or been seriously injured? I can only assume that the foreign eurocrat who made this decision (and many EU laws are made, quite undemocratically, by individual eurocrats) is a fat, greedy, lazy bastard who wants a disabled parking badge for his car.

If the general population knew how much harm the EU has done to our world, armies would be forming in the shires and the heads of eurocrats would soon be decorating park railings throughout the English counties.

24

The average company director now earns £4.3 million a year. Board room salaries have gone up by 73% over the last decade and are now completely out of all proportion to the wages of the people who do the real work. The way to become rich these days is not to become a film star or a singer, or to have a brilliant idea, mortgage your home, soul and family and start your own company, but to join a large international conglomerate, say and do absolutely nothing original, or of interest to anyone, and rise inexorably to the top by mouthing corporate platitudes. In order to do this you need few brains, no talent and little enthusiasm for work. You can become enormously, obscenely rich by robbing widows and orphans and, by meeting the right people at your club. Once you have risen to the top you simply ooze yourself into seats on other company boards so that you can increase your income into the yacht and private jet buying bracket.

One of these professional directors lives near to us in Gloucestershire. As far as I can see he has achieved absolutely nothing in his life except smile benignly, utter endless platitudes and acquire untold wealth. He has a huge, old manor house and a rather tacky modern Rolls Royce and he and his wife are waited on by a housekeeper, a chauffeur, a maid and two gardeners. He was awarded a knighthood as a thank you for giving large chunks of shareholder money to one of the big political parties. These are the rewards the professional nonentity can expect. He is revered by the other villagers, many of whom have trod the same corporate path but with far less success. He wears a three piece tweed suit and a silly hat with a feather in it and looks as if he's been dressed by a wardrobe mistress using props designed for a period drama. His wife carries her stately bosom before her as though it were a fashion accessory, which is honest of her because I suspect she bought her prow in just the same way that she bought her Jimmy Choo shoes and Christian Dior handbag. She's so absurdly posh that if she went blackberry picking (an unlikely possibility, I admit) she'd insist on putting the fruit in a handbag made by Dior or Mulberry. (She'd be bound to pick Mulberry, wouldn't she?)

The local Audi and Mercedes drivers treat him as an old-fashioned Lord of the Manor and probably offer up their virgin daughters on their sixteenth birthdays. 'He's very approachable,' said one local. 'Just like one of us.'

I bloody well hope he isn't like me. I'm waiting quietly for the revolution to start. Such vast and utterly undeserved wealth inequality as exists today must eventually lead to the picking up of pitchforks and the start of a revolution. It will be known in future history books as the 21st Century Pedants Uprising.

I know which side of the barrier I'll be on.

25

A friend of Antoinette's is a well-known author who writes romantic novels. She started writing late in her life and her publishers told her rather bluntly that they were worried that she looked too old to be writing such stories. They solved this problem by hiring a young, out of work actress and putting her photograph on the back of the books. She was quite a voluptuous looking thing, all bosom, hair and legs, and after a couple of years the publishers suggested that Antoinette's friend allow the actress to do some television interviews on her behalf. And so the young actress, using the real author's name, appeared on quite a few television chat shows and became quite a regular on the radio. She looked good, had a pleasant enough voice and always took care to read the books before she talked about them.

Sadly, there has apparently been an unpleasant turn in this seemingly happy story.

'The publishers used to pay the actress a fee for the use of her photograph and another fee to do promotional work for the books,' explained Antoinette's friend. 'In addition, she was allowed to keep all the fees she earned doing interviews. She became quite famous, pretending to be me, and I didn't mind in the slightest. I would have hated having to do all those interviews. I was happy staying at home and writing the books.'

'So, what's gone wrong?' asked Antoinette.

'The young actress told my publishers that since she is now my 'official face and voice' she should receive a royalty. She wants an equal share of everything I earn from writing my books. She threatened to go public with the truth if I didn't agree to her demand.'

Naturally, the author was not happy. It didn't seem fair to us, either.

'What have you done about it?' asked Antoinette.

'I told the bloody woman to go public,' said her friend. 'She will look a fool and lose all her lucrative television and radio work and the publicity will doubtless boost the sales of my books. I also told her that if the unexpected should happen, and the revelation should damage my sales, I will simply announce that I have died and write books under another name.'

'What did she say?'

'I think she was rather alarmed at the prospect of being officially 'dead'. She has apparently told the publishers that she would very much like to carry on with things the way they are. All talk of royalties has been abandoned.'

This curious tale reminded me of a time when I once pretended to be an eminent author of gardening books.

In the 1970s, 1980s and early 1990s I used to tour the country whenever I had a new book out. On each tour I would regularly visit 30 to 40 radio stations and a dozen or so television stations. In between the broadcast interviews I would talk to feature writers working for local newspapers or magazines. Quite often I would sit down in a radio studio and find that the disc jockey or presenter who was about to interview me didn't have the foggiest idea who I was, or what my book was about. He would have a copy of my book on his desk but he would proudly announce that he hadn't had time to read it – or even open it. Despite this rather arrogant attitude, radio stations used to love touring authors. We were, by and large, the most readily available free source of interview fodder. Local politicians and businessmen had not yet discovered the importance of local radio as a promotional medium.

These days, local radio stations have a queue of politicians, lawyers, doctors, accountants and shop keepers all desperate to broadcast and to plug themselves or their business. I suspect that every radio station in the land now has its own earnest young medical practitioner eagerly practising 'radio therapy'. But that's now. Back in the early days of local radio things were very different. Authors on tour were as essential to radio stations as transmitters and coffee machines.

Occasionally, a particularly ambitious presenter would have two author interviewees in the studio at once. The idea behind this rather extravagant and exciting format was that the presenter would talk to both authors and that two visitors would, occasionally, be allowed to talk to each other. Even with this more adventurous type of programme the presenter would frequently not bother to look at the books which were being promoted. He might look at the press releases accompanying the books. But he wouldn't bother to read the books themselves.

It was in these circumstances that I found myself in a radio studio with a well-known writer of gardening books. I was promoting one of my medical books and he was there to talk about his latest book on vegetables, plants and shrubs. You'd know his name but I haven't spoken to him and it would be unfair to name him without getting his permission.

The problem was that right from the start the presenter was mixed up about which one of us was which. He thought I was the writer of gardening books and that the other guest was the writer of medical books. Just before we went on air we both corrected him. But by the time the programme had started he had again forgotten which one of us was which.

'So tell us about your new book,' said the presenter, having introduced me as one of the nation's leading gardening experts. I looked across at the other guest and hesitated for an instant. He smiled at me and nodded, making it clear that he was happy for me to pretend to be him. He quickly passed me a copy of his book. And so, reading from the blurb on the back cover of the book, I rapidly summed up the contents of 'my' book. I then passed my own book to the gardening expert, so that he could pretend to be me and talk about my book as though he were the author.

It worked surprisingly well.

Once we'd started we had to continue, of course. My voice was now that of the gardener and his voice was that of the doctor. Any listeners who knew our real identities would have been mightily confused but the presenter was quite happy. He asked the usual banal questions and we cheerfully fed him the usually banal answers. When you've done a few dozen radio interviews it is remarkably easy to talk about something of which you know absolutely nothing without making this clear to the listeners.

The gardening writer and I had a quick coffee afterwards and then we caught trains travelling in opposite directions. I bumped into him once or twice on subsequent promotional tours but we never repeated that bizarre experience.

26

Lloyds Bank has sent me a new debit card. This one, they tell me, will enable me to pay for stuff without the trouble of entering my PIN number. All I have to do is to touch the card against a shop's little machine. Or, maybe, just wave it about in the general vicinity of the machine. Or, perhaps, just think about waving it about. The cost of whatever I am buying will then be automatically taken from my account. It is, I suppose, all part of the desire to do away with cash. Governments and banks hate cash. It's expensive to move around and handle and, worst of all, it doesn't leave any trace. If I use cash I can buy a penknife or a copy of the 'Morning Star' without anyone in MI5 being aware of it. 'Shop faster, but stay just as safe' claims a leaflet that came with the card. 'You won't be exposed to any greater risk of fraud as your contactless card uses the same high level technology that's behind chip and PIN'.

Huh? Are the people at Lloyds Bank completely clueless? Of course, I will be exposed to a greater risk of fraud. If someone steals my card (or I lose it) the thief will be able to use it to buy stuff without having the inconvenience of having to beat me over the head until I tell him my PIN number. I really do despair. I think that perhaps the well-known Scottish buffoon Fred Godwin is now running Lloyds Bank.

I see, by the way, that Lloyds, like most big companies, are now sending mail in C5 envelopes. I think this is wise. I've been using these bigger envelopes for some time. I am convinced that mail is less likely to get lost when it's sent in a large envelope. It's a terrible waste, of course, but having to send a letter twice is even more wasteful.

27

George Orwell is often given all the credit for forecasting the world in which we now live. But Charles Dickens deserves credit too. Here, for example, is a quote from *Little Dorrit:* 'The Circumlocution Office was (as everybody knows without being told) the most important Department under Government. No public business of any kind could possibly be done at any time without the acquiescence of the Circumlocution Office. Its finger was in the largest public pie, and in the smallest public tart. It was equally impossible to do the plainest right and to undo the plainest wrong without the express authority of the Circumlocution Office. If another Gunpowder Plot had been discovered half an hour before the lighting of the match, nobody would have been justified in saving the parliament until there had been half a score of boards, half a bushel of minutes, several sacks of official memoranda, and a family vault full of ungrammatical correspondence, on the part of the Circumlocution Office.'

Every government department now has its own Circumlocution Office, of course, (HMRC is little more than a large Circumlocution Office) but these days I am reminded of Dickens, and the Circumlocution Office, whenever I am forced to communicate with a utility company or a bank.

28

In Waterstones's book shop I noticed that they are still selling Kindle machines so that people can log on to Amazon and purchase e-Books instead of buying paperback or hardback editions of books. This is one step more destructive than Gerald Ratner describing his company's products as 'crap'. At least Ratner didn't tell prospective customers what to buy instead of the unfortunate product which he had denigrated so thoroughly.

The bookshop staff still insist that they are merely 'keeping up with the times' but I give Waterstones's five years at best and then all their stores will become charity shops selling cheap books and unfashionable clothing. For a bookshop to promote e-Books is as daft as stagecoach makers giving away free leaflets promoting motor cars.

I am constantly amazed at the way that the book business has destroyed itself. Even publishers seem determined to commit commercial suicide. When Sir Allan Lane invented the modern paperback he did so because he realised that there was a market among travellers for small, light, portable paperbacks. He made Penguin books pocket sized so that they would fit into pockets and handbags. But today, paperbacks are huge and if you want to take more than one with you on holiday you'll need an extra suitcase. The cost of posting the books is much higher, too. Modern, heavy paperbacks could have been designed to help boost the sales of e-Book readers. With a kindle device a traveller can get on a train with a library in his pocket.

29

I have recently collected these three wonderful quotations about medicine. I don't expect many of them can be found in dictionaries of quotations.

1. 'Doctors are always working to preserve our health and cooks to destroy it, but the latter are the more often successful.' – Denis Diderot (1713-1784)

2. 'To preserve one's health by too strict a regime is in itself a tedious malady.' – Duc François de la Rochefoucauld (1613-1680)

3. 'Strive to preserve your health; and in this you will the better succeed in proportion as you keep clear of the physicians, for their drugs are a kind of alchemy concerning which there are no fewer books than there are medicines.' – Leonardo da Vinci (1452-1519)

30

Antoinette and I were walking through a quiet Cotswold village when a young boy approached us. He was accompanied by a scruffy, muddy and definitely damp spaniel.

'I bet you a pound that if you throw a stone in the pond my dog will find it and bring it out,' said the boy. He said this defiantly, as though expecting us not to believe him. He held out his hand and showed us a small, flattish stone. We looked around. Sure enough there was a small pond nearby. It was a fairly typical village pond, except that it didn't seem to contain any old bedsteads or supermarket trolleys. Neither of us had spotted it before. Actually, it was so small that I don't think it could have taken offence if you'd called it a large puddle.

I looked at the stone. It was a very ordinary looking stone, which had no distinguishing marks whatsoever.

'But your dog could bring out any stone,' I said, quickly spotting what seemed to me to be the obvious flaw.

'I'll mark it,' said the boy. He took a penknife out of his pocket, opened it and used the blade to scratch a single short line on the stone. He then showed me the marked stone.

'OK,' I said. 'Throw it into the pond. If your dog brings it out I'll give you a pound.'

The boy threw the stone into the pond. It did what stones do in ponds. It sank to the bottom. The dog, not waiting for instructions, dived into the pond, splashed around for a moment in the shallow water at the edge and then disappeared. A few moments later it emerged with a stone in its mouth. The boy bent down, took the stone from the dog's mouth and showed it to me. He pointed to the scratch mark. I gave him a pound.

'How on earth did he train the dog to do that?' Antoinette asked me.

'I don't have the foggiest idea,' I replied.

Half an hour later we were sitting in a café when the boy came in, followed by his muddy, wet dog. He bought a packet of crisps and a can of cola from the girl behind the counter and then left. She was obviously pleased to see him disappear before the dog made too much of a mess.

'Brilliant dog,' I said to our waitress.

She grinned. 'He got you with the scratched stone, did he?'

'He did,' I answered. 'Why are you grinning?'

'He gets loads of people with that trick,' she said. 'The dog makes him a small fortune.'

'But it's an impressive trick,' I responded.

The woman shook her head. 'It isn't a trick,' she told us. 'The bottom of that pond is strewn with stones which have a little scratch on them. He spent hours scratching stones and throwing them in. I doubt if you'd find a stone in that pond that doesn't have a scratch on it.'

She hurried off to attend to another pair of customers.

'He'll go far, that boy,' said Antoinette.

October

1

Driving out of Weston-super-Mare onto the M5 we discovered that the motorway was blocked solid. There were thousands of cars, parked bumper to bumper on all three lanes, all going nowhere. Even the hard shoulder and the approach road were blocked. It seemed crazy to drive on and to add to the mass of vehicles going nowhere and doing nothing except waste fuel and pollute the atmosphere. And so, as a socially responsible citizen, I slowly tried to reverse back up the approach road to find another route out of the town. I'd only driven a couple of dozen yards down the slip road so it wasn't far to go and it did seem the sensible thing to do. Inevitably, however, a car overtook me, and drew alongside with the passenger side window down. The face of an angry woman glowered at me, holding up what looked vaguely like a warrant card but since I wasn't wearing my reading glasses could well have been a membership card for the now sadly defunct Desperate Dan Pie Eaters' Club.

'Police!' she shouted, in the way that most women of her age, class and mental agility might shout Bingo!

She wasn't wearing a uniform but I could tell by her face that she really was a policewoman and hadn't bought her warrant card on the internet. Not even a traffic warden could have pulled a face like that.

'Reversing up a motorway slip road is an offence,' she snapped. 'Join the queue and damn the planet. We're talking traffic law here – much more important than common sense or saving the planet.'

She didn't say the last couple of sentences, of course, but she might as well have done. Rules are rules and even the really stupid ones must be obeyed.

I have a strong suspicion that common sense will soon be a criminal offence, punishable with a long prison sentence and, quite possibly, a good beating too.

And so I took the truck out of reverse, put it into first, tucked in behind the unmarked police car, joined the queue and did my bit towards melting glaciers and drowning polar bears.

No one on the planet can be quite as dim-witted and aggressively stupid as a Government employee with a nice shiny rule to enforce.

For the umpteenth time, I found myself wondering why road designers don't build motorway approach roads in such a way that it is possible to see the motorway before you join it. (I assume someone designs the damned things but maybe I am being naïve. Maybe, a bunch of navvies make roads simply by dumping tarmacadam down wherever they think a road would look nice. It honestly wouldn't surprise me.)

Afterwards Antoinette wondered if some interfering busybody might have filmed my small adventure and put it on YouTube. It would not surprise me in the slightest. The world is, it seems, crammed to the gunwales with people who love to sneak and tell tales and do what they see as their duty to the jack-booted functionaries of the Great State.

Well, rot them all I'm too old and tired and I don't give a damn. If it is my destiny to become a YouTube star then so be it. Bring it on, as I think someone once said.

2

I saw a book on sale today which claims to tell me how to use my iPhone properly. The book had 683 pages. That says it all, doesn't it? You buy a damned phone and to find out how to use it you have to buy, and read, a 683 page book. How long before kids are taking O level mobile phone? (Please don't anyone write and tell me if they already are. I don't want to know.)

3

A local newspaper contains a large advertisement promoting literacy classes for people who cannot read. It's a wonderful idea. But there is, of course, a flaw the size of Mount Everest in promoting literacy classes this way.

I was reminded of a story I was recently told about a racecourse near here. The public address announcer told racegoers that a hearing aid had been found and that the person who had lost it should go to the secretary's office to collect it. Sadly, no one turned up because the only person in the crowd who didn't hear the announcement was the person for whom it was intended.

4

A local policeman is reported to have been running a strippergram service. For a modest fee he would go to parties, hen nights and so on and strip off his uniform. There are plenty of other gentlemen providing this service but this one really was a policeman – and the uniform he removed was also real. His stage name was apparently 'The Copper with the Whopper' and I understand that the Chief Constable, who apparently took a dim view of this piece of imaginative moonlighting, has put his foot down. In future the women of the area can hire a stripping policeman in the doubtless comforting knowledge that he will be a fake.

5

Last spring we planted several dozen ornamental trees in some of the land behind our boule court (only the very best homes, you understand, have a properly built boule court). The trees have done incredibly well. They are all now about ten to twelve feet tall. They all flowered and the plum trees had plums while the cherry trees had cherries. The birds ate all the fruit, of course, but that is by the by.

The problem is that although the trees have done well the grasses and weeds around them have done well too and today I decided that I really needed to strim around them to give them a little space to, well, breathe. So I filled the strimmer tank with the strange mixture of petrol and oil which it prefers, followed the manufacturer's starting instructions and did my best to avoid the doubtless scary warnings. After pulling the darned starter cord about 15,000 times (give or take two or three) I gave up, kicked it and sat down on the ground to do a little quiet cursing. The nearest garden machinery workshop is about 20 miles away so this meant two 40 mile round trips and two half days lost.

(I would have to take the strimmer in to be repaired and since they would almost certainly not be able to fit me in there and then I would have to go back another day to collect the damned thing. I could have asked them to collect and return it but since the strimmer is relatively light and we have a damned great truck available I would have found this too embarrassing.)

While working my way through my regular litany of curses, specially designed for garden machinery which won't start, it suddenly occurred to me that I could, perhaps, try to mend it. I fished out the manufacturer's manual and leafed through it. Sadly, I couldn't find a troubleshooting page but I did discover that the machine contained a plug thing. Now I've seen plug things when I've been watching the man from the AA trying to repair the car so I know what they look like.

I looked around to see a) if I could find it and b) if it was accessible for a man with large hands, a collection of hammers and a screwdriver. I'd like to be able to report that I came across it straight away but that would be a downright lie. I only found it when I had given up and kicked the machine so hard that a little rubber cover thing came off the plug thing.

My next step was clearly to take out the plug thing and wipe it on my overalls. I've seen oil stained mechanics do that in films. At this point I had a brainwave: I remembered that I had removed a good selection of useful looking tools before I had given away our elderly BMW seven series. I rummaged around, found the tools and discovered a spanner thing which looked as if it might fit the plug thing. It did. And minutes later I had the plug thing in my hand.

I know that the professionals wipe these things on their overalls, or on an oily rag, but I had neither so I wiped it on a paper handkerchief and my jacket sleeve. I then put it back into position and used the spanner thing to make sure it was fastened tightly. I then replaced the rubber cover thing and gave the machine another kick for luck.

(I don't know why this is but I have discovered that all equipment, whether mechanical or electrical, is masochistic in nature and responds well when given a good thump. It has sometimes occurred to me that the human body might also respond similarly. How many mysterious symptoms would disappear if the doctor simply gave the patient a good bang with a hammer?)

I then tried the starter handle again.

You could have knocked me down with quite a small stick when it started. What an amazing sound. I had mended the strimmer! Unfortunately, it was almost dark and too late to do any actual strimming. But I did feel rather pleased with myself.

I told Antoinette that from now on she could call me 'Sparky' and gave instructions that in future she should preface as many conversations as possible with the line: 'When Vernon was cleaning the plug thingy on the strimmer…'.

6

For several years an old man called Leonard Pilbeam managed to persuade people in the village to do all his chores for him without any charge. One man cut his grass and his hedges, a woman did his shopping, another did his washing and ironing and so on and on. They did these things not because they liked him (Leonard, a former accountant, was a very unlikeable character) but because he led them to believe that he was rich and that they would figure prominently in his will. Occasionally, he would offer them a little money for their services but they always refused, not because they didn't want any financial reward but because they preferred to wait for the big pay out which they believed would come when he died. He actually told one woman that she could choose between having cash in her hand each week or a prominent place in his will. She, like the others, knew that he had no relatives and told him that she preferred to be 'remembered' in his will. The word was that Leonard was probably worth a million or more and so even a fifth share would be quite a tidy tax-free sum. His house alone, five good bedrooms and just over an acre of good land, had to be worth the best part of a million. Maybe more if the right buyer could be found.

Today, the owner of our village shop told me that Leonard Pilbeam had died and that his will had been read. There was much disappointment and bitterness among those who had nurtured hopes. Their names were all in the will, and so, as promised, they were all remembered, but there was little material consolation for their years of labour. They shared a line of thanks in appreciation of their efforts.

It turned out that Leonard had sold his house ten years earlier, through one of those equity release schemes which allow the former owner to remain in the property until his death. All the money which had been released had gone. And the small pension Leonard had received from the accountancy firm where he had been a partner had died with him. It is apparently expected that the sale of Leonard's furniture and personal belongings will, with a little luck and a following wind, produce just enough money to pay the undertakers and the solicitor. The villagers who had worked so hard for him had to be content with having their names in the will.

7

Leonard Pilbeam's death reminded me that a friend of mine who is a GP recently told me about a dilemma he had faced. He was called, late at night, to the home of an elderly patient who had been seriously ill for several months. The patient, who had cancer, eventually stopped breathing at around 11.30 p.m. It was at this point that the dilemma became apparent. The man's son took my friend aside and asked him if it would be possible to put the following day's date on the death certificate. He was very honest about the situation and explained that just under seven years earlier his father had given him all the shares in the business the family owned and ran. Under the tax laws the gift would be free of inheritance tax once the seven years was up. If the death certificate was dated on the day that the man had died then the business would have to be sold, and a lot of local people would probably lose their jobs. But if the death certificate was given the following day's date, the full seven years would have passed and there would be no inheritance tax due. The business would remain in the family's hands and no employees would lose their jobs. My friend said that this was one of the most unusual, and difficult, dilemmas he had ever had to face. There was absolutely no legal risk because no one would ever know, or be able to prove, exactly when the old man had died. It was a purely moral quandary.

'What did you do?' I asked my friend.

'I said I needed a drink,' he told me. 'The son and I each had a malt whisky. It was a very good malt and I always treat such whiskies with great respect. They're to be sipped, not gulped. We sat there for half an hour or so, I suppose. When I'd emptied my glass I took the death certificate book out of my bag. I always carry the book with me so that if a patient dies at home I can give the relatives the certificate there and then, and make the process as easy as possible for them. I then filled in the patient's details and when I was about to complete the form I turned to the son and asked him if he could tell me the date. He looked at his watch and told me. I then filled in the date and handed him the form.'

'He was happy?'

'I think so. He shook my hand and gave me the rest of the bottle to finish at home. He said he thought his father would have wanted me to have it.'

8

Hackers have stolen the details of over 600,000 French and Belgian customers of Domino's Pizza. The details stolen included names, addresses and favourite pizza toppings. The thieves could have got the names and addresses from the telephone book so it must have been the details of the pizza toppings that they were after. This is yet more evidence that computer hackers are not like the rest of us.

9

I have an awful suspicion that Amazon has decided to employ only low-grade zombies to deliver their orders. We are now having so much trouble with deliveries that I have all but stopped buying through the Amazon website. Software on the site tells me that during the last six months I purchased 231 books, DVDs and bits and pieces of office equipment through the website. Well, they will be lucky if we get to 31 orders during the next six months because at the moment my first port of call will, in future, be eBay. Three times in the last week we have been told that orders have been delivered when they haven't. And parcels clearly addressed to us are being left at locations throughout Gloucestershire; abandoned in an apparently random manner. The couriers don't seem able to follow simple instructions. Why is it so damned difficult to find people who are willing to do jobs with care and thought? I suspect that I'll be back to Amazon before long but for the moment they're standing in the corporate corner wearing a dunce's cap.

10

Friends of ours who live next to a school tell us that nearly all the children attending the school arrive by car. Every morning the streets around the school are clogged with vehicles as parents fight to drop their children as close to the gates as possible. Many of the children live no more than half a mile away. What on earth is happening to our world? It is much safer, in every possible way, for children to walk to school than it was a generation ago. And it is safer than it was for the generation before that. Children are far less likely to be molested or attacked now than they were even a decade ago. What parents don't seem to realise is that children who are taken everywhere by car will, inevitably, be fatter and unhealthier than they would be if they were encouraged to take a daily walk.

These same friends both wear colourful bracelets made out of tiny rubber bands. The bracelets have been made by their daughter. The couple even wear the bracelets when they go to work. The coloured bands are now sold in just about every shop in the country and the rubber band industry must be making a good deal of money out of a product which might have been considered to be on wobbly legs. The joke, however, seems to be on parents. I asked one of their children why there was such a craze for these things.

'There isn't,' replied the little girl. Who is seven in body but at least 18 in mind.

'But shops sell them everywhere and kids love them!' I protested.

'No,' she countered. 'Parents think that kids ought to love them. But I wouldn't be seen dead wearing a bracelet made out of rubber bands. Nor would any of my friends.'

'But you make bracelets out of them!' I pointed out.

'Only to keep my parents happy,' she answered. 'They like to think I like playing with them because they're sort of arty crafty. They think it's healthier to make rubber band bracelets than to go on Facebook or mess with my phone.' She grinned. 'I make tons of bracelets,' she said. 'I can turn them out in no time. Then I give them to my parents and they wear them so that I'm not disappointed.'

11

An industrialist who has been awarded a knighthood is known to be a peeping tom. People who know this are surprised that he wasn't given a peerage.

12

We visited friends. They have had their kitchen completely re-fitted with some astonishing looking equipment. 'What's this cool looking thing?' I asked, pointing to a large grey machine.

'It's a fridge,' replied the friend, drily.

13

An old man who lives near to us is in a hospice. He is dying but he has come to terms with this. He is nearly 90-years-old and content that he has lived his life to the full. We asked if we could bring him anything. He smiled and shook his head. 'I've got more books than I can read and more DVDs than I can watch.'

'No special foods?' asked Antoinette.

'I don't have much of an appetite,' he told us. 'But they feed me very well here.'

We sat and talked for a while. Antoinette talked to him about what was happening in our garden. She told him about the antics of the squirrels and the activities of the badgers. He nodded and murmured. He was interested, enjoying what she told him. Suddenly, he looked up.

'Did you have a good conker crop?' He asked. He knew that our big horse chestnut tree had nearly died but that I had managed to nurse it back to good health.

Antoinette looked across at me.

'Marvellous,' I told him. 'We have enough conkers to keep a whole school full of small boys extremely happy.'

'In my day,' he said, sadly. 'And in your day, I have no doubt.' He sighed. 'The boys these days don't seem interested. They don't play conkers do they?'

'Not much,' I agreed.

'Too busy with their computer games.'

I nodded.

'I used to love the feel of a horse chestnut,' he said. 'The shiny nut, straight out of the prickly casing.' He smiled, remembering.

We talked a little more and when he was tired we left him.

'Are there any conkers left on the tree?' asked Antoinette as we got into the car.

'I think so,' I told her. 'I'll look as soon as I get back home.'

I managed to find half a dozen fruits, still in their casings, still on the tree. I picked them and put them into a brown paper bag Antoinette found. Then we drove back to the hospice. Our friend was asleep but I gave the bag to one of the nurses and asked her to give it to him with our love. She promised to put the bag in his room, so that he would see it when he woke up.

He died a day later and on the table beside his bed were the carefully opened fruit casings. The matron told us that he had one of the shiny conkers in his hand when he died.

14

Our BMW X3 has developed a crack in the windscreen. It just appeared. One day the windscreen was clear (apart from the evidence that it is stored out in the open, underneath a large sycamore tree which is home to a family of magpies with loose bowels) and the next morning there was a two inch crack. The crack wasn't caused by a stone flying up and there were no chips in the windscreen to suggest that the cause was anything other than a fault in the glass.

Gradually, the crack has lengthened and worked its way across the screen. A few days ago I decided that it was time to have the faulty windscreen replaced. I telephoned the dealer from which we'd bought the car, and booked it in for a service and windscreen replacement. This morning, one of the mechanics picked up the car and drove it over to the garage. This afternoon a man from the garage telephoned and asked if I wanted to know the cost of a new windscreen or if I just wanted them to go ahead and replace it and then send me the bill. I said I didn't think I ought to have to pay anything since the crack was clearly a result of a fault, rather than a result of an accident, or a stone being thrown up. The man from the garage then told me that he had found two small stone chips in the glass and that since he believed these to be the cause of the crack, the windscreen would not be replaced under the car's warranty. I was astonished at our bad luck. Clearly what had happened was that while being driven from our home to the garage two small stones had landed on the windscreen and marked the glass. One had landed very close to the crack and the other had landed right on it. How unlucky can you get?

I told the man from the garage to leave the windscreen as it is and to send the car back to us. With that sort of luck we might as well put up with the cracked windscreen.

When the car was delivered back to us, serviced and cleaned, the driver who had brought it hurried away before I could talk to him about this astonishing incident. There were indeed two marks on the windscreen – one close to the crack and one right on it.

15

It took me fifteen minutes to reset my driving position in the BMW. Why, I wonder, do drivers from the garage always have to change every possible position? I can understand that they might have to move the seat forwards so that their little legs can help their tiny feet reach the pedals, but do they really have to change the inclination and the lumbar support?

Once I'd managed to get myself into a moderately comfortable position (I seriously doubt if I will ever be able to get it back to the pleasant, comfy position I had before) it took me another five minutes to turn off the radio. The mechanic who brought the car back had obviously been a deaf and enthusiastic aficionado of Radio One.

The idiots who designed our car were, like the designers of Windows software, overcome by their own cleverness and unaware that making things more complicated just because you can isn't always a good idea. Sometimes, less is more.

The BMW engineers have equipped the car with 7,000 functions which I will never want to use but if I want to turn on the fog lamps or use the rear window wipers I have to stop, park and fish out the manual. The radio and CD player are a total mystery. And so now I am sadly aware that for as long as we own it our car will start to play Radio One whenever I press the starter button.

16

A reader has written to admonish me for the fact that in my first diary (*Diary of a Disgruntled Man*) I moan about the British and American Governments. I should, he says, settle back and enjoy life, instead of criticising the people who run the country. He says my book made him laugh out loud but contains far too many moans. He also complains about the criticisms in my book *Stuffed!*.

Sadly, I'm afraid I suspect that this reader is one of the reasons that people like me spend our lives writhing around in spiritual pain. Is there anyone over 50, with a decent quantity of functioning brain tissue, who genuinely believes that the world is now better run, and more agreeable, than it was two or three decades ago? Is there one leading politician, anywhere in the world, who can justly be described as a Statesman? Is there one leader of anything who isn't a screaming psychopath doing whatever he does simply to boost his own standing and fill his own pockets?

It is, I'm afraid, cryptorchid folk like my whingeing reader who are the problem.

If more people were prepared to stand up and tell the truth – that the world is being badly run by psychopaths advised by crooks and charlatans – then the world would be a much better place.

My reader is right in that I would doubtless have a more relaxing time if I just sat back and enjoyed my life with Antoinette; basking in the joy I get from our garden, and our collection of books and films.

But someone has to stand up on the parapet and scream abuse at the people who are making such a damned awful mess of running the world.

And I've appointed myself.

17

A man died recently of a heart attack. As far as his family, friends and colleagues were concerned he had been in excellent health. But when his wife examined the To-Do list on his mobile phone she found the following entry: 'See doctor about pains in chest'.

The entry had been written four weeks before the man's death.

18

About 25 years ago I constructed an original list of collective nouns (ones I had made up) for a book I wrote called *The Complete Guide to Life* (under the pen name Edward Vernon). Everyone knows that a collection of fish is a shoal and that a group of birds a flock. Most people know that groups of geese, dogs, horses and cattle are collectively known as a gaggle, a pack, a string and a herd. But no one had previously created collective nouns for specific, groups of people. I rediscovered my list this week and I've been adding to it. Here is the new, improved and expanded list:

A hamper of assistants
A congregation of clergymen
A galaxy of actresses
A pride of expectant fathers
A knot of scouts
A shower of weather forecasters
A swarm of heating engineers
A congestion of children
A clump of labourers
A drove of chauffeurs

273

A clutch of car mechanics
A collection of philatelists
A ring of proctologists
A batch of cooks
A press of laundrymen
A girdle of corsetieres
A quantity of surveyors
A parcel of postmen
A cast of sculptors
A band of rubber workers
A tuft of trichologists
A wealth of publishers
A stream of urologists
An embarrassment of parents
A flourish of magicians
A cluster of diamond cutters
A ring of jewellers
A posse of vets
A flounce of divas
A bunch of florists
A nest of mothers
A stack of booksellers/librarians
A corps of pathologists
A cup of bra makers
A congress of prostitutes
A concentration of students
A body of undertakers
A chest of transvestites
A company of representatives
A set of osteopaths
A dossier of policemen
A sheaf of administrators
A pile of gastroenterologists
An aggregation of biochemists
An association of psychologists
A drift of skiers
A clutch of physiotherapists
A school of nurses
A meeting of social workers

A herd of audiologists
A convergence of opticians
An issue of journalists
A brood of midwives
A community of public health officials
A cell of cytologists
A branch of foresters
A line of geneticists
A chain of chemists
A growth of endocrinologists
A cloud of spiritualists
A catch of obstetricians
A mass of oncologists
A smear of laboratory technicians
A promenade of chiropodists
A gathering of dress makers
A camaraderie of photographers
A host of bacteriologists
An order of waiters
A pyramid of archaeologists
A giggle of teenage girls
A gawp of teenage boys
A hold of sailors
A grip of luggage handlers
A slump of economists
A grievance of defendants
A whinge of consumers
A bore of mining engineers
A nerd of IT workers
A bosom of typists

19

I bought a pile of books today from my favourite second-hand bookshop in Cheltenham. Among them was a local history book which contained a section dealing with a lawyer called William Prynne who was a Protestant extremist with strong views on women's hairstyles. He wrote that 'our English gentlewomen are now grown so far past shame as to clip their hair like men and make this whorish cut the fashion of the times'. When he'd finished getting into trouble for that bit of fun Prynne published a book called *Histriomastrix* which was lucky enough to be declared both subversive and blasphemous. These days that would have got him a TV contract, a column in *The Guardian* and valuable serialisation rights in one of the Sunday tabloids. He would have had to put up with some pretty scathing one star Amazon reviews, but by golly he'd have been rich beyond his dreams.

But things were different back then, and the unfortunate Prynne was debarred, fined £5,000, put in the pillory twice (once in Cheapside and once, for an encore, in Westminster) and then imprisoned in the Tower of London. As if that wasn't punishment enough he also had both his ears cut off. But Mr Prynne didn't allow such petty inconveniences to silence him. Once people had stopped throwing rotten vegetables at him, and his ears had stopped bleeding, he wrote another book on the same theme. The result was that the authorities (still several laughs short of a good sense of humour) fined him another £5,000, put him into the pillory again, branded him and stuffed him into the dungeon at Carnarvon castle. They also ordered that his ears be cut off for a second time. (Perhaps they'd grown back. Perhaps he'd had plastic surgery. Perhaps they didn't do a proper job the first time.)

When the Restoration came in 1649 the adventurous Prynne was released and happier times lay ahead. He moved to Cheltenham, married a Cotswold girl, and lived for another 31 years saying 'I beg your pardon, would you repeat that?' a good deal and having nowhere to rest the arms of his spectacles. I don't believe there is any record of the type of hairstyle his new wife favoured.

20

I cut myself shaving this morning. It was a minute cut but by the time I had bathed the wound and covered it with a suitable old-fashioned fabric sticking plaster (if a sticking plaster doesn't make you say 'ouch' when you remove it then there is really no point in putting it on in the first place) the blood that had seeped out had gone everywhere. I doubt if I had lost more than a quarter of a teaspoonful but even that was enough to soak a tie, a shirt, a pair of trousers, a jacket, an overcoat, a hat that was hanging up in the front porch, a carpet, a packet of paper tissues, an oil painting that was hanging on the wall, a blanket, the lawn mower, a pair of socks, a rug in the boot of the car, a clock and two apple trees. I hate to think how much mess would have been made if I'd lost a whole teaspoonful.

21

I've wasted another hour of my life dealing with a bunch of bureaucrats. The damned creatures are everywhere these days – as ubiquitous as cockroaches in an NHS hospital kitchen. But at least it is not yet illegal to annoy them with a little light bureaucrat baiting. Worrying bureaucrats (in the same way that a dog worries sheep) is an essential pleasure and a natural instinct and it should not be repressed. There are lots of variations but here are some of my favourite:

1. Ask for a copy of the official complaints procedure. All bureaucrats (except those working for the NHS) are terrified of formal complaints. NHS bureaucrats don't give a damn about complaints because no one ever takes any notice of them. If the complaint is serious the patient will be dead and so that's that.

2. Send one page of what is obviously a two page letter. Make sure you send it by recorded or special delivery.

3. Enclose a cheque for a small amount of money when no one has asked you for any. (This is a good way to elicit a response. They will have to return your cheque.)

4. Write two letters saying precisely opposite things and post them on the same day.

5. Add an extra letter or figure to the reference you are asked to quote on your replies.

6. Make constant references to a previous letter that you never wrote.

7. Make constant references to a previous letter that they never wrote.

8. Make constant references to a named but imaginary individual. I like to give my imaginary individuals good solid names like Ditchfield and Woodhead.

9. Add a postscript to your letter saying that you have sent a copy to the chairman of the board and to Mr Hoskins. There doesn't have to be a Mr Hoskins and you don't actually have to bother sending a copy to the chairman.

10. Enclose an invoice with your letter and request payment within seven days. The invoice should be for the inconvenience you have been caused. I usually make mine out for £1,500,000 since this is a nice round sum and likely to attract attention.

22

For some years now I have been unable to fit all the junk I feel I must carry into my pockets. I have, therefore, invariably carried a shoulder bag when leaving the house. Today, I decided that the bag had become too heavy and so I emptied it out onto the carpet so that I could try and decide what was essential and what could be safely discarded.

Here are the contents: seven pencils, three notebooks, a copy of a paperback by George Mikes, a French dictionary, a make-up bag containing a collection of essential medicines, an Epipen for use if Antoinette, I or anyone else suffers an anaphylactic shock reaction, a handful of AA and AAA batteries, two pen refills, three dice, a portable electronic chess game, an emergency sewing kit, a folding umbrella, two packets of paper handkerchiefs, a packet of wet wipes, a digital camera, a spare disk for the camera, a small book to help me identify trees, a recipe for shortbread, a packet of mints, a penknife, a spare pair of reading spectacles, a spare pair of shoelaces, a cigarette lighter, a street map of Monte Carlo, another spare pair of reading spectacles (in case I lose my usual pair in which case there would be no spare pair), a disintegrating packet of cough sweets, some eye drops for use during the hayfever season, a button from a jacket I no longer own, six paperclips, a small stapler, a packet of spare staples, a pair of sunglasses, a map of London, a train time table for Eurostar, a brochure advertising a taxi service in Paris, a USB storage device, a jeweller's loupe, a comb with very few teeth, a spare bunch of keys for a building I sold several years ago, some bird food in a small plastic bag, a hand held fan for use on really hot days, a small telescope for looking at birds, a handful of euros, an MCC membership card, a small metal model of a Bugatti T50 motor car, a Filofax, a packet of extra paper for the Filofax, a Leatherman, a small wind up torch and two plastic shopping bags in case I buy anything I haven't already got. I threw out the comb, the cough sweets and the street map of Monte Carlo and put everything else back into the bag. To my dismay the bag does not seem a good deal lighter.

23

Every town in the Cotswolds seems to have at least one festival. Nowhere has as many as Cheltenham, which is the Queen of Festival Towns, but most self-respecting places have more than one. Even tiny villages have them. They seem to have taken over from fetes, revels and carnivals and they are nowhere near as much fun. Good old-fashioned fetes, carnivals and revels were all designed as celebrations; with stalls, side shows, Morris dancers, maypole dancing, proper old-fashioned skittles and a good many other traditional events. These are now considered unacceptable because they celebrate English tradition and now that England is no longer a country it is politically incorrect to remember, let alone celebrate, anything English. In contrast, modern festivals all seem to be terribly serious affairs. The people who organise them do so to make money, of course, and so they tend to be earnest and quite devoid of any real sense of fun. By far the worst are the literary festivals which are invariably so po-faced and dull that they would put most sensible people off books for life. I used to get invited to speak at them quite often but always made my excuses and did not go. These days I receive no invitations at all and this is a Good Thing because it means I don't have to waste time and energy thinking up excuses.

24

A good friend of mine, a successful author, has taken his e-Books off Amazon after discovering that the American site will not remove reviews which are factually inaccurate or just plain libellous. He insists that at Amazon the whole business of dealing with authors has been delegated to a 16-year-old assistant deputy intern on a work training scheme, complains that the emails he receives from Amazon are usually incomprehensible but invariably contaminated with a strong whiff of patronising superiority and says that if there was some way to rank Amazon he'd give them one star. And, probably, the bullet.

25

A young friend of Antoinette's told us that she has passed another GCSE examination. She takes one a year just for fun. She now has passes in Greek, Maths and Religious Studies. She says she's looking for a job as a bookkeeper to a Greek priest. She has diabetes mellitus and told us that her favourite flower is the sweet pea. When I asked her why, she just smiled. It was minutes before the penny dropped. Antoinette got it straight away.

26

An Australian came into a local pub where Antoinette and I were having a drink. There wasn't any doubt about his nationality. The size, the tan, the blond hair and the accent were enough; he didn't need a bush hat with corks dangling from the brim. He ordered a pint of lager.

'You should have a word with Sebastien,' the barman said, putting a glass under the appropriate tap. He struggled to get his tongue around the name. 'You two have a lot in common.'

The Australian looked at him and raised a blond eyebrow. 'Why's that?' he asked.

'He's from France,' exclaimed the barman, turning on the tap and starting to fill the glass.

'I'm from Australia,' said the Australian, unnecessarily.

'Of course you are,' said the barman, concentrating on his work.

'So what have we got in common?'

'You're both foreign, aren't you?' said the barman.

The Australian looked at me. I looked at him.

'So, what's wrong?' demanded the barman, looking at each of us in turn. 'What's wrong?'

27

There are now 260,000 people in the UK who suffer so badly from anxiety or depression or both that they are unable to attend work and are, therefore, claiming benefits every week. Very few of them are receiving medical treatment for their alleged condition. Mental health problems are now the commonest, and fastest rising, type of disability and have overtaken old, traditional excuses such as backache. Most of the 260,000 are malingerers but there is an easy way to sort them out from the genuinely ill. Anyone claiming unemployment benefits because of a mental disorder should be required to spend one day a week as a day patient in a mental hospital, where they could spend their time with people who have genuine mental illness – and see how they are treated. (Not much worse than the days of *One Flew over the Cuckoo's Nest*, I admit, but no better either.) One or two might actually feel guilty and realise that their malingering helps ensure that there isn't enough money available to provide decent health care for the mentally ill. Most of the rest would be shocked into accepting that they are, after all, fit for work and would rather go to the office or the factory than spend any more time in a mental hospital.

28

In Brazil, in March 2009, Prince Charles warned us all that the world had 'only 100 months to avert irretrievable climate and ecosystem collapse'. He is now, I fear, in real danger of looking a right royal plonker. The really embarrassing thing, however, is that Charles hasn't done anything at all to help deal with the problem except to fly hither and thither in an oil guzzling private plane, repeating the nonsense he has been told by pseudoscientists who wouldn't know a fact if it stood up and bit them on the nose. I'm sure he means well.

29

A woman in our village is called Ms Jacqui Dick. She is an accountant but very snobbish and is engaged to a man called Nigel Head. He is the second son of a not very wealthy farmer and he has a job in a bank so all is lost. Ms Dick has apparently always wanted to have a double barrelled name. She thinks that any children of their prospective union will travel further and higher in life if they have two surnames connected by a hyphen. She is a young woman of limited experience but great determination and the rumour in the village is that she is insisting that her name come first when their new surname is minted. Good luck to them, say I. I'm rooting for her and I hope she wins the argument. The world is a sad and dark place and we are all in need of light entertainment.

30

A friend of Antoinette's has a husband who is much older than her and she is forever worried that her husband will one day develop

Alzheimer's disease. Her father suffered from this most cruel of disorders and she lives in dread of the day when her husband might wake up in the middle of the night and demand to know what she is doing in his bed. And so, having read that it is possible to delay the onset of dementia by keeping the brain busy, Antoinette's friend decided that they would spend a few minutes each day learning to memorise cards. 'I'll do it with him,' she told Antoinette, 'so that we can share the experience. We can turn it into a bit of a fun.'

Today, in Cirencester, Antoinette saw her friend and asked her how the card memorising was going. The friend blushed deep red and looked very embarrassed. 'Oh, we gave that up,' she said, rather dismissively.

'Was there a problem?' asked Antoinette, solicitously.

'Not really,' replied her friend. 'Well, sort of. In a way. But not quite what I'd expected.'

Antoinette took her into the café above the antique arcade and bought her a cup of tea and a toasted teacake.

'I got an old pack of cards and two pieces of paper and two pencils and we sat down at the dining room table and I counted out seven cards,' she said. 'I laid them down in front of us and told Jeff (Jeff is her husband) that he had to try to remember the values and suits of the seven cards. He looked at them for about two seconds and then said he was ready and what did we do next. I told him that we had to memorise the cards and that when we'd done that I would turn them over and we both had to write down the values and suits of the seven cards. He said he knew what the cards were and that he was going to put the kettle on while I memorised them too.'

'Oh dear,' said Antoinette. 'And I suppose that when it came to it he couldn't remember any of the cards?'

'No, not at all,' said Antoinette's friend. 'I spent another three or four minutes memorising them and then...' She paused and hesitated.

'What happened?' asked Antoinette.

'I could only remember three of them.'

'And Jeff? How did he do?'

'Oh, he remembered all seven of them. He'd only looked at them for a couple of seconds but he knew them backwards and forwards. He didn't get any of them wrong.'

'Oh well,' said Antoinette. 'At least you know he hasn't got Alzheimer's.'

'No,' said her friend. 'But now I'm a bit worried about whether I've got it...'

31

The Royal Mail has such a bad reputation for 'losing' packets and parcels that almost everything worth more than ninepence now has to be signed for by the recipient (When referring to the Royal Mail, of course, the word 'lost' is a synonym for 'stolen'. The thieves have become blatant. Last week we received an envelope which had one end torn open so that the contents could be extracted. The thief, having stolen the valuable part of the missive, had then put the torn envelope back into the system and it had been duly delivered.) Postmen must spend half their lives standing on doorsteps while house owners who are tardy risers must struggle downstairs in nightwear and dressing gown. Those who go out to work must spend hours queuing at the local sorting office to pick up their parcels. Life would be so much easier for everyone if the Royal Mail could be persuaded to restore the simple, reasonably priced and reliable service which once made it the envy of the world.

November

1

We drove to Longleat and had an absolutely splendid day as paying guests of Lord Bath. Whenever we go there I am always impressed by the number of wonderful things there are to enjoy. I love driving through the parkland and watching the lions, the giraffes, the tigers, the rhinos and the wolves. They all have far more space here than animals could possibly have in a zoo and I really think that even the most virulent animal rights campaigners would be hard pushed to complain about the way the creatures are treated.

As we drove through the monkey enclosure I kept moving at 20 mph so that the monkeys wouldn't jump onto the car and tear off the windscreen wipers but, inevitably perhaps, the monkeys proved themselves to be far cleverer than I had anticipated. When they realised that we were travelling too fast for them to jump onto the car they took a short cut across the grass and then sat down on the road in front of us. Naturally, we had to stop. And then they had their fun tearing at the windscreen wipers. The score was clearly monkeys 1, Vernon 0.

What is the attraction of windscreen wipers, I wonder? Maybe the monkeys just enjoy being mischievous. Or maybe they are paid a retainer and banana bonuses by the windscreen wiper industry. Nothing in this world, or any other, would surprise me.

We spent the rest of the day wandering around and visiting all our favourite spots. In the butterfly house we spent ages watching the leafcutter ants. One was carrying his leaf in the wrong direction and only realised his mistake when he was stopped and told to turn round and go the other way. In the walled garden we examined the gravestones of dozens of family pets and admired a statue to the family's favourite dwarf entertainer. We admired the human sundial (if you stand in the correct spot your shadow will tell you the time) and enjoyed the hidden, tucked away exhibition of family bygones. I really do think that this is probably my favourite part of Longleat. A dozen huge glass display cases contain the family's Victorian and Edwardian gadgets, toys, sporting equipment, medicine boxes and heaven knows what else. Everything passes the William Morris test:

it is beautifully made and eminently functional. I suspect that most visitors miss this part of the estate but in its unique way it is one of the most revealing and entertaining museum exhibitions I've ever seen.

2

I am no Luddite. I had a mobile telephone when they looked like house bricks and I had a computer when the language was Basic and the printer was a noisy dot matrix creation. I have, however, resisted e-Books for a long while; not because I disapproved of the technology or because I really enjoy the sight, feel and smell of real books (which I do) but because, as an author and a publisher, I was convinced that e-Books would mark the end for professional authorship. (I was also convinced that they would kill off publishers, agents and booksellers but since I consider that all three are parasitic trades which we can well do without I wasn't too bothered by that.)

The main problem with e-Books is that they are distributed via the internet and internet users have, from the very beginning of time, been accustomed to getting everything for free; often regarding copyright as something 'evil', to be resisted. I worried about authors losing control of their copyright (or, to be more precise, I worried about me losing control of my copyright) because although musicians can make a living doing live gigs and selling T-shirts those really aren't options which are open to the average professional author. (Most musicians have little choice but to make their money by going on the road. The royalties paid by music providers on the internet are truly pathetic. A company called Spotify announced that it paid artists as little as $0.006 per song and Bette Midler revealed that nearly 4.2 million plays on the Pandora site earned her just $114.11 in royalties. Antoinette and I wouldn't eat very well if we had to rely on my flogging tickets to public readings or selling clothing with my picture emblazoned on the front.

But I have given in and, as I have already noted, I am having all my existing books converted to e-Books. Since Amazon pretty well has a monopoly on e-Books we're starting with them. I really cannot see any sort of future for traditional publishers and small publishers, who relied on selling most of their books through the mail, are doomed. If Royal Mail had set out to destroy small publishers they could not possibly have made a better job of it. I realised that we were in serious trouble when I took a sackful of book parcels to my local sorting office only to be told that because all the parcels were headed overseas they would have to be taken to a post office. And so we had to stand in line and, eventually, answer questions about the contents for every single parcel. Fifty times we were asked the same questions and fifty times we gave the same answers. The people in the queue behind were understandably cross and I think we were lucky to escape with our lives. After that Royal Mail put up its prices for books posted to addresses in the UK and the price rise, which was far above the rate of inflation, finally did us.

3

American readers are beginning to discover my seven Bilbury novels and one or two have written kind reviews and already given the first book the full five stars. Unfortunately, however, the first review which appeared is headlined 'Why are the other books in this series not available on Kindle!!!???' The review is unfortunate because all seven books are available and the reviewer clearly just couldn't find them. I wrote to Amazon asking if it might be possible to change the heading or, at least, to ask the reviewer to amend the heading. But they wrote back to tell me that the review does not break any or their guidelines (inaccuracy clearly doesn't matter) and so they cannot change it and will not inform the reader about his error. So, although all seven books are available the first in the series, *Bilbury Chronicles* now carries a permanent stigma: an inaccurate notice suggesting to readers that the other six books aren't available. Not surprisingly this review has brought sales to a halt. I'm not sure how this helps anyone. Maybe someone at Amazon needs to take a good, hard look at their policy about reviews. Worse still this policy makes life very easy for internet trolls – who have, I suspect, already done irreparable harm to the reputation of the internet as a whole.

4

Staff in NHS hospitals will no longer feed patients who are too frail or weak to feed themselves. The auxiliary staff aren't allowed to touch patients because that would upset the nurses and the nurses won't feed patients because they regard it as a demeaning activity. Just how or why it is demeaning to give food to a sick person who cannot feed themselves I cannot imagine but too many modern nurses seem to have been trained according to new principles of caring which seem to me to have more in common with Reinhard Heydrich than Florence Nightingale. Most spend their days filling in forms, messing around with computers and pretending to be terribly important. (Unison, a terrible trade union which seems to have completely lost the plot as far as hospitals and patient care are concerned recently complained that 45% of nursing staff have to look after eight or more patients during their shift! Writing in the 'Spectator', Jane Kelly pointed out that Florence Nightingale and 38 volunteers looked after 18,000 seriously injured men in the Crimea.)

Friends of ours who have a relative in an NHS hospital are so worried about the fact that nurses will no longer do any caring that they visit at every mealtime and feed their relative themselves. They take in their own food because the hospital food is patently unfit for human consumption. Even starving rats would probably turn their noses up at the unhealthy slop served in NHS hospitals these days.

When these relatives knew they would be unable to visit for a few days they dragged one of the official harridans away from her office and asked if it would be acceptable for them to send in a paid nurse three times a day. The hospital harridan was most indignant and stated categorically that this would not be allowed and that if a hired nurse arrived she would be sent away with rather more than a flea in her ear.

I understand the dilemma. When my mother was terminally ill in hospital she desperately needed regular physiotherapy treatment. The hospital physiotherapists could not or would not provide any more than a vague and rudimentary service and I asked if they would allow us to send in a private physiotherapist. The hospital staff were appalled and said that they definitely would not allow such a thing. They could have hardly been more shocked if I had suggested sending in a troupe of Black and White minstrels to give a matinee concert.

Our friends have solved their dilemma by hiring a nurse and telling her that when she visits the hospital she must do so in her own clothes and that if anyone asks who she is then she must tell them that she is a friend of the family.

5

The supermarket chain Tesco hasn't been doing well lately and so the boss has been sacked. His reward for not doing a terribly good job is a payoff package totalling just £21 million. The company could have hired 1,500 check-out assistants for a full year for that amount of money. When are companies going to stop handing out lorry loads of shareholders' cash to executives who didn't earn (or deserve) the mountains of money they've already received? Since everyone with a private pension or savings in an investment trust or unit trust probably owns shares in Tesco this sort of indecent and indefensible generosity hurts us all. The FTSE 100 index is now almost precisely where it was 15 years ago (meaning that shareholders have made no money at all) but during that time executives have awarded themselves huge pay rises. Fifteen years ago the average chief executive received 47 times as much as his or her average employee. Today, the average chief executive (and most of them are very average) receives 143 times as much as the average worker in the same business.

6

I boycott all companies which use pop up adverts to advertise their products. If everyone else did the same there wouldn't be any pop up ads. No company is going to continue with an advertising technique which doesn't work.

7

A dear friend of mine has just published his first book. He spent eighteen months writing it. The very first review he received on Amazon gave his book one star. 'This is not my cup of tea,' was the reviewer's only comment. The book will now die unless other readers give the book a fairer review. I wonder if reviewers who destroy a book so lightly realise just how much harm they are doing. And why do so many reviewers give a book a bad rating not because it is a 'bad' book but because it is 'not their cup of tea'? I have seen books and films destroyed by reviewers because the packaging wasn't considered satisfactory or because there was some problem with the delivery. And reviewers often criticise books because the book doesn't 'look right' on their phone, kindle or computer. Few realise that the whole process of converting a book into an e-Book is fraught with difficulty and that a book which appears perfect on one device will look distorted on another device.

8

I made the silly mistake of looking at my wikipaedia entry today. (I know that's not how it is spelt but it is how it would be spelt were it spelt properly). It's a nice piece of fiction but bears little resemblance to my life as I know it. One of the oddities of this wretched site is that living people (other than the person who set the whole thing up who is called Jimmy Wales and who has edited his owns wikipaedia entry) are not allowed to make any corrections and must wait until they are dead to correct inaccuracies. The spotty 14-year-olds who write and edit this stuff apparently believe they know my life better than I do. I never asked to have a damned wikipaedia entry and I wish to heaven I could remove the damned thing. Why do the teenage idiots who write and edit this appalling site tend to put in only the unpleasant or libellous references? One article to which they refer, and which appeared in the appalling *Independent on Sunday* newspaper, contained so much rubbish that the editor of the paper printed a letter of correction from me. The article, possibly written, in my opinion, at the behest of drug company lobbyists, caused so much embarrassment to the publisher at the time that it helped lead to the editor being fired. I noticed that the last person who corrected my entry on wikipaedia did it last Christmas Day. What sort of sad bastard spends his Christmas Day messing about with wikipaedia entries? The sort of sad, geeky bastard who doesn't have a life of his own so must mess with the lives of other people, that's who.

And who gave these cowardly, sad bastards (most of them male and most of them too young to go out of doors without their mums) the right to remain anonymous? Every time they write a word they should give their name, age, experience and reason for thinking they have the right to fuck with someone's life. It's the same with the sites which invite people to write reviews. Most allow reviewers to hide behind daft fake names. How many brain cells does it take to think up the name 'Buyer' and 'Book reader'? If I did reviews and wanted a fake name I'd at least have the imagination to call myself Adolf Hitler or Karl Marx.

The miserable, humourless, self-important little twats who review anonymously should have the courage to put their names on what they write. Then, on wikipaedia, we'd get things like this: 'My name is Christofer Moody and I am nine but nearly ten. I will be your judge and jury for today. I will mess with your life early today because I have to do sports at school today and I need to find my gym bag or Mummy will be cross. I hate sports because all the other boys and girls laugh at me and call me weedy so when they grow up I will mess with their lives too and then they'll see.'

Obnoxious little kids who've never even heard of *Lord of the Flies* rule the internet these days and, therefore, rule our bloody lives. This is no hyperbole. Astonishingly, 80% of five-year-olds own or have regular access to an internet device. They are growing up tweeting, blogging, posting embarrassing pictures of themselves – and writing reviews. They already assume that they are important people and that the world is interested in their eating habits, their bowel movements and their opinions on things about which they remain woefully ill-informed. They expect everything to be free and are perfectly happy to steal anything that isn't offered free.

Oh how I wish I could remove my name from all search engines and all websites – especially google and wikipaedia, two of the most evil and irresponsible and harmful companies on the planet.

Meanwhile, I've decided that I'm going to start suing some of these bastards. Get them and their mummys and daddys into court and watch the little toe rags squirm.

I feel better now.

The Princess put a reference to the letter of correction on my Wikipedia page. She didn't change anything else at all. Within hours the reference to the letter of correction had been removed. But the reference to the egregiously inaccurate 'hatchet job' article remained.

9

I'm thinking of writing a guide book for beggars. Indeed, I have high hopes that I might be able to persuade one of the newly formed universities to create a degree course based on my work. And, inevitably, there will be a massive opportunity to claim EU grants which will make us incomparably rich. The book and course will have to be called something other than 'begging' and I'm rather keen on the idea of labelling it *Spare Change Reclamation Processing* because this sounds very official and important. In Chapter One I will explain that since very few people in Britain speak English these days there really isn't any point in learning the local language. Indeed, I will recommend that beggars learn a more useful language – Polish or Romanian for example. In Chapter Two I will teach students that they must never say 'thank you' when given money since this suggests to the donor that the recipient is satisfied with what he has received. As a result the donor might give less the next time round. In Chapter Three I will explain that it is possible for a beggar to increase his or her income by the judicious use of a dog, baby or small child. Research has shown that a beggar can increase his income by 68% by having a dog by his side and by 92% if there is a baby or sad looking child in the vicinity. I will also explore and explain the advantages of dog or baby sharing.

10

I watched a *Big Issue* salesman retrieving copies of the magazine from a nearby waste bin. He is clearly going to recycle these unwanted magazines. This isn't the first time I've seen this happen. I suspect that many of these salespeople sell each magazine several times. I have for some years been convinced that the magazine's editors make sure that the publication contains absolutely nothing anyone would want to read with the intention of making it easier for salespeople to make extra money this way.

11

I discovered today that at one point in history Idi Amin and Carlos the Jackal were both in exile and were living in the same apartment building. Can you imagine that? 'What are your neighbours like?' 'Oh they're very nice. We've got Idi Amin just down the hall and Carlos lives in the flat above.' You wouldn't want to say anything if Carlos was making a lot of noise, would you?

We watched a film the other day about mad Ugandan President Idi Amin and the young, gauche, cocky Scottish doctor who became his personal physician and then his special adviser and then the lover of one of one of his wives. It was promoted as a sort of true story though we subsequently discovered that Amin didn't have a young white Scottish doctor at all – let alone one who became a special adviser. The writer made him up. Still, Idi Amin was real so that bit of the film was true. And Uganda exists, so that bit of the film was true too.

12

I bought two paperback books by American author Nelson DeMille today. One was printed in the year 2000 and the cover price is £9.99. The other was printed in 2010 and the cover price is £6.99. That's deflation in action. (For the record the two books are about the same length.) Things are going to get much, much worse for publishers. Many are now facing a massive pricing dilemma. The cost of actually making a book (printing, binding, etc.,) has soared in the last few years. But pricing a book has become a real dilemma. If you charge enough for a 'proper' book to make a profit then what do you charge for the e-Book? If you charge a pound or two less for the e-Book then everyone will complain that you're being greedy. There are no printing, binding or transporting costs with e-Books. And booksellers can't return unsold copies for pulping. But if you charge considerably less for the e-Book then the sales of 'proper' books will collapse at an even faster rate. It's a problem that is going to end in tears. I predict that within five years there will be very few old-fashioned publishers left. The commercial model just doesn't work anymore. And there will be very little demand for literary agents either. Most authors now realise that they can self-publish their own e-Books just as well as big publishers can do it – and they can keep all the money instead of having to make do with a tiny percentage. And if you're publishing your own books what on earth do you need an agent for? I suppose a few agents who specialise in selling foreign language and film rights will survive. But most literary agents will very soon have to start looking for proper jobs – and they're going to have to start working for a living. What a shame.

13

We drove to Tetbury for the day. It's only a few miles away for us and even closer for Prince Charles and his sister Princess Anne who both have splendid estates near to the village.

Tetbury originally made its money out of wool and although I can hardly remember it I know that an early commodity market was held under the Market Hall back as far as the 12th century. I wonder if there was any rigging or price fixing?

Tetbury has been well preserved and remains pretty well unspoilt. Many of the local shopkeepers have tales to tell of members of the Royal Family popping in for a bit of this or some of that. The lady who used to work in the local newsagent delighted in telling us about the times Princess Diana visited with young William and younger Harry.

Sadly, like most towns these days, the best shops are those run by charities although the Prince of Wales does have a splendid and appropriately up-market shop in the town. It's odd to think of the heir to the throne being a shopkeeper, though neither he nor Camilla seems to spend much time behind the counter.

We pottered around for a while, picking up old books and stuff we really didn't need and then had coffee in the Snooty Fox, an ancient Cotswold coaching inn opposite the Market Hall.

14

An 18-year-old entrepreneur has launched a 'hen hotel'. For a mere £1 per chicken per night he will look after pet chickens while their owners are away on holiday. So if you've got a dozen chickens and you go away for a fortnight the whole deal will cost just £168. I wonder who gets the eggs? Or do they just count as a perk.

15

I overheard a child talking to her mother about the death of a much loved pet. 'Well, at least no one can hurt him now,' said the child. 'But no one was trying to hurt him,' said the mother, puzzled. She did not understand that what had been the child's fear had now become her consolation.

16

A man is reported to have lent his wife to two friends who did not have sexual partners of their own. Greater love hath no man than he lay down his wife for his friends. I don't know whether much of this goes on in the Cotswolds but I do remember reading that in 1835 a local farmer called Joe Thompson sold his wife at Gloucester market. He sold her and a large dog as a job lot. The two had been married (the farmer and his wife, not the farmer and the dog) just three years earlier but things had not gone entirely according to hopes and expectations. 'She's been a born serpent,' said the farmer, who doesn't seem to have been a naturally skilled salesman, when talking to a small crowed of potential buyers. 'I took her for the good of my home, but she has become my tormentor. A domestic curse. A nightly invasion and a daily devil.' After these preliminaries the farmer really got going. 'Avoid troublesome women as you would a mad dog, a roaring lion, a loaded pistol, cholera, Mount Etna and any other pestilent thing in nature,' he warned what was by now a considerable crowd.

Rather surprisingly, considering this rather negative advertising, a city gent called Henry Mears paid 28 shillings for the wife and the dog and the deal was done. Maybe Mr Mears was swayed by the fact that Mr Thompson did say that his wife could both read and milk cows. I don't know whether she could do both these things at the same time but I rather doubt it since in those days milking was usually done in dingy barns and at times of day when the natural light was often very poor.

17

I've been involved in a correspondence with the BBC's Natural History Unit about a programme they broadcast about the Red Squirrels Trust Wales. The programme praised the Trust for their efforts in trying to promote and expand the population of red squirrels but, as usual, the BBC failed to tell the whole story. The Red Squirrels Trust Wales, which is funded by the lottery, boasts that it boosts tourism to Wales by promoting the red squirrel. 'Red Squirrels Boost Tourism' they claim.

And it is the touristy attraction of the red ones that is probably the only significant difference between red squirrels and grey squirrels. The bottom line is that although the red probably looks cuddlier, and employs excellent public relations people, both colours of squirrel damage trees. Indeed, in the past the red squirrel was slaughtered in vast numbers by people (mainly in Scotland) who believed it damaged forests. It was this slaughtering which led to the downturn in the number of red squirrels. Today, ironically, there are six red squirrel charities in the UK and it's not difficult to argue that six is at least five more than are necessary. I very much doubt if the

Government (which controls the Charities Commission) would allow anyone to found a grey squirrel charity (although I intend to try).

What the BBC forgot to tell its viewers was that as part of its plan to promote the red squirrel (and help local businesses) the Red Squirrels Trust Wales is busy killing grey squirrels. The 'wrong' coloured squirrels are caught in traps and 'allowed to venture out from the wire trap into sacking'.

What happens then?

'The squirrel is then moved into a corner of the sack and with the head positioned carefully within the corner, killed humanely by a single blow to the back of the head.'

This is conservation as practised by the Red Squirrels Trust Wales, supported by the Lottery and promoted by the BBC Natural History Unit.

It's superficial and, in a squirrelly sort of way, definitely racist.

When I wrote to the BBC to complain about their promotion of such a thuggish organisation someone called James Smith, the series producer for Springwatch, replied.

'We did mention in the film that the grey squirrels had been removed from Anglesey to enable the reintroduction of the reds to take place, although we did not go into the specifics about how this was achieved.'

I wrote back suggesting that the BBC owed its viewers an apology. 'I doubt if many of your viewers will think kindly of an organisation which puts squirrels into a sack and then kills them by bashing in their heads,' I wrote. I also pointed out that the fact is that red squirrels do just as much damage as grey squirrels and are not a threatened species.

But the BBC refuses to acknowledge a huge blunder. Three loud boos for the once respected (and once respectable) BBC Natural History Unit.

18

One of the local villages always holds its carnival later in the year than all the others. They are, I suspect, hoping that their unseasonal timing will help them stand out from the crowd. Antoinette and I attended and were very impressed. For a tiny village the locals always put on a good show and make a great effort. There were only six floats in the carnival procession (all consisting of very heavily decorated tractors and trailers) so the organisers carefully ensured that there were large gaps between the floats. They also sent the whole procession round the village three times guessing, quite rightly, that this would confuse those watching, and convince at least some of them that the procession was longer than it was. As they passed the field where they had gathered before the procession started, each float made some changes to its appearance to ensure that the spectators were confused still further. The five mermaids who had been on the Disneyland float changed places with the six Jack the Rippers who had been on the float dedicated to crime and criminals and the local beauty queen, who had been sitting on a magnificent throne on the Father Christmas float, moved over to a less impressive dining chair on the Glorious England float which she shared with the local band of Morris dancers.

The local squad of majorettes and flag twirlers (average age a hopeful 39 and average weight an equally hopeful 12 stones) marched at the front of the procession and impressed everyone with their skill, daring and courage. They wore red fishnet tights bought from a sex shop in Gloucester. It is one of the problems of life that the hourglass figure is difficult to attain. To reach and maintain the essence of female loveliness a woman must eat. Indeed, she needs a hearty appetite since the curves of the breasts and buttocks are comprised of fat not muscle. But there remains always the problem of the bit in the middle, to which the only honest answer is corsetry, and so the majorettes all wore costumes made primarily out of discarded corselettes which had been dyed red.

The majorettes were followed by four trumpeters, two trombonists and three drummers who described themselves as the district's leading brass band (it is, in truth, the only brass band for quite a way in any direction but at times like this one should be generous and not picky). They played a medley of tunes which would have doubtless been recognisable if they had been identifiable. However, the band made up in volume for what they perhaps lacked in skill.

After the carnival had finished there were donkey rides and a pig roast (fortunately, they got this the right way round and didn't end up with pig rides and a donkey roast) and three farmers organised a display of their farm equipment.

Antoinette and I contented ourselves with several large glasses of the vicar's traditional, and justly famous, mulled wine.

It was a chilly evening and, not for the first time, there were some who felt that organising a carnival at this time of the year might not be the wisest way to attract visitors.

19

We're in Paris and I've been reading *Who the Devil Made It?* by Peter Bogdanovitch. Antoinette bought it for me because she knows how much I enjoy Bogdanovitch's books. This one, which is over 800 pages long and weighs about as much as Alfred Hitchcock after a large meal, contains interviews with 16 legendary film directors – including some of the very earliest filmmakers.

In one of Bogdanovitch's books I read a wonderful story about Clint Eastwood. I can't remember the book, the film, or the director, but at one point, early in a film he is making, Eastwood is expected to shoot one of the bad guys. And he is supposed to do so effortlessly and quickly.

Just before they shot the scene, Eastwood asked the director if they shouldn't include a scene to establish that his character was fast with a gun. The director said that this wasn't necessary. 'They know you're fast, Clint,' he apparently responded. I thought this wonderfully telling. When making movies with big stars, directors always have to remember the star's film reputation. Cary Grant never died and always had to get the girl. John Wayne was often gruff and bad-tempered but invariably a good guy at heart; decent and honourable. Dean Martin was always a drinker. Eastwood was always quick with a gun.

The irony is that in reality, Eastwood was not, apparently, all that quick a draw. When Eastwood and the magnificent Lee van Cleef were making the classic film *A Few Dollars More*, the crew organised a quick draw contest between the two. And Lee van Cleef won the competition.

Film buffs who have studied movies frame by frame reckon, however, that Lee van Cleef wasn't the fastest of them all. That honour apparently (and rather surprisingly) goes to Glenn Ford.

I don't think big John Wayne came anywhere on the list. But then his characters often used a rifle rather than a handgun.

20

I had to ring Lloyds Bank today to check on something in my account. Naturally, before anyone was prepared to tell me anything I had to take a special Lloyds Bank examination on my account. The first question was: 'How much was paid into your account three days ago?' I explained that I could not possibly answer that question since I now only receive statements when the moon is green and is in one of its rare Sage Derby phases. I also pointed out that a couple of dozen foreign publishers and various odd organisations are kind enough to put small sums of money into my account at all sorts of strange and unpredictable times. The woman at the other end of the phone line told me sternly that Lloyds Bank expects its customers to know how much has gone into or out of their account on any given day. I asked her how they are supposed to know this but she couldn't answer that.

She then said that she would ask me two more questions.

She wanted to know how much had recently been withdrawn from the hole in the wall machine and the size of the overdraft on the account. I got the first question correct but failed the second question when I told her that I did not have an overdraft facility. Having told me that I had failed she refused to tell me anything about my account, so once again I could not do anything with my own money. I didn't know whether to cry or scream so I screamed. I have no doubt I will be disciplined for this.

I discovered later that someone at Lloyds has, for reasons best known to him or herself given me a £100 overdraft facility. I don't remember anyone asking me whether I wanted this or telling me that it been done.

21

Every time the police raid a celebrity's home they somehow manage to leak it to the press before they leap into their cars. When one recent raid took place the police admitted afterwards that they had 'worked with the BBC' in advance of the raid and that as a result the BBC had a news crew at the property and an expensive licence payer funded helicopter hovering overhead.

The result is that reputations are ruined even if no evidence turns up, no one is charged and there is no trial.

It has been proved beyond doubt that people believe headlines and rarely bother with the small print. If people see a headline which says 'Nick Clegg is an Alien' they will believe that Nick Clegg is an alien even if there is absolutely no evidence. Moreover, if the headline is 'Nick Clegg denies that he is an Alien' those who see the headline will still believe that he is an alien. (I am not, of course, suggesting that Nick Clegg is or is not an alien. I have not been made privy to such knowledge.)

When the police announce that someone is being investigated they destroy that individual's reputation – whether the individual is guilty or innocent. Is that really what is meant these days by British justice?

I look forward to the day when a rich celebrity sues the police for leaking information to the press. I seem to remember that a number of journalists were arrested for associating too closely with police officers. Doesn't the law work the other way round?

22

I am getting increasingly annoyed by film companies who cram advert after advert onto their DVDs, and then make it difficult or impossible to skim through them to reach the feature. It is bad enough being treated as a thief and hectored by advertisements warning me of the terrible things which will befall me if I purchase a counterfeit tape or feel the urge to show what I have purchased to a bunch of lonely men on an oil rig or a group of sick children in a hospital ward. But the advertisements for the film maker's other products have been a real nuisance. Some DVDs even contain advertisements for stuff such as chocolate, anti-personnel hand grenades and gambling holidays in Las Vegas. Three times this week we have sat down to watch a film and then spent fifteen to twenty minutes trying to get to the point where we can press 'play'. Last night we took so long to find our way through the mass of warnings, threats, promotions and advertisements that we decided we needed to put on the kettle and make a cup of tea. So by the time we finally did sit down to watch the film we'd planned to watch it was too late. Oh, how I miss the good old days of video tape. Life was so much easier then.

23

The internet has damaged critical writing permanently. The non-fiction books I have written have always been intended to challenge assumptions and expose inaccuracies and lies. Thirty years ago it was possible to write books like this because those whose vested interests were being damaged could not easily destroy a book's sales. A drug company might be able to arrange for a bad review in one newspaper, or bribe an interviewer to write a dishonest and unflattering profile in another (both these things have happened to me) but not even a large, powerful multinational newspaper could control everything. A bad review in one newspaper might dent the sales of a book but it wouldn't kill the book completely. Things are very different now. One troll can kill a book stone dead in five minutes. All he or she has to do is to write bad, one star reviews on all the major outlets – but especially Amazon. I very much doubt if my books *The Medicine Men*, *Paper Doctors*, *The Health Scandal* and *Betrayal of Trust* would find a publisher today. Drug companies, and the medical establishment will, of course, find that a cheering thought. These days, reviewers don't even have to read the books they destroy. One troll, who did his best to destroy my book *Oil Apocalypse*, seemed proud of the fact that he hadn't read a word of the book, though he had seen an advertisement for it. (It is, I suppose, possible that his determination to destroy my book might have been linked to the fact that he'd written a book on the same subject and was perhaps upset that his book wasn't selling as well.) And so authors and publishers are no longer writing or publishing books which offer strong, original views or which challenge popular assumptions. My book on vaccines and vaccination (*Anyone Who Tells Vaccines Are Safe and Effective is Lying*) was hammered in the UK and the USA the moment it appeared on Amazon. I had spent years researching the book and many months writing it. The anonymous critics didn't bother to try to explain why they disapproved of the book – they just gave it one star and made sure it would never have a chance. I suspect that they were drug company employees – hired to protect industry profits. It is commercially far too dangerous to spend years researching and writing a complex book, and finding a way through libel laws and other legislation, if you know that the day the book appears a lobbyist for the industry or cause you have attacked will hire someone to write scurrilous or spiteful remarks on half a dozen websites and so wreck the book before its life begins. It's so much easier to add another diet book to the mass already available.

24

Amazon has been taking 30% tax from my earnings in America and I had to obtain a special code number from that country's Internal Revenue Service so that I could apply for exemption from this taxation. A very helpful lady helped me with the form and when I thanked her and told her that it had been much easier than I had expected she burst into peals of laughter. I then used my new special number on a tax form issued on the Amazon site for e-Book authors. I managed to fill in the form but I confess that I didn't understand most of it. I'm now not sure whether I have managed to make myself exempt from American taxes, joined the French Foreign Legion or bought a pandamonium. No doubt time will tell. (A pandamonium, by the way, is a little known musical instrument, usually played by a black and white bear.)

25

A reader has written to me asking how often I 'trade' shares. The answer is that I never trade shares. I buy investments that I hope I can hold for years. I buy and sell quite infrequently and I am probably one of the least popular customers of the brokers I use. I always think an investor is probably in trouble if he gets a Christmas card from his broker. Buying and selling shares costs a good deal of money for, in addition to the trading costs, and the spread between the buy and sell prices, there are taxes to be paid. A man I know who lives in Monaco is constantly buying and selling shares. Indeed, he writes a successful newsletter in which he encourages his readers to buy and sell shares on a daily basis. He does OK (though I am pretty certain he doesn't do anywhere near as well as he likes to pretend) but he only gets away with constant trading because he doesn't pay any taxes when he buys or sells. The people who run Personal Assets, one of the most successful investment trusts in Britain, change the trust's portfolio so infrequently that I suspect they have to look up the phone number for the company's broker whenever they want to do a deal.

26

A few weeks ago Antoinette and I signed up as executive producers for the village drama group's latest extravaganza. We don't have to do any 'producing', of course. Our titles are purely honorary and, as with the movies, we 'bought' them; acquiring them in return for donations of £50 each towards the cost of costumes and scenery. I suspect you have to stump up a little more than £50 to be named as an executive producer on the latest Tom Cruise epic but the principle is the same. We get our names on the programme and as long as we don't offer too much advice we are entitled to attend all cast meetings, rehearsals and post-production parties. A grand outlay of £100 between us is a small price to pay for the privilege of being allowed to sit at the back of the village hall during rehearsals. And, of course, we had tickets for tonight's grand opening.

The play the group chose to perform is *Macbeth*. Only the prompter and assistant wardrobe mistress (the same person) wanted to do *Macbeth*. The director and cast were split. Half wanted to do *Charley's Aunt* and half wanted to do *The Importance of Being Earnest*. Because the half wanting *Charley's Aunt* wouldn't agree to do *The Importance of Being Earnest* and the half wanting to do *The Importance of Being Earnest* wouldn't agree to do *Charley's Aunt* and some idiot had introduced a voting system based on a version of preferential voting devised by the prompter's husband they ended up with *Macbeth*.

Here's a list of our top ten favourite things to have happened so far.

1. The actress playing Lady Macbeth (an assistant in a branch of Boots who is also a keen first aider and a perfect example of the over-confident amateur who can turn a live patient into a corpse faster than a doctor can say 'For God's sake don't...') refused to go on stage for her dress rehearsal because she didn't like the dress she was expected to wear. She complained that it was black, shapeless and unfashionable and refused to go on until the wardrobe mistress had pinned up the dress to just above her knees and lowered the neckline to show an indecent amount of cleavage.

2. On dress rehearsal night no one could find any fake blood for the scene where Macbeth murders King Duncan and so the actor playing Macbeth, who thinks he looks like the late Bob Hoskins but doesn't

because he is fatter, taller and always looks puzzled, as though not quite sure where he is or why he is there, hit the actor playing Duncan on the nose thus producing a seemingly unstoppable supply of real blood. The fun really started when one of the three witches (a Health and Safety officer at the local council, and if ever anyone suited the part she was playing then she clearly does) demanded that the hall be cleared because of the possible AIDS risk associated with the presence of blood on scenery and costumes. The actor playing Duncan (who is, in real life, an estate agent) objected strongly to this and said something about not being a 'bleeding poofter'. This upset the stage manager, who does something with computers. He is a homosexual and he lives with the actor who is playing the ghost of Banquo, who works in tree preservation and who is, of course, also a homosexual. The rehearsal ended early with everyone going home, most of them sulking.

3. One of the three witches, a woman who has been a committed and enthusiastic vegetarian for nearly two months, insisted that the script be changed to accommodate her views. It took an hour and three quarters for the cast to agree on the necessary changes. I was struggling so hard to stifle my laughter that I missed most of the changes but I do remember that 'tongue of dog' became 'ear of corn', 'eye of newt' became 'eye of black pea' and 'sow's blood' was changed to 'milk of soya bean'. No one offered to consult the playwright about any of these changes.

4. During one of the early rehearsals, we were sitting in the auditorium together with the actor who is playing Malcolm (Malcolm is a taxi driver when he isn't a thespian) when he leant across and whispered to us: 'You'll like this bit. This is where I come in. I'm really good.' He then sat back and waited for his own entrance. It wasn't until Antoinette quietly explained to him that the show was live and that he wasn't watching a DVD that he got up, leapt up onto the stage and made his entrance from an unusual direction. The taxi driver, who has a sharp and savage wit, was a constant source of entertainment. During rehearsals one evening he had a row with one of the witches. He complained that she had left the village hall's solitary lavatory seat down. 'It was,' he said, 'a deliberate act of typically aggressive matriarchal behaviour.' I can't possibly write down her reply.

5. When the curtain went up this evening there was quite a commotion at the back of the hall when a local quantity surveyor noticed that his living room curtains (which his wife had told him had been taken to the dry cleaners) were being used as a backdrop. The actresses playing two noblemen called Ross and Lennox (the play contains very few parts for women) had to go outside through the fire door, run round to the back of the hall and drag the surveyor outside. They then had to threaten him with a breach of the peace charge (they are both policewomen in real life) before they could persuade him to go home.

6. During the dress rehearsal the director (who is a vet who specialises in treating large animals because he can't stand the sort of people who own dogs and cats) had a meltdown. I can't remember everything he said but I did manage to write down this gem: 'I don't care who says the lines, or even in what order, but it would be nice if someone said most of them before the curtain fell.' His wife, a GP who was there to provide moral support, had to take him home and sedate him. He would, I suspect, have been distraught to know that the rest of the dress rehearsal went smoothly without him.

7. At some point between the dress rehearsal and tonight's first night someone decided that it would be a good idea if the witches could sit around a real fire. Whoever had this bright idea lit the fire in a large iron wok and obviously assumed that the risk of the fire spreading would be minimal. Unfortunately, the second witch leant a little too close to the fire when dropping in the liquorice allsorts which had somehow become part of the recipe though to be honest I don't remember Shakespeare saying anything about liquorice allsorts. It was one of the other witches, the third witch, who noticed that the second witch's wig had caught fire and it was generally agreed that the problem could have been dealt with if the second witch had simply been told to rip the wig off her head. The three witches complained that the deputy assistant stage manager (the 18-year-old son of the prompter, who is, coincidentally of course, studying 'Macbeth' at school) was a little over zealous in throwing a bucket of water over them all.

8. Five minutes before the start of tonight's performance the actor playing Macbeth (the man who thinks he looks like Bob Hoskins but doesn't, who is a school master who teachers maths and religious knowledge to young hooligans who probably don't have any interest

in either) decided that he needed to wear his spectacles while on stage. Everyone pleaded with him not to do this but he was adamant, claiming that he was worried that if he didn't he might bump into the props or knock down some scenery. The director said he'd rather he bumped into the props and knocked down the scenery but his words fell on stony ground. The spectacles are horn rimmed.

9. The actor playing Macduff, (a man who owns a shop selling cushions and who wears wide, flowered kipper ties, the ones that were made by Mr Fish of Carnaby Street and were popular in the 1960s) had three pints of beer before the performance in order to give him courage. He looks like Russell Brand, the self-important drug addict who thinks he is an entertainer but who is about as funny as diarrhoea on a long train journey. Unfortunately, the three pints of beer meant that he had to leave the stage twice in order to visit the loo at the back of the hall. During his lengthy absences the three witches, still soaked, came on stage and filled in by singing an impromptu version of *Where Did Our Love Go?*, the song made famous by the Supremes. The fact that all three of them knew the words suggested that this was not, perhaps, quite the impromptu performance it appeared to be.

10. The actress who played Lady Macbeth dived into her death scene with great relish. She collapsed right at the front of the stage and draped herself over a chair. Unfortunately, because she had by this time shortened her dress another foot or so, it was immediately clear to the entire audience that she was not wearing any underwear. Several parents immediately stood up and dragged their children out of the hall. They made no attempt to do this quietly. The actress has something of a reputation for exhibitionism, and has twice before suffered serious costume malfunctions (once while playing a nun in the *Sound of Music*).

All things considered, Antoinette and I consider our first experience as producers to have been highly successful. We will certainly be prepared to cough up our £50's for the next production. We were particularly pleased to discover that, like most of the people who describe themselves as 'producers', we didn't actually have to do anything at all. Local drama society productions are, I believe, the only place where it is possible to see genuinely impromptu performances these days. Even on the last night of a run the actors will still be making stuff up as they go along.

In the old days it used to be possible to hear proper repartee when politicians were on the stump, dealing with hecklers. These days any member of a political audience who dares to open his mouth will be leapt on by a bunch of ugly bouncers and dragged outside. He will probably be beaten up and almost certainly be arrested for speaking without a licence. And there is no such thing as an ad lib on television. I was not surprised to discover recently that the bon mots uttered by the three men in cars on Top Gear are carefully scripted beforehand. Even when they're driving through the jungle there is, so I'm told, a script girl standing somewhere out of shot, making sure that the 'boys' say just what they're supposed to say.

Our actors and actresses are keeping the art of the ad lib alive and very well.

27

We passed by Dr Jenner's house in Berkeley (it's not far from Berkeley Castle which has a marvellous butterfly house) but it was (like the Castle and its magnificent butterfly house) closed. Much of Gloucestershire closes during the lengthy off season.

Dear old Dr Jenner is widely and rightly considered to be a medical hero for the experiments he conducted on vaccination, though these days any doctor who did what he did would be locked up, struck off the medical register and viciously attacked in *The Guardian* and *The Sun*.

The proponents of vaccination regard Dr Jenner as a hero but, as usual, they overlook the salient facts. The truth is that things did not go quite as smoothly as the vaccine supporters would have us believe.

Jenner tried out the first smallpox vaccine on his own 10-month-old son but tragically the boy remained mentally retarded until his death at the age of 21. Jenner wisely refused to have his second son vaccinated.

Oddly enough the doctors, health visitors and other vaccine industry pimps who talk so knowledgably and admiringly about Jenner and his work never seem to know any of this.

England's last court jester, Dicky Pearce, is buried in Berkeley churchyard. He died while halfway through a performance and

Jonathan Swift, of Gulliver's Travels fame, wrote this rather miserable inscription for the poor little devil's tomb:

Here lies the Earl of Suffolk's fool,
Men called him Dicky Pearce,
His folly served to make folks laugh
When wit and mirth were scarce.
Poor Dick alas is dead and gone
What signifies to cry?
Dickys enough are still to come
To laugh at by and by.

28

An Irish reader tells me that plans for Country and Western singer Garth Brooks to hold a series of five concerts at Croke Park in Dublin have been abandoned. Dublin City Council decreed that they would only allow concerts on three days so two of the concerts would have to be held as matinees. Brooks rightly and sensibly cancelled the whole lot rather than do two daytime gigs. A staggering 400,000 people had bought tickets and were planning to travel to Dublin for the concerts but the council refused to give permission because locals had reportedly complained about the possible noise and disruption. The fiasco is reported to have cost the teetering Irish economy around £12 million. (There was actually some confusion about how many people had complained. Indeed, there were suggestions that fake objections had been made, or that one person had complained more than once, or that absolutely no one had complained but that someone in a cheap suit was worried that there might be complaints.)

The point surely is that if you buy a house close to an absolutely enormous stadium it might be reasonable to expect that there will be shows and performances and occasional noise and disruption. The people living close enough to be disrupted will have paid less for their homes because of that risk of disruption.

The same thing happens all the time and it is becoming a nightmare for the owners of sporting and entertainment venues. Motor racing circuits which have held races for decades are being told by local councils that they can only allow racing on a few days a year lest residents, who have just moved into the area, be annoyed. It seems to me that if you buy a house within sound of Silverstone or

Brands Hatch or Goodwood or any other racing circuit then you know what you're buying into and if you don't like the noise of racing cars you should buy an undoubtedly more expensive house somewhere else.

I wrote some time ago about a vicar who received a warning visit from a council officer after a woman who had just moved into her home moaned about the noise of the church bells. The church had been ringing bells for 400 years.

29

I made two cups of coffee today. I was quite pleased with this example of domestication and handed Antoinette a cup with a certain amount of pride. She took a sip, grimaced and looked at me.

'What did you make this with?' she asked gently, clearly puzzled.

I picked up the jar and showed her.

'That's a powder for making gravy,' she told me with some sadness. She pointed to the label which said Bisto. 'I like gravy,' she said quickly, reassuringly. She paused. 'But I was sort of hoping for coffee. Expecting coffee.'

I examined the jar and peered through the glass at the contents. 'The jar looks like the coffee jar,' I explained. I apologised.

'I suppose, if I'm honest, a cup of Bisto was just rather a surprise,' said Antoinette, kindly.

30

A reader sent me a link to an internet program on which, it is claimed, three experts discuss whether it is safe to eat genetically modified food. My reader asked for my views. Simple. There are no experts because no-one has done any research on whether genetically modified food is safe or not. So anyone with an opinion on the subject is merely guessing.

December

1

According to *Fortune* magazine a chemotherapy drug called Yervoy costs $120,000 for four injections. The company which makes the drug, Bristol, defends this extraordinary price by claiming that it 'reflects the survival benefit'. Can we assume from this that drug companies are now going to price their drugs according to whether or not they work? If the drug works well then it will cost a good deal of money and only very rich people will be able to afford it. If the drug is no bloody use at all then it will be very cheap and everyone, even poor people who don't deserve to be kept alive, will be able to afford it.

2

'There's a drink in it for you,' one of our neighbours told a workman who had been asked to do some extra work. The workman stayed for three hours, completed the task and then reported to our neighbour to collect his reward. He was not well pleased when he was handed a two pound coin. 'That'll buy you a pint at the supermarket or half a pint at the pub,' he was told.

The neighbour concerned, who does something unspeakable in London and travels there every day by train, is notable for having a very small, snub nose and every time I see him I wonder if he knows that the French author François Rabelais once claimed that the length of a man's nose depends upon the softness of the nurse's breast. He claimed that if a child's nurse has breasts like a feather pillow then the child's nose will grow and keep growing whereas a child fed by a small-breasted, hard-bodied woman will have a snub nose. I must mention this to our neighbour sometime and ask if he was breast fed and if so whether he can remember the size of the feeder's bosom.

The neighbour's wife, is a callipygian humbug with such an extensive supply of varicose veins that if she wanted to cover them up she would need 50 square yards of aluminium siding. She collects tasteless and worthless knickknacks which she stores in glass cabinets and dresses in clothes made out of a synthetic material which would probably be untouched by a nuclear blast and would doubtless remain uncreased if left crunched up in a ball for a century. She is the spitting image of a British politician called Vince Cable. I sometimes think that they might perhaps be the same person. I've certainly never seen them standing side by side. She paints terrible water colours and boasts of having had an exhibition in Paris though I have been told that the exhibition consisted of her hanging a few daubs from the railings around the Luxembourg Gardens.

I do hope she doesn't ever read this diary. Not that there's much risk. I don't think reading is her strong suit.

3

A rather nasty looking thug who threw a pensioner over a fence has been fined. No prison. No need for an economy sized tube of KY jelly, or a year's supply of soap on a rope. This is, I fear, typical of the way old people are treated in our society. Doctors and nurses working in the NHS are given carte blanche to kill old people (through a form of legalised murder known as the Liverpool Care Pathway) and it seems that bullies of all descriptions are now allowed to throw old folk over fences just as if they were black sacks full of unsorted rubbish.

The truth is that you can now do pretty much what you like with an old person and the State will quietly look the other way. The NHS has become a National Homicide Service; keeping down the State's pension liabilities by killing off pensioners.

At least we oldies know where we stand.

We are the new second class citizens.

But there is an upside.

I am making a list of people over the age of 65 whom I dislike, and I will be throwing them over fences quite soon. I will be allowed to throw Gordon Brown over a fence in just two years when he is 65. Come to think of it we could all throw Gordon Brown over fences. But let's not stick at ordinary garden fences. Let's take him to Aintree and throw him over the Grand National fences. Hundreds or maybe thousands of people whose lives were ruined by Brown's absurd economic policies could line up at all the big famous fences, Becher's Brook, the Foinavon fence, the Chair and all the rest of them, ready to toss Gordon the Moron over the spruce. Oh boy this is going to be fun. And Tony Blair will be 65 in 2018. I can hardly wait.

Sometimes the only way to deal with bad news is to look at it from a slightly unexpected angle.

4

Whenever we leave our home in the Cotswolds (which, I confess, we do with increasing reluctance unless we are heading for Paris) we pass a modern pink bungalow with a dry stone wall outside it. This is not, of course, intrinsically unusual. Just about every house in the Cotswolds has at least one dry stone wall. We have at least a mile of the stuff ourselves. What makes this particular wall different is that the owner of the house, a retired NHS administrator, has, for a year or so, been steadily rebuilding his wall himself. In heat, rain, sleet and snow he has been out there picking out stones for size and colour, and then fitting and adjusting them with all the care and deliberation of a Savile Row tailor measuring a bad-tempered, gun-toting client from the Levant for a silk suit.

The stone wall man is a miserable, difficult bastard who has, over the years, annoyed us a good deal. He has, for example, often taken delight in telling delivery drivers not to try driving their van down the lane to our house. He has wrongly told them that the lane is too narrow and that they will get stuck.

He is a very pedantic, literal minded man. A few years ago he was wrongly told that he was dying and the doctor advised him that he should put his affairs in order. I am reliably informed that he took this literally and spent an entire weekend writing down the names of all his past girlfriends and trying to make sure that he put them all in the correct order. He apparently caused considerable annoyance by telephoning former mistresses and asking them if they could remember the precise dates during which their relationships existed. I have no idea why he thought anyone would be interested in such a record of his amatory experiences but it is my experience that people will often do precisely what the doctor tells them to do, however daft it may later appear to be. The diagnosis was wrong, of course but by the time it was clear that he wasn't going to die the full list had been handed to the doctor's receptionist without benefit of an envelope. A district nurse, a clerk at a local bank and the vicar's wife had all

311

appeared on the list though many of those named afterwards insisted that the man's memory had been faulty.

The wall was eventually finished about two weeks ago and Antoinette and I had mixed feelings about this. We were pleased that the objectionable fellow would not be standing in the lane telling delivery drivers to reverse back up the lane, but we were disappointed that we would not see him out there in the rain weighing up the pros and cons of two pieces of dry stone walling material. On balance it was disappointment that was the greater and so we were not ill-pleased to see today that a vehicle of some kind had collided with the carefully reconstructed wall and had demolished most of it. We now look forward to being able to watch the retired administrator rebuilding his wall yet again. With any luck at all we will have a cold and wet winter. Maybe there will be a flurry or two of snow. It is the small delights which make life such fun.

5

I was sitting in the conservatory today, trying to decide whether to go out and do some tidying up in the garden or to work on my new book, when I realised that I had been sitting there so long that it was too dark to go out and too late to start work. Cats do this all the time. They sit and think through their options and then decide that they have spent so much time contemplating the options that the best plan is to do nothing. I call this 'sophisticated prevarication' and I suspect that it is more popular than anyone imagines.

W.H. Davies, the author of *Supertramp* and a one time resident in nearby Nailsworth, once wrote: 'What is this life if, full of care, we have no time to stand and stare?' and I think that I would like to amend the thought.

Sitting and staring is far better than standing and staring.

I would do some research into the whole business of doing nothing if I could be bothered.

6

A lovely couple we know, Charles and Hermione Wilberforce, had a bizarre misunderstanding this week.

He fetches the newspaper every morning, and although the newsagent is less than half a mile away from their home it invariably takes him half an hour or so.

'Why does it take so long?' Hermione asked him one day.

'The old guy who runs the shop likes to chat,' explained Charles.

And it was left at that until one day Charles had a rather bad cold and Hermione told him to stay in the house. 'I'll go and fetch the paper,' she told him. 'I don't want that cold getting worse. And if you go into the shop and cough over that old man he'll probably get it too.'

When she came back from the shop Hermione was in a very bad mood. It took Charles an hour to find out what had annoyed her.

'I thought you said you chatted to an old man in the shop!' she protested.

'I do!' he insisted.

'Well, the assistant who served me this morning wasn't old and he wasn't a man. He was about 19, blonde and very busty.'

For several days the atmosphere in the house was, to say the least, rather frosty. Hermione wouldn't even go back to the shop again to fetch a paper.

However, when Charles was feeling better he decided that he missed his morning walk and his daily paper and he announced that he felt fit enough to walk to the shop again. But he insisted that his wife accompany him.

'I'm going to get to the bottom of this business,' he told her.

Reluctantly Hermione agreed to go along.

And she was genuinely and pleasantly surprised when they found that the person behind the counter was, as Charles had described, an elderly gentleman. A few moments of gentle conversation confirmed that the old man, who owned the shop, had been ill (he too had had a bad cold) and that his granddaughter had been standing in for him for a few days.

'She was very good for business,' he told them, surprised.

'So I expect she'll be working here again,' said Hermione, setting out on a fishing expedition.

'Oh no, I'm afraid not,' said the old man. He seemed rather sad but very proud. 'She's in a rock band with three other girls. They call themselves 'Rockers with Knockers' and they're just starting a tour of the pubs and clubs up north.

'Oh, that's nice,' said Hermione, genuinely delighted. 'I am pleased for her.'

She didn't apologise but she made Charles a huge plateful of cauliflower cheese that evening.

She knows it's his favourite meal.

7

One of our squirrels was sitting on the shed roof when a stream of liquid suddenly appeared from beneath him.

'Oh look,' said Antoinette. 'Piddler on the roof!'

8

Antoinette and I were trying to remember the name of someone we met when we were last in Paris.

'His Christian name begins with C,' I said. 'That's the only thing I can really remember.'

'Christopher? Christophe?'

'No.'

'Clive?'

'No.'

'Cuthbert.'

'What?'

'Cuthbert.'

'I've never met anyone called Cuthbert. No one is called Cuthbert.'

'There was a saint called Cuthbert.'

'I've never met any saints either.'

'Christian?'

'No.'

'Claude?'

'No.'

It went on like this for quite a while.

'Phillipe.'

'That doesn't begin with C.'

'No. But that's his name.' Antoinette seemed certain.

I thought about it and nodded. 'You're right. It's Phillipe. That's more or less what I said.'

'You said it began with a C.'

'Well P rhymes with C.'

I don't know why we bothered trying to remember his name anyway. Phillipe is a male model and as far as I'm concerned men who model are in the same bracket as women who box. He is French and enormously immodest. He once told me that he speaks English like a native and that when we spoke together we should always do so in English because my French is so poor that it distresses him. I agreed with him that he spoke English like a native but told him that he spoke it like a native of France rather than England. I softened the blow, however, by assuring him, in the most patronising manner I could manage, that he spoke quite passable English for a foreigner.

9

The euthanasia argument is in the news again. Some doctors and general purpose campaigners want to be able to kill people off when they are dying, decrepit, expensive, unable to complete an Iron Man Triathalon or in a great deal of pain. Others worry about making killing legal. I'm one of the worriers. I can see all sorts of problems.

As I've become older I've realised that when things can go wrong they often do.

I worry more than I did when I was young because I have more experience of the frequency with which serious problems can occur, and the consequences which can result from unexpected misinterpretations and confusions.

The Government has already given doctors the legal right to kill old people (by starving them to death, or depriving them of fluids) if they are filling a hospital bed that the administrators want to use for a patient requiring cosmetic surgery or infertility treatment.

The killing is called 'adhering to the Liverpool Care Pathway' and that is a phrase Orwell would have been proud to call his own if ever there was one. I can see the government taking advantage of a euthanasia law to get rid of all sorts of patients with chronic or potentially expensive illnesses; assisted dying will metamorphose into something quite different to the gentle and kindly easing the proponents envisage.

Is there anyone in the land who would trust David Cameron or Ed Miliband (or, indeed, any of our dastardly politicians) to decide when they should be 'put to sleep'?

I fear that if a euthanasia law is introduced it will mark the return of the death penalty. But this time we won't be killing the probably guilty; we will be killing the definitely innocent.

One additional problem is that it is utterly impossible to predict when a dying patient will die. Anyone who says they can do so is a fraud, a crook, a cheat and a liar.

The world is full of people who are still breathing and living full lives despite having been diagnosed as being terminally ill.

I heard this week about a doctor in County Antrim, Northern Ireland who was wrongly diagnosed with terminal cancer and told to prepare for death. She was told that she had three months to live. Fortunately, being a doctor, the patient discharged herself, went to a London hospital and was diagnosed as having gallstones. Twenty five years ago I myself was diagnosed as having kidney cancer. I requested a second opinion. The diagnosis was changed.

It wouldn't be difficult to fill a large book with such stories. When I was a GP I saw a number of patients who lived far longer than seemed possible – often because they had a very good reason not to die. One patient, a young prostitute with three small children, was dying of bowel cancer. She survived far beyond anyone's expectations, and simply would not die until she was happy that a good home had been found for her children.

(I remember the night I diagnosed her condition and sent her into hospital for the first time. I had no idea what to do with her three small children. I was on call for the night and living in a bachelor flat so I could hardly take them home with me. There were no neighbours, friends or relatives to care for them. I rang the emergency telephone number for the social services department and the social worker on call told me that he couldn't possibly help. When I asked why he could not come out, collect the children and take them to a children's home for the night he told me that he couldn't leave his telephone in case someone rang with an emergency. I ended up taking the children to a nearby nunnery where I was the nunnery's medical officer.)

The other patient was the wife of an alcoholic playwright and the mother of two teenage children. She had breast cancer but refused to die until her children had grown up. She had secondaries in just about every organ in her body but still she wouldn't die. I remember sending a sample of her blood to the laboratory to be tested. They rang me up and asked me what I was playing at. They said that no one could be alive with the blood readings they'd taken. But she was alive. And she lived for several more years. I just stopped taking blood samples because there wasn't any point.

10

Around £122 billion worth of property in England and Wales (most of it in London, of course) is now held through companies based in offshore tax havens. Why? The only conceivable answer is that the UK is still one of the world's favourite havens for dirty money. Next time my bank tells me that I cannot touch my own money without producing my passport, and filling in a surfeit of forms, because of money laundering regulations I will remind them that we actually live in one of the world's two most notorious and successful tax havens for crooks, thieves and tax evaders. (The other is, of course, the United States of America.)

11

These days there are signs everywhere offering 'free wifi'. With the possible exception of prison food there is, of course, no such thing as 'free' anything. I've just been sent evidence showing that when local authorities offer free wifi they aren't just making their money out of pushing advertisements to those using the service. The local authorities are also extracting all sorts of valuable personal data from mobile telephones, by using technology that targets and tracks phone users in a variety of ways. All this is being done without the knowledge of the people whose privacy is being invaded.

Councils are recording the names, telephone numbers and email addresses of people using the free wifi services. They're also collecting and recording details of the websites individuals are visiting and the apps they are using. The information, which can be used to monitor the behaviour of shoppers (including where they go, who they speak to and what they spend their money on) is of enormous value to a wide variety of companies. And, of course, the councils who spy in this way can also easily collect passwords, bank account information and other sensitive information. Once they've got the information it will be theirs forever.

'We don't give this information to anyone,' said one council spokesman.

I bet they don't. It's far too valuable to give away. Councils need money to cover their vast pension liabilities and this is an excellent way to make huge amounts of money out of unsuspecting residents and visitors.

(And if they're not giving it away and they're not selling it why the hell are they collecting it? What can the council do with a list of the websites you visit or a print-out detailing the contents of your private emails?)

The scary thing is, of course, that most people won't think any of this matters a damn.

12

I had a letter from a reader who wants a copy of our latest catalogue. 'There are one or two of your books I want to buy,' he wrote. 'Obviously I'll purchase them on the internet because I can probably pick them up for 1p each plus postage but a copy of your catalogue would help me decide which I want to buy.'

Our last catalogue cost 70p a copy to produce. And to post a catalogue costs another 60p. And, naturally, I receive nothing when second-hand copies of my books are sold on the internet.

My affection for e-Books grows stronger by the day, though I confess I was concerned today to read that new research shows that people who read e-Books are far less likely to recall the content of the book than are people who read printed books.

13

Antoinette and I have discovered the joy of horse racing on the television. We pick horses and put imaginary bets on them and it's just as much fun for us (though not as profitable for the bookies) as placing real bets. We've learned a little about horses (the most successful ones tend to come from stables where the trainer has been in trouble for doping) and about jockeys (they're all absolutely minute but wrinkled like prunes and the best ones are driven with ambition and as cunning as foxes).

We've decided that the most successful horse trainers are the ones who are smooth enough to persuade very rich people to give them oodles of money to feed and water their expensive horses. We don't believe that a horse can be trained to go faster any more than a washing machine can be trained to wash whiter and horse training is, we suspect, one the most successful sleight of mind tricks ever created and sustained.

And we've discovered that the only owners to make money out of horses are probably the ones who also breed them and can therefore sell the young animals to rich people who want to find an excuse to wear posh clothes and be seen in the winners' enclosures.

Finally, we have discovered that horse racing is, above all, a business where cronyism and nepotism fight for supremacy. Everyone is, it seems, related to everyone else. The jockeys are the children of trainers and the trainers are related to the breeders who are related to the commentators who would like to own horses but aren't Arabs or ex-bankers and so don't have enough money. The tipsters are really confidence tricksters because everyone with more than a teaspoonful of brain knows that if they were any damned good at it they would be living in luxury in the Bahamas or Gstaad instead of writing newspaper columns or tipping on the telly.

Everyone in racing is obsequious to everyone else (except the bookies who merely scoop up the contents of people's wallets) but especially obsequious to the people who have the money because horse racing is, above all else, about the money. It is often described as a sport but it isn't, of course. It's a business and the aim is to take as much money as possible out of the wallets and purses of the dreaming punters and status conscious owners and hand it over to the enormously greedy people who run and control the sport.

But Antoinette and I just watch. And pretend to bet. (I did try to set up an account with one of the big bookies but I eventually gave up. I couldn't work my way through their application forms and gave up when they wanted my inside leg measurement.) And although the programmes on Channel 4 appear to have been made as home movies for those involved in racing (and are, in my view, very poorly produced) they are quite surprisingly entertaining.

14

The end of copyright is near.

There has, for some time, been a growing movement on the Internet which has been led by philistines who regard copyright as something as dirty and unpleasant as a cup of hotel coffee.

Many websites, and web users, simply help themselves to whatever they fancy, reproducing articles and whole books without any concern for the rights of the author. Now, I read that the Quebec Université Laval in Canada has taken this one step further and has decided, all by itself and without any assistance from grown-ups, that members of the university are entitled to help themselves to any newspaper or periodical articles they fancy, and to 10% of all books (including whole chapters), without seeking permission from the copyright holder. They argue that this is 'fair dealing' and that if the copyright holders want payment for their work they can go whistle in the wind because they won't be getting any payment from the Quebec Université Laval. I don't think this is fair dealing at all. On the contrary I think it's plain and simple theft and that the folk who made this decision are rogues, bandits and Philistines. How would the Chancellor of the Université Laval feel about me wandering into his library and tearing out whole chapters from the books on the shelves? How would the university ruffians feel about my helping myself to 10% of their furniture? The argument that copyright holders should be prepared to give their work free of charge to anyone who wants to take it (without the thief bothering to say please or thank you) is one of the most dangerous ones to have ever emerged and it is maintained and spread by individuals who have absolutely no understanding of the creative process or the importance of creativity in the community. Why should the writer or musician be less entitled to a reward for his labour than the chimney sweep or the carpenter, the traffic warden or the tax inspector? If institutions and individuals are in future going to regard copyright as irrelevant, and to simply help themselves to any material they fancy, then there will, inevitably, be no more professional authors. All the books and articles which are written will be written by amateurs who earn their living in other ways. And although I have no doubt that much great material has been written by artists who did not get paid for their work I am equally in no doubt that far more of the good stuff has been produced by people who had absolutely no other source of income. (I find it quite scary that around two thirds of all the e-Books downloaded are free. And this figure is rising rapidly. The majority of e-Book readers do not now expect to pay anything for the books they want to read. Readers' expectations are such that many now take advantage of the facility on Amazon which enables them to read a book and then return it and claim back any payment they have made.)

15

A fellow I know called David is a playwright who specialises in writing dramas about obscure events in history. Several of his plays have been performed outside London but he struggles to make a living and depends largely on his wife's salary as a schoolteacher.

'My agent says I should do something dramatic and contemporary,' he told me. 'He wants me to do something domestic: a drama about real, modern people. But I don't have any ideas. I don't know anything about real people or modern problems. I've spent my life researching stuff from history.'

For a while I really didn't know what to say to him.

He lives in a tiny terraced house with a wife who smokes dope, four teenage children and two huge St Bernard dogs. His two daughters are 16-year-old twins who, although still at school, go clubbing three times a week. They both have boyfriends who are much older than them. Twice in recent months they've held rave parties in a house that creaks at the seams when all the family members are in residence. The older son, who is 19, works in a betting shop and is gay. The younger son is 15 and wants to be a professional footballer.

'I can't write modern drama sort of stuff,' David complained. 'I live in the past. I just don't have any contact with real people so how can I possibly write about the problems they face or how they deal with them?'

When I'd heard all this I knew for certain that I didn't know what to say to him.

16

It has been known for some time that amateurs win tennis and golf matches not by playing wonderful shots but by avoiding playing awful shots. The same thing is, I suspect, true of investing. The private investor is more likely to make money (and to beat the market) by avoiding really bad investments than by discovering marvellous investments which double, triple or quadruple his money.

Success in sport usually means doing the things you are good at, and doing them repeatedly. And that is true of investing too.

It is perfectly true that wise investors will diversify. But really wise investors don't diversify too much; they stick to the sort of investments they understand and when things turn sour, and an investment appears to have been a mistake, they sell as quickly as they can in order to minimise their losses.

17

When I was very young I went to bed the same day I got up. In my middle years I went to bed the day after I got up. These days I get up the same day I went to bed.

18

Today, for the fourth time in a week, a packet which I had ordered from Amazon failed to arrive. The first missing parcel was apparently left at the wrong house. The same fate befell the second missing parcel. The third parcel was, I was told, left at yet another address. And the fourth parcel was left at an unnamed post office somewhere in Gloucestershire. I wasn't overly worried about the loss of the first three parcels (two contained books and one contained new USB storage sticks) but I am angry and annoyed about the loss of the fourth parcel which contained food for the birds and squirrels.

The basic reason for this unhappy sequence of events is, of course, the greed and incompetence of the folk at Royal Mail.

When it became clear that people were going to send far fewer letters, and use email instead, the Royal Mail bosses decided that in order to deal with the fall in income they would put up their prices.

As anyone who has ever run a proper business will confirm this is the single most stupid thing you can do. If a product or a service isn't selling then you have to reduce the price in order to make it more attractive. But the people at Royal Mail appear to have no experience of business and so don't think like that.

The Royal Mail bosses thought that they were going to get rich delivering the parcels sent out by internet companies supplying customers who have bought books, DVDs, clothes, television sets, lawn mowers and caravans by clicking buttons on their mobile phones.

Sadly for Royal Mail things didn't quite work out as planned.

I wasn't the only person to notice that Royal Mail is a lousy organisation, and that the service it provides is both shoddy and expensive. And so a whole host of parcel delivery companies have been set up to provide a service which is still shoddy but is at least cheap. Amazon, which used to provide Royal Mail with a staggering

6% of all its parcel business, has set up its own delivery company (known, for reasons quite beyond me, as a logistics company).

The new delivery companies will collect as well as deliver and they will collect and deliver seven days a week.

And now that the internet companies have discovered the joys of shoddy and cheap they are, not surprisingly, reluctant to go back to shoddy and expensive. They won't send stuff by Royal Mail for love nor money.

Now, Royal Mail may have its faults but its delivery folk do have a pretty good idea of where houses are. They can cope with flats in a high rise building and they can cope with cottages in the country. Postman Pat doesn't have an attack of the vapours if he is asked to drive his little red van down a lane with hedges on both sides.

But the folk employed by some of the delivery companies are ordinary, untrained people trying to earn a little extra money by delivering parcels in their own cars. They pick up a boot load of packets from a depot not far from their home (probably a warehouse called a Logistics Inventory Repository) and they drive around trying to deliver the parcels they've collected. They can cope perfectly well with parcels to no 8 Acacia Avenue, no 10 Acacia Avenue and no 12 Acacia Avenue but Honeysuckle Cottage is something else entirely. And since they are probably paid by the number of parcels they deliver they don't have much interest in making the effort to deliver the 'difficult' stuff.

We live down a narrow country lane with hedges and trees on both sides but the lane isn't too narrow for cars or lorries. Supermarket delivery vehicles manage it perfectly happily, once the drivers have learned to ignore the road signs. I've seen an oil tanker and a bulldozer pass by our front gate and although it is perfectly possible that the drivers were lost they had at least managed to drive along the lane without getting stuck.

But the staff of the delivery companies now taking over from Royal Mail can't be bothered to make the effort to find us and so they dump whatever they're supposed to be delivering at any old cottage. They probably think that a cottage is a cottage is a cottage and that if you have a parcel which is supposed to be delivered to a cottage somewhere it really doesn't matter if you deliver it to a cottage somewhere else. 'It's a cottage, innit?'

All this is, of course, another manifestation of that wonderful thing called progress. We have to buy stuff over the internet because the stuff we want to buy isn't available in shops (or, at least, not in any shops within a 100 mile round trip of where we are) but once we've bought it no one will bring it to us.

19

I'm surprised to see that British taxpayers are forking out around £1,000,000 a year to hire bodyguards for the nation's most famous living war criminal.

In a book I wrote early in Blair's career, just when he was planning to become a war criminal, I predicted that he was sucking up to the Bush administration and planning to take us into a war against Iraq so that he could fix himself up with some well-paying jobs when he had retired from mainstream politics. Well, surprise, surprise, Blair reportedly earns £2,000,000 a year from JP Morgan and millions more from assorted (largely American) corporations. He charges up to £250,000 a time to tell audiences how best to become war criminals and has advised Kazakhstan and Colombia on whatever they felt he could best advise them on. Blair claims, of course, that much of his work is 'unpaid' and that his highly paid work supports his charitable projects. Anyone who believes that baloney is probably not fit to pour milk on their own cornflakes. Since being pushed out of politics Blair has managed to scrape enough cash together to buy a country estate for £4,000,000, a London townhouse for £3,650,000 and three other London homes. So why isn't the blood-soaked Blair told to pay for his own damned bodyguards?

Mind you, if they lock the bastard up (a la Rudolf Hess) I'd be happy to pay for the guards and the gruel.

20

Two keen chess players were sitting in front of a roaring log fire, hunched over the board. The fire was giving out an enormous amount of heat and the players must have been very hot. 'Look,' said 'Antoinette. 'Two chess nuts roasting by an open fire.'

21

It always amuses me when I find books which have been placed in the wrong category – not by accident but deliberately. Hunting around in an old bookshop in Cirencester today I found a copy of Ernest Hemingway's novel *Across the River and into the Trees* which had been carefully placed in the Natural History section. A pal of mine swears he once found an Austen in the classic car section in a bookshop in Manchester. I doubt if this is true, however. I don't think there are any bookshops in Manchester. Actually, come to think of it, the classic car section wouldn't be a bad place to hide her damned books. Jane Austen wrote unreadable tosh and if she had been male she would have been long ago forgotten.

22

Companies in Silicon Valley in the USA are organising 'Digital Detox Camps' where participants surrender their cell phones and laptops and agree to give up social media for a while. The aim is to enable them to 'experience life off the grid'. Honest! Why don't the silly beggars just turn their damned phones off? Or put them in a drawer? Turning mobile phone usage and 'social media' into an addiction problem is truly pathetic. (And why, just out of idle curiosity, do so many dumb celebrities take nude pictures of themselves with their phones and then seem surprised when the pictures go viral? Do these people still not realise that nothing done with a mobile phone or a computer is private? Taking nude pictures or embarrassing pictures on a mobile phone is the same as putting them on Facebook or offering them online. And it is as daft as managing your bank account online.)

23

A friend confessed to me today that he always gets confused about the meanings of the words 'tautology' and 'oxymoron'. I suggested that he remember the phrase 'whingeing Scot' as a synonym for 'tautology' and the phrase 'generous Scot' as a synonym for the word 'oxymoron'. He pointed out that this is probably politically incorrect and even illegal and warned me that I should not repeat the remarks. I told him I was joking. He said that these days that is no excuse. I suspect that he is right.

24

We were watching a DVD of Poirot's *Christmas* (a regular Christmas Eve routine for us) and I'd put the film on pause while I put another log on the fire and Antoinette went into the kitchen to switch on the kettle.

'It's chilly in here,' called Antoinette from the other room. 'Would you turn the central heating up a couple of clicks?'

When I was satisfied that the log I'd put on the fire was settling in nicely I walked across to the thermostat which controls the central heating boiler providing heating for the rest of the house. I was surprised to see that it was turned up quite high. I instinctively reached for the nearest radiator. It was cold. Stone cold. I went upstairs to the small room where our boiler lives, alongside the hot water tank, our collection of step ladders and a huge cardboard box full of candles, lamps and torches. The boiler, which normally makes a satisfying hum when it's working, was silent. It was also cold. I peered at the display panel. It didn't look good. I pressed the start button to try to kick the boiler back into life. Nothing happened. I turned off the electricity supply and then turned it on again in the hope that this might trigger some response. Nothing at all. Our boiler wasn't working.

The irony of this did not escape me. In the film we had been watching Poirot discovers, one Christmas Eve, that the central heating system in his flat has failed and cannot be repaired until after the holidays. In order to escape from his cold flat he accepts an assignment at a country house where they do have heating. We were now in exactly the same position except for two things. First, we didn't have a job in a country house to go to and second, we did have a boiler insurance policy which provided us with cover even over bank holidays. I rang the service number and was told that someone would call round the following morning.

We then went back into the living room, piled more logs onto the fire, and settled down to watch the remainder of Poirot's Christmas adventure. The log fire and the gas fired AGA cooker in the kitchen kept the whole house surprisingly warm.

'Why do all these odd things happen to us?' I asked Antoinette, when I'd poured us both a glass of supplementary warmth.

'You should be grateful that they do,' she pointed out. 'If they didn't what else would you find to write about?'

25

A kindly British Gas boiler repair man came, found the fault and used his laptop computer to order a spare part. These days all repairmen seem to come equipped with computers, mobile telephones and heaven knows what else. They lug around huge numbers of bags containing all their equipment. He told us that the parts supplier would put the replacement whatever it was in a taxi and have it delivered to the reception desk of a nearby hotel so that he could pick it up later. I was impressed by this rather crafty way round the fact that all the usual offices and depots were closed for Christmas.

Antoinette made the repair man a cup of tea and gave him a plateful of chocolate biscuits to keep him going. Half a century ago, before breathalysers, I'd have offered him a glass of something more exciting and he would have left us happier and rosier if not safer.

He saw the row of medical textbooks on the shelves next to the boiler room and asked if I was a doctor. (I suppose it was either that or a hypochondriac.) I confessed that I was. In the old days people who knew I was a doctor used to tell me their medical problems; these days people who know I am a doctor tell me about their terrible experiences with the medical profession. Everyone seems to have a horror story to tell.

The engineer told me that he had recently visited his doctor and that after he had been in the surgery for exactly three minutes, and had detailed just one of his three symptoms, the doctor had looked at his watch and said: 'Your time is up!'

I was appalled at this. Every doctor should know that the second and third problems a patient reports (known in the trade as the 'while I'm here, doctor' symptoms) are often the most important ones.

In addition, every doctor should know that symptoms are invariably linked and it is always wise to try to find one diagnosis to cover all of a patient's symptoms.

'So what are you going to do?' I asked him.

He told me that he had made three separate medical appointments for the following week: one appointment for each symptom.

26

When I was so young that I could watch television without the subtitles switched on I remember being given a new digital watch. I didn't have the foggiest idea how to start it, how to change the time or how to do anything with it other than strap it on my wrist. I was working as an assistant to a GP at the time and he told me to wander into the waiting room and find a six-year-old.

'They always know how to make these things work,' he told me.

I tried this and he was absolutely right. The kid I picked might have been seven and he could have been five but he was round about six and he knew instantly what to do to make my watch work. He fiddled with the little buttons on the side and I had a working watch. He tried to explain that there was a stop watch but he lost me there. I was so thrilled I gave him a prescription for some medicine to cure his worms and asked his mum to bring him back twice a year when the clocks changed. You couldn't do that these days, of course. You'd end up being vilified as some sort of horological paedophile.

I was reminded of all this when I read in the news that six-year-olds understand modern technology as well as all adults but that by the time they reach the age of 15 it's all downhill. Apparently, most people hit their peak at that age and after that they're in trouble when faced with new gadgets and new devices. I've thought this was probably the case for some time and I was delighted to see that it's true. It's remarkably cheering to know that the snotty little bastards in shorts, who know so much about mobile phones and laptops, will be as lost as I am by the time they're 16 or so.

I enjoyed my time working with that old GP. He was barking mad but rather fun. He used to stay interested in his work by setting himself unusual challenges. For example, he would sit down at the start of a Monday morning surgery and announce that he was only going to prescribe red medicines. I remember he spent an hour ringing local chemists and trying, unsuccessfully, to find a red antibiotic.

He had a bit of a breakdown later in life (long after I'd left his practice) and got into a little trouble with the authorities. He went off to play golf one Friday and left a huge bowl of medical samples on the table in the centre of the waiting room. He'd put a handwritten sign by the side of it saying 'Help Yourself'. The authorities got to hear about this from an aggrieved councillor who happened to be a patient. They weren't sure what to do because no one could find anything suitable in the regulations but my erstwhile employer was quietly encouraged to retire shortly afterwards.

27

A bull escaped today and somehow found itself running around a local shopping centre. Heaven knows how this happened. I expect a hoodie had bought one as a status symbol, probably to outdo his mates who had nothing scarier than bull terriers on their leads. The authorities failed miserably in their attempts to catch the beast but eventually the animal caught sight of himself in the window of a shop selling ladies unmentionables. He charged at his own reflection, smashed through the glass, collected two horns full of bits of and pieces of silk and lace and knocked himself out when he crashed into the shop's back wall. It took hours for a large team of men in yellow fluorescent jackets to get him out of the shop and take him away. The good news is that he was apparently unhurt by the experience. I cannot, however, help wondering if he might not develop psychological problems as a result of his experience. There will be much chuckling if the cows get to hear about his lingerie festooned horns.

28

My wife, Antoinette, is a coke addict. We neither of us feel the need to be ashamed of this. These are modern times and the world has become accepting of these little foibles. Antoinette confessed today that she has tried to break the habit but she simply cannot get through a day without drinking one, or possibly two, cans of the damned stuff.

29

A friend of ours went to a party and won a prize for having the best 1960s outfit. We congratulated him but he was not in the mood for congratulations. 'I didn't realise it was a fancy dress party,' he told us, glumly.

30

The dramatic society of which Antoinette and I are producers is doing a pantomime this year. They are going to present a version of Dick Whittington. There has been much discussion about whether or not there should be a cat. The actor who played Macbeth in the play of that name, and who is a school teacher, insists that Mr Whittington never had a cat. He says that when he was Lord Mayor,

Mr Whittington had his portrait painted in his posh ceremonial robes (as mayors are wont to do) and the artist put in a skull for the mayor to hold. The skull, a symbol of mortality, was very much the thing at the time. Everyone who had their picture painted ended up holding a skull, or having a skull at their feet or in the background. Later on skulls went out of fashion and so an art dealer who couldn't sell the damned picture painted out the bony, fleshless cranium and painted in a cat. Hence the story of Dick Whittington and his cat. There were many boos when the teacher related this story and it was agreed by a majority vote that Dick would have a damned cat now whether or not he had one then. Bugger history. A local spinster known to all and sundry as Miss Haversham has offered the society the loan of her mackerel tabby and this offer has been accepted.

31

And so another year bites the dust and very soon God will have a fresh one ready, waiting and ripe for consumption. This evening, as is our tradition, we will watch Jeremy Brett as Sherlock Holmes plunge to his death over the Reichenbach Falls in Switzerland. Tomorrow evening we will watch the indestructible Holmes return to life and a new beginning. Our personal traditions provide us with much comfort and soothing continuity in a world where tradition has become a dirty word and too many of those in power insist that change is the same thing as progress.

We hope you enjoyed this book. If you did then we would be grateful if you would post a favourable review on Amazon.

Dr Vernon Coleman is a qualified doctor and professional author who has written over 100 books which have sold more than two million hardback and paperback copies in the UK alone. His books have been translated into 25 languages and sold around the world. Many of his books are available as Kindle books on Amazon. For more details about available books please see his author page on Amazon. For free articles etc please visit http://www.vernoncoleman.com/

A few reference articles referring to Vernon Coleman

'Volunteer for Kirkby', – *The Guardian*, 14.5.1965

'Bumbledom forced me to leave the NHS', – *Pulse* 28.11.1981

'Medicine Becomes Computerised: Plug In Your Doctor.' – *The Times*, 29.3.1983

'Home Diagnosis', – *Practice Computing*, February 1983

'Computer aided decision making in medicine', – *British Medical Journal*, 8.9.1984 and 27.10.1984

'Doctor with the Common Touch', – *Birmingham Post*, 9.10.1984

'Sacred Cows Beware: Vernon Coleman publishing again.' – *The Scotsman*, 6.12.1984

'I'm Addicted To The Star', – *The Star* 10.3.1988

'Our Doctor Coleman Is Mustard', – *The Sun* 29.6.1988

'Reading the mind between the lines' – *BMA News Review*, November 1991

'Doctors' Firsts', – *BMA News Review*, 21.2.1996

'Portrait of a doctor in the doghouse was unfair' – *Independent on Sunday*, 21.4.96

'The big league of self-publishing', – *Daily Telegraph*, 17.8.1996

'Doctoring the books', *Independent'*, – 16.3.1999

'Conscientious Objectors', – *Financial Times magazine*, 9.8.2003
'You have been warned, Mr Blair' – *Spectato*r 6.3.2004 and 20.3.2004

'Food for thought with a real live Maverick', – *Western Daily Press* 5.9.2006

'The doctor will see you now', – *Independent*, 14.5.2008

Note 1: Professor Vernon Coleman gave evidence to the House of Lords Select Committee on animals in Scientific Procedures (2001-2) on Tuesday 12.2.02

Printed in Great Britain
by Amazon